The Indus Script
and
The Ṛg-Veda

The Indus Script
and
The Ṛg-Veda

EGBERT RICHTER-USHANAS

MOTILAL BANARSIDASS PUBLISHERS
PRIVATE LIMITED • DELHI

First Edition: Delhi, 1997
Second Revised Edition: Delhi, 2001

ISBN: 81-208-1405-3

Also available at:
MOTILAL BANARSIDASS
236, 9th Main III Block, Jayanagar, Bangalore 560 011
41 U.A. Bungalow Road, Jawahar Nagar, Delhi 110 007
8 Mahalaxmi Chamber, Warden Road, Mumbai 400 026
120 Royapettah High Road, Mylapore, Chennai 600 004
Sanas Plaza, 1302 Baji Rao Road, Pune 411 002
8 Camac Street, Kolkata 700 017
Ashok Rajpath, Patna 800 004
Chowk, Varanasi 221 001

Printed in India
BY JAINENDRA PRAKASH JAIN AT SHRI JAINENDRA PRESS,
A-45 NARAINA, PHASE-I, NEW DELHI 110 028
AND PUBLISHED BY NARENDRA PRAKASH JAIN FOR
MOTILAL BANARSIDASS PUBLISHERS PRIVATE LIMITED,
BUNGALOW ROAD, DELHI 110 007

CONTENTS

PRELIMINARY NOTE

The numbers of the seals and tablets of this book have been taken from A Concordance to the Indus Inscriptions and A Concordance to the Texts in the Indus Script, Helsinki 1973 and 1982, published by K. Koskenniemi, A. and S. Parpola and by K. Koskenniemi and A. Parpola respectively (Finnish concordance I and II). The initial numbers 0,1,2 refer to Mohenjo Daro, 3 and 4 to Harappa, 5 to Chanhu Daro, 6 to Lothal, 7 to Kalibangan, 8 to smaller sites, 9 to the Near East. The number in brackets following the number of the Finnish concordance refers to the illustration of the seal or tablet in the Corpus of Indus Seals and Inscriptions (CISI) I and II, Helsinki 1987 and 1991, published by A. Parpola and J.P. Joshi (Vol. I) and A. Parpola and S.G.M. Shah (Vol. II). M refers to Mohenjo Daro, H to Harappa, Ch to Chanhu Daro, L to Lothal, K to Kalibangan. Smaller sites have been indicated by their full name. If the seal or tablet is not contained in the corpus, only the number of the Finnish concordances is given. In the few cases, when it is not found in these concordances either, the number has been supplemented by me and indicated with a star. Most of the motifs from Mohenjo Daro, especially those that are difficult to read, have been transcribed and discussed in the monograph of U. Franke-Vogt, Die Glyptik aus Mohenjo-Daro, Mainz 1991, referred to with Franke-Vogt. In the case of the Akkadian seals Boehmer stands for R.M. Boehmer, Die Entwicklung der Glyptik während der Akkad-Zeit, Berlin 1965, and Frankfort for H. Frankfort, Cylinder Seals, London 1939. The characters of the Indus script have been reproduced as computer graphic on the ground of the first Finnish concordance. I thank Dr. Urs Widmer from the PC-laboratory of the Bremen university for his assistance in this field. The Sumerian characters have been reproduced in the same way. The Sanskrit and the Akkadian letters have been rendered according to the international rules of transcription. The Vedic accent has been omitted, however, as it is of no importance for the present investigation. Saṃdhi, junction of final and initial letters, has generally been separated and indicated by a long stroke after the preceding letter. The translations of the Ṛg-Veda and other sources are from the author, if not stated otherwise.

The seal impression on the cover has been reproduced from a photograph in H. Mode, Das Frühe Indien, Stuttgart 1959. Its number in the concordances is 2522. For the reading of the inscription cf. p. 114.

PREFACE

Upwards the root, downwards the twigs,
thus the eternal aśvattha tree is said to be,
whose leaves are the Vedic hymns;
who knows it, is a knower of the Veda.

—*Bhagavadgītā 15.1*

This book has not come into being in one step. Chapter II, IV, V, VII, VIII and IX were originally written in English as separate articles and then published in German in *Der Komische Mensch und die Indus-Kultur* together with other articles. Two years later they were printed in their original language in *The Cosmic Man and the Tree of Language,* enlarged by the chapters I, III, VI and X. This collection was published in revised form in Delhi in 1997 under the title of the first chapter. Now they appear in the second revised edition together with a chapter on the swastika.

The nucleus of the second chapter was presented in a lecture at the Conference of the Association of South Asian Archaeologists held in Berlin in 1991. The original version of the Xth chapter was published in *Ancient Science of Life* XII.3-4, 1990, p. 320-326. The last chapter is based on a lecture held at the 3rd World Archaeological Congress at Delhi in 1994. It has been placed at the end, because the swastika is not only found throughout Indian history, but also in the West. It even occurs in the form of a bird in the Easter Island script. [1]

---

[1] Cf. tablet Tahua, line B3. All tablets of the Easter Island script were published together with a sign-list by Th. Barthel, Grundlagen zur Entzifferung der Osterinselschrift, Hamburg 1958. They can also be found in the internet. For the meaning of the swastika-sign in the Easter Island script cf. E. Richter-Ushanas, Die Schrifttafeln der Osterinsel, in print [2001]. Examples of my reading of the two scripts have been presented in the internet in Two Systems of Symbolic Writing, http://www.zfn.uni-bremen.de/~ushanas

One of the aims of the former books and lectures was to show that there is a cultural relation between the Indus civilization and the Indian tradition already in the time of the R̥g-Veda. In the course of the printing of the German edition, I discovered phonetic values for an obviously bilingual seal from Failaka. The discovering demonstrated that the Indus inscriptions are not only symbolically related to the R̥g-Veda, as I had demonstrated in *Der Fünfte Veda/The Fifth Veda* in 1992, but that the Veda also offers a phonetic reading of a great number of seals.
The disadvantage of the previous editions was that the phonetic and the logographic reading of the inscriptions often pertained to different hymns. This unfavourable state of affairs has been removed now, because the inscriptions including that of the Failaka seal are not read syllabically, but logophonetically. In this way, a greater part of the Vedic hymn, sometimes a whole verse even, is preserved. The progress is mainly due to the study of the Easter Island script I was engaged in in the last four years, because it destroyed the prejudice I had against the practicability of word scripts.
The basic rules of the reading of the Indus script have to be modified according to these improvements:
1. The language of the script is an early type of Vedic Sanskrit, which we may call Gandharvic. At that time prefixes and suffixes were still treated as separate words as in isolating or agglutinative languages. Many words are non-Āryan, but of Sumerian or Austrian provenance. The word-divisions are often made in a similar way as in the later Vedic etymology. Homophony and synonymy are largely made use of. The copula is not written.
2. All signs, including the number-signs, are originally names or attributes of gods, whose totality is represented by the most frequent sign U which I call cup-sign (cf. chapter I.1). It often indicates a finite verb. On account of its multivalence it can be used like a joker.
3. The direction of the script is normally from right to left. The few exceptions are correctly indicated in the Indian concordance.[2] Sometimes an

[2] Cf. I. Mahadevan, The Indus Script, Bombay 1977.

inscription can be read from both sides. In longer inscriptions consisting of two or three lines the reading generally starts from the bottom and may also be boustrophedon. On tablets with two, three or four sides the inscription can start on any of the sides.

4. The script is logographic. Compound signs can refer to several words or a sentence. The motif of a seal or tablet can also be treated as a logogram. Many signs have diacritic strokes that can form a new sign with the corpus of the basic sign. Geometric signs have a concrete meaning, too. Many signs have several meanings in correspondence to the different possibilities of their pictographic interpretation. There are no determinatives as in the Sumerian and Akkadian writing.

5. The man-sign is used for males, the teeth-sign  that was explained as a comb by A. Parpola is used for females.[3]

6. To make larger use of homophony long and short vowels are often treated alike, nasals and semi-vowels may be dropped or added. Cerebrals can be represented by dentals and vice versa, aspirates by non-aspirates. This is due to Prakrit influence.

7. There are several pictograms with the same or nearly the same value as is obvious from the concordances. Vice versa different words can be written by the same sign. This phenomenon is known from the Sumerian pictographic and the Akkadian cuneiform writing. It is quite normal for a symbolic script. The second rule has economic, the first may also have local and historical reasons. On account of this rule, the same Vedic verse can be written by different pictograms and different verses by the same pictograms. Nevertheless, the phonetic value of a pictogram is constant in the frame of its pictographic possibilities of interpretation. The multivalence is necessary, as otherwise the number of signs would increase too much, but it makes it often very difficult to-day to find the most appropriate Vedic verse. Of great help for the deciphering are identical bigrams and sequences, even though they do not always lead to the same translation.

---

[3] Cf. Decipherment of the Proto-Dravidian Inscriptions of the Indus Civilization, Copenhagen 1969, p. 29. The word for comb is identical to the female organ in Greek and Latin. Cf. V. Pisani, Kamm und Scham, in: Antiquitates Indogermanicae, Gedenkschrift für Hermann Güntert, Innsbruck 1974, p. 285.

8. Number-signs and similar geometric signs can be used as simple or combined numbers or they can have pictographic values. The long stroke can represent the wind or the earth, for instance (cf. Sign-dictionary). Generally the number-sign precedes the sign it belongs to The single stroke can also be read as ten or any multivalence with zero at the end. In the same way two strokes can be read as twenty, three strokes as thirty and so on. Ten, hundred and thousand is sometimes written by the woman-sign and its derivatives, the two banner-signs. Thousand can also be written by the number-sign for twelve. In relation to counting, that was regarded as an art like the game of chess and of dice (cf. chapter IX), long strokes denote the fingers, short strokes the teeth.
9. Pronouns are written by the equivalence of the word they refer to or by a number-sign. For this purpose only the short strokes are used.
10. Every sign can be a noun, a verb or an adjective. Abstract nouns are written by a concrete homophone. There are no special signs for the plural or the dual except repetition of a sign or the use of a stroke-sign
11. The main motifs of the seals refer to the caste the owner belongs to (cf. chapter II) and to the god that is addressed in the inscription. The unicorn indicates a brahmin and the gods Agni and Soma, the elephant, tiger and zebu indicates a king or Indra, Rudra, Mitra and Varuṇa, the rhino and the crocodile a landlord or Viṣṇu and the Dawn, the water-buffalo a servant or a minor god.
12. If no corresponding verse can be found in the Ṛg-Veda, only an approximate translation can be given. The reason lies in the symbolic value of the signs. Like in other symbolic writings; the actual meaning depends on the context, but often the inscriptions are too short to discover it. Therefore the deciphering of the Indus script will never come to an end. Everybody working in this field can only turn up fractions of the whole.
Like the hymns of the Veda, the signs of the Indus script can be compared to the leaves of an aśvattha tree. The tree as a whole is equal to the language of Sanskrit, hence all its leaves are Sanskrit words, though they are related to different roots and stems and branches. The aśvattha can also make other trees his host. Then Sanskrit or other words are found on such a tree, though they do not belong to it originally.

The tree of language and the signs of the Indus script are identical to the body of the cosmic man. Of language the seer says in ṚV I.164.45:

Language is divided into four parts,
they are known to the enlightened brahmins;
three parts are deeply secret, nobody stirs them up,
the fourth part of language is spoken by men.

Similarly we hear of the cosmic man in ṚV X.90.3cd:

One part of him are all beings,
three parts are the immortality in heaven.

That means that the Indus script is based for a great deal on intuition and that the same quality is required for reading it. The process of deciphering an inscription or a motif can be compared to contemplation and meditation. It takes much time often, until the deeper layers are revealed or reveal themselves. Even when the deepest layer is reached some secret may be left that is inexpressible. The Indus writers who are identical to the first Vedic seers and priests could also have developed a letter script, but they preferred to use a logographic writing, because the word is a better vehicle for expressing their ideas.

Needless to say that for driving the vehicle of this language a lot of philological equipment is necessary, too. No car can be driven by intuition alone, but it is not necessary for the reader to be conversant with Sanskrit. On account of their pictographic value many signs of the Indus script can even be understood by an illiterate, if he is conversant with the tradition of the Vedic seers. I am myself not an expert of Sanskrit, but have studied this language for the purpose of reading philosophical and poetical works in the original. With the help of the ability gained from the study of Sanskrit I studied Sumerian, Akkadian, Hebrew, Greek, Latin, Arabian, Hindī, Bengalī, Tamil and other languages in the course of time.

In the beginning of the year 1994 I was in India for two months and discussed the issue of this reading of the Indus signs with scholars of Sanskrit and other persons working on the same field. Notably, I have to thank I. Mahadevan, the compilator of the Indian concordance of the Indus script, and S.R. Rao, the excavator of Lothal and other Indian sites, for spending a couple of hours with me in discussing some of the main problems of my proposal. In addition, I am obliged to S.R. Rao for pointing out to me a lot of new material, which I probably would have overlooked otherwise. Of course, this approach to the deciphering of the Indus script would not have been possible without the Indian and the Finnish concordances.

The conception of the cosmic man cannot be confined to any scientific method, though I have almost only quoted scientific literature. For modern science stands rather helpless in front of the associative way of thought of ancient societies that we cannot avoid to become acquainted with, when we study their writing systems. I have mentioned this to save the reader from too quick a conclusion regarding the compatibility of modern and ancient philosophy. On the other hand, somebody who is not ready to accept the hypothesis of a relation between the Indus civilization and the Ṛg-Veda, with which I started my investigation more than ten years ago, cannot make modern science responsible for it.

Another field that could lead to dissension, is the role of women and of virginity in particular in the Indus civilization. It is obvious from the motifs of the seals and tablets that the Indus people venerated a high goddess like the Sumerians and that they had priestesses, too. Moreover, there are many signs with female character in the Indus script. Certainly, women had much more religious and social freedom at that time than in the later Āryan society. This may not please some people in India. On the other hand, women had to play their part in a sacred order including the sacred prostitution that is known form Mesopotamia. This will not suit the moral codex of many people in India and the West as well. But whatever our standards are, we should at least be ready to accept that the way of life of such a remote society in comparison to our own must be different, and that this society should not be held responsible for our deficiencies.

Bremen, in November 2000

I. THE INDUS SCRIPT AND THE ṚG-VEDA

1. The historical background

Like the Sumero-Akkadian pictographic writing the Indus script has been engraved on seals. The Sumerians and Akkadians used cylinder seals, whereas in the Indus Valley stamp seals prevail. Far more important for the reading is, however, that in case of the Indus Valley, there are only these seals and a few terracotta tablets and graffiti, there are no inscribed clay tablets of larger size as they have been found in Mesopotamia. Accordingly, the inscriptions on the Indus seals are very short, on an average they consist of only. 5 signs.[1] The longest inscription has three lines with 9 + 10 + 8 signs (cf. chapter I.5), no single line has more than 12 different signs. The total number of the Indus inscriptions that were excavated so far is not very high either. Including the graffiti we arrive only at about 4000. The Akkadian seal inscriptions can be read phonetically. They contain mostly names of persons and gods and the vocation writer (dub.sar).[2] It is clear from these readings that the Akkadian seals served predominantly like a signature or visiting card for their owners, but they were also used as amulets. That means that the pictograms can be interpreted symbolically, independent of their phonetical value. The amulet character of the Mesopotamian seals is evident from Salomo's Song of Songs in the Old Testament, where the young woman says to her lover in chapter 8.6:[3]

Set me as a seal upon your heart,
bind me as a seal around your arm,
for my love is strong like death,
mighty like the hell is the fire of my womb.

---

[1] Cf. Finnish concordance I, p. x.

[2] Cf. H. Frankfort, op. cit. p. 8. For the translation of these seals cf. D.O. Edzard, Die Inschriften der altakkadischen Rollsiegel, AfO XXII, 1968.

[3] For the interpretation of the text cf. E. Richter-Ushanas, Eros und Mythos, Das Hohelied Salomos, Bremen 1996; O. Keel, Das Hohelied, Zürich 1986.

We can deduct hereof that the name of the woman was written on the seal. The name in ancient times was nothing profane, but was equivalent to the innermost being of its bearer. In the Old Testament, death, hell and love have almost lost their pictorial meaning, as it had for the Mesopotamians and still has for the Indians. This meaning is reflected in the motifs of the ancient seals. Today we attribute a real value to worthless things like used telephone cards, but we have difficulties to understand that an ancient seal had more than a fanciful value, that it could even protect its owner. It is not accidental, if today the economic purpose of the seals is emphasized, but the real import of a certain phenomenon can only be judged from the cultural environment of a peculiar time and place. Economic relations and activities were part of the religious life in the archaic cultures.[4]

That Indus seals are mentioned on Akkadian lists of merchandise as imports from Meluḫḫa,[5] is a further proof that they had a high value. But their economic purpose stands far behind their magic function. This holds true even if they were found on rubbish places, as such places had a religious function in the worship of Śiva and are known as being inhabited by ghosts. Instead of thinking of the economic purpose we should try to transcend the confinements of our present-day civilization and try to anticipate the conditions of an earlier and geographically remote culture. This does not mean that the data collected in the archaeological reports should be neglected. Since the Indian tradition has always kept in memory its earliest testimony, the Ṛg-Veda, it is indispensable to study this tradition, as it cannot be precluded a priori that it contains at least traits of the Indus culture and religion.

This continuity of this tradition was recognized by the first excavator of the Indus civilization, J. Marshall, but only in regard to the post-Buddhist era. The Ṛg-Veda was excluded from any comparative study of the Indus script in the West so far, as it is generally believed by

[4] Cf. H. Haarmann, Universalgeschichte der Schrift, Frankfurt 1990. He lays particular stress on the religious function of the Indus script.

[5] Cf. W. Heimpel, Das untere Meer, ZA 77 (1987).

Western scholars that the circumstances depicted in this corpus of hymns are suitable to an India of about 1500 ante, i.e. after the end of the big Indus cities. This makes it improbable for them to accept that the Veda was influenced by this urban society. Indian scholars have a different opinion in this matter, because of the general belief that the Veda is older than every other tradition, including the Indus civilization. It is not very likely, however, that a tribal society gave birth to an urban and fell back to its original level after its decay. On the contrary, it is much more probable that the Vedic society and religion were influenced by the Indus culture, even if the dating of Western scholars is right: the spirit of this tradition cannot be confined into borders like a dammed up river only to be released 1000 years later. That the Vedic society remained untouched and uninfluenced by the Indus culture is even less probable, if it came into being already 1000 years earlier than the date stated by most Western scholars, as M. Winternitz contended.[6] Earlier, H. Jacobi arrived at a similar date.[7]

Jacobi's results are based on certain astrological data obtained from the Ṛg-Veda itself, especially from ṚV X.85.13. This verse describes the time, when Sūryā, the daughter of the sun, sets off to be married to the Aśvins, the twin-gods of the Veda:

> *The wedding procession went ahead*
> *which was dismissed by Savitṛ (the father);*
> *in the lunar mansion Aghā the bulls are killed (sacrificed),*
> *in the lunar mansion Phalgunī she (the bride) is brought home.*

Jacobi believed that the marriage of the daughter of the sun was celebrated ritually at the time of the summer solstice, i.e. in the time of maturity. The two stars of the nakṣatra or lunar mansion Phalguṇī culminated around 3000 ante according to the nakṣatra-list he attached to his paper. This means according to him that spring-time, i.e. the

[6] Cf. History of the Indian Literature, Delhi [3]1990, p. 288.

[7] Cf. Über das Alter des Rig-Veda, in: Festgruß an Rudolf v. Roth, Stuttgart 1893, p. 68-74 (Kleine Schriften, Wiesbaden 1970, p, 258).

seed-time, when human marriages preferably take place, began in the lunar month Vaiśakha. The bulls were generally killed in the month before, when the lunar mansion Aghā, called Maghā in later nakṣatra-lists, culminated. The modern Indian calendar was invented about 400 post our era. Almost the same date, 3102 BC, was appointed then as the beginning of the Kali-Yuga.[8] In Bhāgavata Purāṇa XII.2.31 (written down in the first millennium after our era) we read in this regard:

When the Seven Seers enter the lunar mansion Maghā,
then the Kali-Yuga consisting of 1000 (divine) years begins;
when the Seers go from the lunar mansion Maghā to Pūrva Aṣādhā,
then the Kaḷi-Yuga starts, from the Nanda-days onwards.

Nanda is the name of the auspicious days of the fortnight and of Kṛṣṇa's father. At the death of Kṛṣṇa begins the Kali-Yuga, the iron age, for the Purāṇa. According to the ancient doctrine of the four ages that is also found in Babylon, but goes back most probably to the Indus culture, the Kali-Yuga consists of 432,000 years.[9] The year 3101 is simply a projection like the year 3713 ante, where the Julian calendar started.[10] This calendar, named after Julius Caesar, who reformed the Roman calendar, would have ended in the year 3267 post our era. Its total length was 7980 years. This date is explained by W. Kubitscheck[11] as the sum of 28x19x15, referring to the cycle of the sun, the moon and the indictions - the years, when the income tax was levied in the Roman empire.

These dates were combined with regard to the conception that creation starts, when all planets including the sun and the moon are in conjunction or stand in one line from the terrestrial point of view. The Indian astrology is based on the same idea. Therefore it lets the Kali-Yuga start at a date, when sun and moon meet in the middle of

---

[8] Cf. J.F. Fleet, The Kaliyuga Era of B.C. 3102, JRAS 1911, p. 479.

[9] Cf. B.J. van der Waerden, Das große Jahr und die ewige Wiederkehr, Hermes 80, 1952, p. 129-155.

[10] Cf. Fleet, op. cit. p. 675.

[11] Cf. Grundriß der antiken Zeitrechnung, München 1927, p. 44.

the zodiac in the summer solstice. The Seven Seers mentioned in the Purāṇa are identical to the constellation of the Great Bear, but here the seven planets are referred to. The constellation of the Maghās culminated in the beginning of the lunar month Āṣādha, i.e. about 3000 ante, shortly before the summer solstice, the Pūrva Aṣādhās will be in conjunction with it around 12,000 post our era. This agrees approximately with the end of the Great Year formed by the apparent precession of the spring-point.

Since the year 3101 is said to be the time of Kṛṣṇa's death, it must also be the time of the composition of the largest Indian epic, the Mahābhārata. Its apparent antiquity was quite in tune with the intention of the Indian astrologers to make the Ṛg-Veda and the whole Indian tradition appear older than that of the Greeks and the Romans. The Indian philosophers have always attached great importance to the remote antiquity of their tradition. This is also evident from the belief that the Veda came forth from the mouth of Brahmā in the beginning of creation, a belief that is not shared by the Vedic seers themselves, however. In their opinion, it was the Veda and not the Mahābhārata that was composed in the beginning of the third millennium.[12]

There are references to an older spring-point in Mṛgaśiras (Orion) around 4500 ante and even earlier in Punarvasū around 6000 ante, as was pointed out by L.B.G. Tilak.[13] For Jacobi, these references were reminiscences only. They are of course convincing to those who are in

---

[12] A.D. Pusalkar arrived at the same time by counting the dynasties mentioned in the Purāṇas from Manu onwards. Cf. History and Culture of the Indian People, Bombay [4]1965, Vol. I (The Vedic Age), p. 273. With regard to the relations of the Aryans and the Indus culture P. suggests a reappraisal of the question "with an open mind" (cf. Ṛg-Veda and Harappan Culture, in: Mélanges d'Indianisme, Paris 1968, p. 592,594).

[13] Cf. The Orion or Researches into the Antiquity of the Veda, Poona 1955, and J. Deppert, Rudras Geburt, Wiesbaden 1977, p. 179. The same standpoint is advocated on the ground of linguistic discoveries by S.S. Misra, The Aryan Problem, Delhi 1992. Even if some Āryans lived in India already at this time, it does not mean that the whole Ṛg-Veda is of equal age.

favour of the utmost antiquity of the Veda, but their historical value is similar to the statement of Kṛṣṇa in Bhagavadgītā 10.35, where he says that he is the Mārgaśīrṣa among the months. Nobody would ever infer from this statement, that the Gītā was composed in 4500 ante. It is nothing but a reference to the constellation of Orion that has always been the greatest and most impressive constellation in the northern hemisphere. In the Brāhmaṇas, it was therefore affiliated to Prajāpati.[14]
That even Jacobi's moderate opinion did not find much approval among Western scholars is also caused by the idea they have of the Vedic society, which they believe is a rural community like that of the early Greeks, with whom it is tied by linguistic bonds, too. It is maintained that such a community need not come into any contact with the urban community of the Indus civilization, even if they were contemporanian.[15]
The notion that neither cities nor other instruments of an urban society have been mentioned in the Veda is mostly based on the dictionaries. They are not always reliable. It may be that the assumption that the Veda deals with a rural community has resulted in suitable word-renderings. Sri Aurobindo and Swami Dayananda have arrived at totally different readings. Even if the terms of the dictionaries are applied, we come across several inconsistencies. How can it be explained, for instance, that a 'flying' merchant who is the son of a seer is mentioned thrice in the Veda? Not alone that it is difficult to explain that the son of a seer could be a merchant, what does it mean, that he was able to fly? Was he a travelling merchant or could flying be a synonym for sailing? H. Zimmer states that in the Veda ships were used only for travelling on rivers or for crossing them,[16] but there are several passages, where

---

[14] With reference to J. Bentley, M.R. Yardi dates the Gītā on account of this verse to the period of 699-452 B.C. Cf. The Bhagavadgītā as a Synthesis, Poona 1991, p. 12. Perhaps the Orion is mentioned in the Gītā to make her appear earlier than the Buddha.

[15] Cf. F.R. Allchin, The Legacy of the Indus Civilization, in: G. Possehl, South Asian Archaeology Studies, Oxford 1992, p. 332.

[16] Cf. Altindisches Leben, Berlin 1879 (reprint Hildesheim 1973), p. 255.

ships are mentioned in relation to the ocean, notably in ṚV I.25.7 and in connection with the Aśvins. It is also difficult to explain that hymns of the sometimes high poetical and philosophical standard of the Ṛg-Veda could be composed by simple herdsmen or their priests. Moreover, the description of women in the Veda does not fit into a rural community, but very well into an urban.

It must be pointed out here that meanwhile cities of the same size as or even bigger than Mohenjo Daro have been excavated at Dholavira in Gujarat and at Dwārkā at the coast of Kathiawar that are dated back to 1500 ante.[17] In later time, the city of Dwārkā became the home of Lord Kṛṣṇa, but the original town is drowned now, as is told in the Mahābhārata. That the original town was inhabited by relatives of the later people, is also obvious from their writing that was a sort of Brāhmī (cf. chapter I.6). The Vedic word pur translated in Grassmann's dictionary as 'fortified place' could also have meant city.[18]

A city could of course have oversea trade connections. The first written testimony of the Vedic gods was found in a Hittite contract that has been dated to 1350 ante our era (cf. chapter II). This is difficult to explain, if the first hymns of the Veda were composed approximately at the same time or still later. In addition, it is highly unlikely that the comprehension of the Indus script was lost all of a sudden after the decline of the Indus cities. Though the production of seals became difficult or impossible then, the pictograms could and were also written or painted on pottery, bangles and perishable material.[19]

It is further maintained that the Veda was transmitted orally and that it is hence quite unreasonable to expect renderings of the Indus seals therein, as I maintain to have found them, but it was G. Bühler already, who gave vent to the expectation that the "argumentum ex silentio", the conclusion that a script does not exist, because it is not mentioned,

---

[17] Cf. Dawn and Devolution of the Indus Civilization, New Delhi 1991, p. 152.

[18] W. Rau's argumentation in regard to this point is not convincing. Cf. Zur vedischen Altertumskunde, Mainz 1983, p. 36.

[19] Cf. S.R. Rao, Lothal and the Indus Civilization, London 1973, p. 160.

might be abandoned in this field. Even in modern India, Bühler continued, the written word is not mentioned in spite of its being used for a long time, since it is regarded as inferior to the oral communication of a teacher.[20]

The written word is not regarded as authoritative, since it can easily be misunderstood. This is equally true for a word or a letter script, since the possibilities of misinterpretation are the same.

There are also terms for to write and writer in Vedic times. Bühler mentions lipi for script and lipikara for writer in Pāṇini's grammar III.2.21,[21] but several words denoting to write and writer can be found in the Ṛg-Veda itself, they have only not been recognized as such on account of deficient entries in the dictionaries. Thus Ṛbhu, the name of three Vedic artisans, can be explained as writer. Its root rabh is related to Greek rhaptein, to knit together, and glyphein, to write, from which hieroglyph, sacred sign, is derived. Synonymous and homophonous with rabh is the Sanskrit root grabh corresponding to Greek graphein for to write, and glyphen. The word for writing in classical Sanskrit, lipi, is derived from the same root. Grabh is not used in this sense in the Veda, but we come across the roots rī, to let flow (the line of writing) and ṛṣ, to pierce. From the latter root ṛṣi, seer, singer, is derived. It is synonymous with the root rad, to scratch that was explained as to write by Geldner.[22] Another root that can be used for to write is piś, to carve (in stone).

The signs may have been called 'pada', foot, like the quarters of the Vedic verse. This can be a pictographic meaning of the most frequent pictogram  that served as a marker for the end of a verse or a quarter (pada) of it. In the symbolical language of the Veda this sign may be compared to a cup or vessel. The grail of the revived Celtic mythology (cf. chapter II) has its origin here.

In several hymns, the Ṛbhus are said to have made the single cup of the creator Tvaṣṭṛ into four. This can be explained in relation to the standard (cf. § I.7) or the quarters of the universe and the yugas, the cosmic periods,

---

[20] Cf. Indische Paläographie, Straßburg 1896, p. 1,2.

[21] Ibid. p. 3.

[22] Vedische Studien III, Stuttgart 1901, p. 26.

but it could also contain a hint to the development of the script that consisted of one sign in the beginning as on early Harappa graffiti and in Neolithic cave paintings.[23] According to Vedic counting, four is identical to 400, which is approximately the number of signs given in the Finnish Concordance I (cf. sign-dictionary). The highest number of different signs in a line that we find on the Indus seals is 12 corresponding to the months of the year and of the divine years of a kalpa or world period of four yugas. If the number of 13 signs, corresponding to a 13th month, is found in a few cases, this is due to repetition. The statistic average number of five signs of the inscriptions is quite near to the four cups of the Ṛbhus.
It is possible that the invention of the Ṛbhus was influenced by the older Sumerian pictographic writing, since the Indus pictograms have many similarities with it. This assumption is especially supported by the fish-sign, whose phonetic value can be traced to the Sumerian word for fish, ḫa or ku (ku_6). The Sanskrit root kū, of which kavi, seer, is derived, is of uncertain meaning. Perhaps it is a Sumerian loan-word. The Sumerian fish-sign was the starting point of my phonetic deciphering (cf. chapter I.2).[24]
By making the single cup into four the Ṛbhus became immortal like the gods. This could mean that writing was highly estimated in old Vedic times, though Tvaṣṭṛ, the god of the priests, did not accept the new invention at first according to a certain tradition. The priests might have been appeased by reserving the art of writing for them.
Divine and urban origin is also ascribed to the modern Sanskrit script, the Devanāgarī, (the script) of the town of the gods, and the Brāhmī script standing chronologically between the Indus script and the modern Sanskrit script. The Brāhmī got her name from the goddess of wisdom who is the daughter of god Brahmā. Brahmā is identical to the Vedic Tvaṣṭṛ. It is generally believed that the Brāhmī alphabet is based on the

---

[23] This origin of the script is also suggested by B.B. Lal mostly on the ground of the comparison of the mature Harappa script with graffiti from Rahman Dheri. Cf. Antecedents of the Signs used in the Indus Script, in: G. Possehl, op. cit., p. 45.

[24] That the sign depicts a fish is proved by early Harappa graffiti from Rahman Dheri (cf. Corpus of Indus Seals and Inscriptions II, p. 377) and by the crocodiles with a fish in their mouth similar to the pictogram.

Old Semitic alphabet going back to the Phoenicians who are said to have taken it from the Egyptian still pictographic letters. It is more likely, however, that they derived it from the Indus script, whose geometric signs have much more similarity with the Brāhmī alphabet than the Egyptian (cf. chapter X). This does not mean that the Indus script became a letter script at the end, as S.R. Rao contends.[25]

If the date of the origin of the Veda can be inferred from the astrological data contained in the Veda itself, we can expect similar hints from the Indus seals. This is indeed the case with seal 2347 (M-311) that I have already investigated in this regard in the logographic translation of the Indus inscriptions.[26] The motif of this seal is a centaur with additional elements that can be affiliated to the 12 main constellations of the zodiac. It does not make much difference, whether we look at it from the Vedic or our point of time, since the Indian names of the constellations are easily adaptable to the precession of the spring-point. Some alternations in the present names of the constellations are inevitable, however. The name of the sign of Scorpio, for instance, whose counterpart is not to be found on the seal, has to be changed into that of the neighbouring sign of the Snake Carrier, because the scorpion is an attribute of the goddess Ištar, whereas the Snake Carrier can be regarded as a form of Lord Śiva. Cancer has no equivalence on the seal either, but the pig-tail of the person indicates that it represents a priest (cf. the seven persons on seal 2430), i.e. somebody who is able to write. The time for writing and studying was the rainy season beginning with this constellation. The symbols of the constellations and the planets are also found in the Indus script (cf. chapter III.2).

Further astrological information is obtained from the cylinder seals 7733 (Sibri-2), 7731 (Sibri-3) and the graffito 8025 (Daimabad-5). On seal 7733 a zebu is attacked by a lion whose jaw is wide open. A man in a kino tree holding a club and a knife in his upraised hands follows the lion. A crocodile at the top and the bottom complete the scenery. On the other seal from Sibri simply a zebu and a lion standing opposite each other are depicted. On

[25] Cf. Dawn and Devolution, p. 200. For further discussion cf. chapter I.6.

[26] Cf. The Fifth Veda, p. 23.

the graffito 8025 a tiger is jumping on a bull from behind. On the reverse a file of six lozenges and an extra stroke is inscribed.
In the astral context, the six lozenges with the extra stroke represent the Seven Seers, the crocodiles the goddess of Dawn, Uṣas, the zebu the era of Taurus. It is attacked by the new era in form of the lion. Leo represents an older age than Taurus, but it is a symbol of the devouring time in general and a fire-sign like Aries, the following era. The tree may be explained as the cosmos and the man in the tree as Rudra or Śiva. The era of Aries, identical to the nakṣatra Bharaṇī, began around 1500 ante according to Jacobi's list. The archaeological date of the seals and the graffiti is given as late Harappan.
The sign  on the top of the cylinder seal 7733 reappears with slight difference on Kuṣān coins as the monogram . It corresponds to the Indus sign . On several Kuṣān coins a man with the head of a bird is engraved representing the Avestan Ḫravana (Sanskrit svar, Persian pharo), effulgence. He often appears together with the goddess Ardoxšo beside him who is represented by the teeth of the upper part of the monogram.[27] The sign may also represent Śiva's and Poseidon's trident, as flames and waves are both similar to teeth. Śiva's weapon is hinted at in ṚV II.33.11. The Vedic word for it is trir-aśri, three-edged (ṚV I.152.2). A similar trident is held by a priest on tablet 3303.
One may further object that it is not very likely that the Indus inscriptions are contained in the Ṛg-Veda, for its language, called Sanskrit since the time of the Buddha, was Āryan, whereas the so-called priest-king (Marshall, pl. XCVIII) and other human figures from Mohenjo Daro have rather negroid or even mongoloid features. However, the founders of a high civilization can also be credited with the ability of creating a ceremonial language like Sanskrit from the natural languages of that area.

---

[27] Cf. R. Göbl, Dokumente zur Geschichte der iranischen Hunnen in Baktrien und Indien, Wiesbaden 1967, Vol. 4, pl. 17, 106. The monogram is also found on a coin with the image of the four-armed Manao Bago, the 'Lord of Dream'. Cf. H. Humbach, Methodologische Variationen der arischen Religionsgeschichte, in: Antiquitates Indogermanicae, p. 195.

That the invention of this language was beyond normal human capacity was also felt by the authors of later Vedic literature, for according to the Maitrāyaṇī and the Taittirīya Saṃhitā[28] it was Indra, the king of the gods, who made the language of the Asuras[29] *distinctive*. This was necessary, it is told, since it was originally *singly* (eka-dhā), *turned back* (pratīci) and *indistinct* (avyāvṛtta or avyākṛta). These features could be interpreted as isolated, focused on the end and non-flectioning, as they are found in the Dravidian languages today. According to Śatapatha Brāhmaṇa III.2.1.23-24 the gods robbed the language from the Asuras that is called *enigmatic* (upajijñāsya) and *mleccha* (barbaric) in this passage. Since the language of the gods is Sanskrit, the language of the Asuras they have robbed must have been Sanskrit, too, at least it must have been a dialect (prākṛit) similar to Sanskrit.[30]

It is likely that mleccha is the reimported form of Meluḫḫa. Like asura in the later portions of Vedic literature, mleccha has a negative connotation in the Brāhmaṇa. Mleccha does not occur in the Ṛg-Veda, but we find the synonymous mṛdhra (vāc) instead, said to be the language of the Dasyus, the enemies of the Āryan people who composed the Veda. On account of their black complexion and their flat nose the Dasyus could easily be transformed into demons, called asuṛa in the later portions of the Veda, but according to Indian mythology the Asuras and the Devas were generated by the seer Kaśyapa, only the mother was different. The same would hold good for the Dasyus. It is very likely

[28] For the original and a French translation of the text cf. S. Levi, La Doctrine du Sacrifice dans les Brāhmaṇa, Paris 1966, p. 35.

[29] P.L. Bhargava points out that the word 'asura' meant originally mightiful and that it became a name of the enemies of the gods only in the latest hymns of the Veda. Cf. Vedic Religion and Culture, New Delhi 1994, p. 23. A similar result is arrived at by W. E. Hall, Asura in Early Vedic Religion, Delhi 1986, p. 98. Hence asura in the negative connotation cannot refer to the Harappan gods. This is also clear from ṚV X.124.

[30] This is suggested by Keith/Macdonell in their Vedic Index of Names and Subjects, Delhi 1982 (reprint), vol. I, p. 181.

that the Dasyus lived together with the Āryans in the Indus cities.[31] The name 'ārya' is a synonym for noble in classical Sanskrit, but in the Vedic time it simply denotes the ruling class, whose members could act morally good or bad. From the view of the Dasyus, their activities were generally bad.

Hitherto, it was not possible to explain the name of the Dasyus, but with regard to the Indus script it can be derived from the root daṃs, that has two meanings according to Grassmann, to bite and to teach. The first meaning is also found among the renderings of the root 'rad' that was used for to write according to Geldner (cf. note 22). Writing in that time was often done with the tooth of an animal. Therefore it was compared to biting. This meaning is also contained in the Indus sign for woman. Their ability to write made the Dasyus more powerful than the generally illiterate Āryans. This could be the real reason, why the Āryans fought them and tried to annihilate them.

In III.2.4.3-6 of the same Brāhmaṇa we read that Language (vāc) is sent by the gods to the Gandharvas, since they are known for their attachment to women, in exchange for the Soma they have in possession. When she leaves the Gandharvas with the Soma, the gods and the Gandharvas follow her. They agree eventually not to hold her back by force, but to allow her to stay with that party she feels most attracted to. In order to entice her, the Gandharvas recite the Vedas and the gods play and sing, whereupon Vāc goes to the gods, because playing and singing is natural to women.[32] In the later tradition, however, the Gandharvas are the musicians and dancers of the gods, whereas the reciting of the Veda is part of the sacrifice for them. In the singular, Gandharva is the name of a superhuman being in the Ṛg-Veda who guards the Soma. As a superhuman being he is similar to the seers and yogis of the Indus cities (cf. chapter III.2).

Like the quarters and the cosmic man as described in ṚV X.90.3 language has four parts. Only one part is spoken by men. This part must originally have been the language of the Asuras called Mleccha by the

---

[31] It is not very likely, that the Dasyus are identical to the Bactrian Dahas, as the Russian archaeologist V. Sarianidi contends, because they belong to a later time.

[32] Cf. S. Levi, op. cit. p. 33.

Śatapatha Brāhmaṇa, but which should be called Gandharvic, since it were the Gandharvas who recited the Veda first. It cannot be much different from Vedic Sanskrit. Sanskrit is an elaborated language, as its name implies. It got its name only in post-Vedic time, but it was obviously from the beginning the language or vāc of the poets, different from the language of the common people called bhāṣā.[33] This must have been a Prakrit language like Pali that was used by the Buddhists for the same purpose. The Veda consists of an older and a younger part. It is possible that the older hymns were translated into Sanskrit from a Prakrit language, and that only the younger were originally composed in Sanskrit. This would imply to give up the idea that Sanskrit is older and higher than any other language and that the Āryans are the supreme race. The original elaboration of Sanskrit could have taken place at the time of the manufacturing of the first Indus seals around 2500 ante. This would then also have been the time of the composition of the first Vedic hymns in this language, but it is possible that a number of them was composed earlier already in a 'natural' language. [34]

Another confirmation of the relation of the Veda and the Indus script is the method of Indian etymology, applied in the Brāhmaṇas and Upaniṣads. It is quite different from the rules of modern science. According to this method an abstract word is substituted by a concrete homophone. The same method is found in the Atharva-Veda.[35] It is also applied in the homeopathic treatment of the Āyur-Veda that belongs to the Atharva-Veda. Since the same method is applied in the Indus script, the authors of these later texts must have learnt this from the priests of the Indus civilization.

---

[33] Cf. Keith/Macdonell, op. cit., vol. I., p. 103.

[34] J. Gonda held the view that "besides the 'official' brahmanical texts and rites, unorthodox currents, rites and 'literature' existed and that the brahmins at an early period incorporated a number of these texts in their own collection." Cf. The so-called secular, humorous and satirical hymns of the Ṛg-Veda, in: Orientalia Neerlandica, Leiden 1948, p. 348.

[35] Cf. N.J. Shende, The Religion and Philosophy of the Atharva-Veda, Poona 1985, p. 11.

There are several theories about the decline of the Indus cities. Many scholars believe that they were destroyed by invading Āryans and that this encounter is reflected in the slaying of the demon-snake Vṛtra by Indra.[36] If the older parts of the Ṛg-Veda and the Indus civilization are contemporary, the fight between god and demon could have been part of the New Year festival as in the Near East. Vṛtra is then not the representative of the Indus civilization, but of the dark half of the year, of the night, of cold and dryness. This supposition is confirmed by his name, meaning encloser. According to the Veda he encloses and obstructs the waters and the light and prevents fertility when lying like a snake on the hill (the clouds), his abode. Indra, his opponent, the god of the monsoon-rain and lightning, kills the snake, drills up the hill or clouds with his thunderbolt and set the rivers and streams free. The historical encounter belongs to a later time, when the Āryans fought against the Dasyus (cf. chapter I.5).

The most detailed description of the myth is given in ṚV I.32. In verse 12 of this hymn Indra is said to have become the hair of a horse-tail, when he was caught by Vṛtra at his chin. That means that Indra bears the features of a horse here, but very often he is compared to a bull, too. The same ambivalence is found with the unicorn (cf. chapter I.2). Indra is a representative of this animal and therefore he belongs to the Indus civilization as well as to the Vedic. ṚV I.32 does not only reflect the phenomena of the seasons. Verse 8 says that Vṛtra is lying at the feet of the waters he formerly has enclosed, and that the waters rise to his mind (manas). It is also possible to read manas as Manu, the name of the Indian hero of the Great Flood. Then the sentence would render that Vṛtra was overflowed by *Manu's waters*.

From both renderings we can infer that there must have been a much greater inundation as the yearly floods on account of the monsoon in summer or the melting of the ice of the Himalayas in spring. Rao mentions in this connection two great floods in 2000 and 1900 ante our era and explains them as caused by tectonic disturbances.[37] D.D. Kosambi who believed in the theory of the Āryan invasion thought that an inundation took place,

---

[36] Cf. B. and R. Allchin, The Birth of Indian Civilization, Harmondsworth 1968, p. 153-156.

[37] Cf. Lothal and the Indus Civilization, London 1973, p. 179,180.

because the Āryans pierced up the dikes the Indus farmers had built to prevent the waters from receding too soon after the monsoon.[38] It is more likely, however, that the land became silted after a natural inundation and was abandoned deliberately, because it became infertile.

Like against the mighty demon-snake Vṛtra Indra fights against the fortified places or pur of the Dasyus. ṚV VI.27.5 mentions 130 Vṛcivats who were killed by Indra at (the) Hariyūpiyā. Whether this is the name of a river or a place, it can anyway be regarded as the Vedic name of Harappa (cf. chapter I.7). In ṚV I.133.2,3 Indra fights against witches and the vulture Piśāci living at an 'armaka', a place 'with sherds', i.e. a deserted place. In ṚV X.155.4 he destroys amazons with one breast and a *rusty vagina*.[39]

On account of such activities Indra is called *destroyer of fortified places* (puraṃdara), whereas he lives safe in his city Amarāvatī, the 'town of the immortals'. The name is not mentioned in the Veda, but a similar place was certainly known to the poets. In ṚV I.154.5 Indra's and Viṣṇu's abode is called pāthas, which could be explained as a fortified place, in ṚV I.155.1 the two gods are said to stand on the back of the hills. This recalls Vṛtra lying on the hill. In I.154.4 Indra's and Viṣṇu's abode is described as the place where pious men enjoy the Soma. The same is said in X.135 of the place of Yama, the god of death.

In the name of Mohenjo Daro, which can be translated as 'hill of the death', the Vedic equivalent of cannabis, muñja-grass, is preserved. This may also be the root of the name of the Mohānas, a clan of fishermen living in this area nowadays. So there are several reasons to identify the abode of the gods and not the abodes of the Dasyus with the Indus towns, whose citadels were built on a hill. Furthermore, skirmishes like those with the Vṛcivats or the ravage of fortified places cannot explain the destruction of big towns inhabited by thousands of people.

---

[38] Cf. Ancient India, New York 1965, p. 71.

[39] Amazon is derived from Sanskrit ama-jani, aggressive or violent woman. The root am means to advance and to injure. It is later used for the accusative ending and is equal to the Indus sign ↑ (cf. chapter X). Amazons may have lived in the Indus Valley, before they immigrated to Asia Minor.

Normally, natural catastrophes or epidemics do not prevent a people from coming back to their abandoned or destroyed houses. Even if the walls of the Indus towns were corroded by nitre on the same scale as in Sodom and Gomorrha, this does not explain, why urban life has stopped all of a sudden in an area as big as the Indus Valley.

If we imagine that some of the authors of the Veda were among the founders of the Indus cities, it is not to be expected that the Veda deals with them, as if they were enemies. Indeed, the Veda remembers the former gods and seers with respect and veneration. There is, however, a behaviour that the Veda treats with contempt. This is greed and covetousness personified in a Dasyu people called Paṇi. A similar behaviour is given as the reason for the Great Flood in the Gilgameš epic. It was found with the class of the merchants in the ancient cities as well as it is found in the modern. If the merchants were too covetous to look after the public affairs, the towns would corrode from within, as it were. On the other hand, the merchants were the builders of the ships that are essential for the development and survival of an urban community. Ships, however, are modelled after the structure of temples, as we know from the epic of Gilgameš.

Similarly, it is evident from the story of the Great Flood in the Śatapatha Brāhmaṇa that the spiritual survival of a culture depends on sacrifice and that egotism is the root of its destruction. There seems to be no remedy against it apart from building an arch, as it was done in former times. The ship is not only an image of the temple, but also of the cosmic man called sacrifice in the last verse of the Puruṣa-hymn X.90.16:

> *Through sacrifice the gods sacrificed the sacrifice,*
> *these were the first laws;*
> *thus these mighty beings reached the sky,*
> *where the former gods, the Sādhyas, are.*

The Sādhyas can be related to the Indus river called Sindhu (with the root sidh) in the Veda. It seems likely that they are identical to the Gandharvas and Aṅgiras, the godlike beings, who were the founders of the Indus civilization. This would explain why there were gods earlier to those that invented the first laws.

After the arch had reached land again, the former culture was re-established. Therefore many features of a tribal society are missing with the Āryan inhabitants, instead we find features of a colony that has lost its motherland. This is corroborated also by the excavation of the inundated Dwārkā. From this observation it can be inferred that the civilization of Manu that had started in about 3100 ante together with that of Harappa was re-established in about 1500 following the decline of the Indus civilization. Afterwards, the Śatapatha Brāhmaṇa was written, where the Great Flood is described for the first time in Indian literature.[40] Together with Manu the Vedic seers were reborn.

Though there was certainly a Great Flood at the end of the ice age, a similar catastrophe at the beginning of the Harappan culture would not have fulfilled the effect attributed to it, since there was no overcrowding of human population at that time, whose destruction is the main aim of this catastrophe. In the Purāṇas we are informed that there was a Veda before and after the Great Flood. They are not identical, as the Indian tradition will have it, but the younger Veda was remodelled on the older according to the necessities of the time.

Now Indra, who was formerly a rain-god with some relation to war, becomes a war-god with some relation to rain, and the Asuras become the opponents of the gods like the Dasyus of the Āryans. From the same reason, the Mahābhārata in its present form must have been composed approximately two centuries before the Christian era. Indeed Alexander has the features of the divine nature of Lord Kṛṣṇa and of the devilish nature of Duryodhana, who is said to be an embodiment of the Asura Kali, the demon of the present Kali-Yuga, but who was an Āryan by birth. By these considerations it is clear, I think, that a correct description of the Indian history is impossible without being aware of the notion of reincarnation that can be traced back already to the Indus civilization (cf. chapter I.7).

---

[40] The time of the Brāhmaṇas according to astrological data found therein ranges from 1820 till 860 ante. Cf. A.B. Keith, Rig-Veda Brahmanas, New Delhi 1981, p. 49. Keith refers to A. Weber's Indische Studien V.64.

2. The evidence of a bilingual

For any decipherment a working hypothesis is necessary to begin with.[41] With the help of the hypothesis that the Indus seals contain mantras of the Ṛg-Veda I was able to translate practically all the inscriptions logographically. There remained a great amount of ambiguity in regard to the pictographic as well as to phonetic value of the signs, however. A bilingual would allow us to state with security, which language was spoken in the area of the Indus Valley at that time. With regard to the shortness of the Indus inscriptions the greatest hope to find one is to discover a name written in two languages. This has already been helpful in deciphering other scripts like the Egyptian. The only name that is known in this field is Meluḫḫa[ki], the Akkadian name for the civilization at the Indus river. The name appears on an Akkadian cylinder seal that has been interpreted by M. Tosi[42] and A. Parpola.[43] The signs of the name being written vertically on the seal are equal to 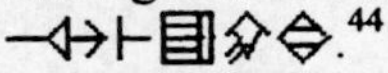.[44] The syllable ḫa is rendered here by the sign  that originally meant a fish. In the same position a fish is found in the second line of the inscription of the Failaka seal 9702, included in Tosi's article (Aachen, fig. 99), that is reproduced on the following page:[45]

---

[41] This method is also enjoined by M. Jansen. Cf. Non-contemporaneity of the contemporaneous in the Indus Culture, in: G. Possehl, op. cit., p. 200.

[42] Cf. Die Indus-Zivilisation jenseits des indischen Subkontinents, in: Vergessene Städte am Indus, p. 119 (fig. 97/Boehmer 557).

[43] Op. cit. (1994), p. 132. For the illustration of the seal cf. p. 77 of this volume.

[44] For the correct reading and explanation of the Akkadian signs I thank R.K. Englund, Berlin.

[45] The seal was first published and explained by P. Kjærum, Failaka/Dilmun, Aarhus 1983, p.119 (fig. 279).

Parpola, following Kjærum's explanation, takes only the five pictograms in the upper line as an inscription, which he renders as 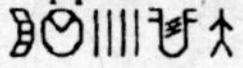 in the Finnish Concordance II (read in the direction from right to left of the impression). Since the position of the man-sign is at the end normally, in particular when it follows a cup-sign, we shall try to read the signs from left to right here or from right to left of the original as rendered under the image. This would also agree with the Akkadian way of writing. The three pictograms of the lower line can be identified as Sumerian. If the first two signs of the first line are in correspondence with the first sign of the second line, we may obtain a bilingual of the name of Meluẖẖa as indicated by the fish-sign. Since the fish-sign renders ẖa, the other signs of the second line must be read as 'ma/me' and as 'luẖ/laẖ'.

The equivalence of 'me' on the Akkadian seal is a pictogram that is explained in A. Deimel's *Sumerian Dictionary* as a mouth with an outstretched tongue. Obviously, the lower part of the sign can be interpreted as a mouth. It is also a rendering of the second sign of the first line, where the lips are expanded and the face is turned upside down. The tongue is missing, instead we find two lines that can be interpreted as rows of teeth. The line at the right corresponds with the first sign of the upper line. As an Indus sign, it must be written with parallel curves on both sides that are connected with each other at the end and in between. Nevertheless it could be interpreted as a row of teeth like the similar sign  that is regarded by Parpola as the pictogram of the comb, but which means woman, because the comb is a symbol of the womb or the vagina dentata (cf. Preface, note 3). The comb with its teeth is not only associated with beauty in the Veda and the goddess of Dawn in particular, but also with swallowing. It has the same capacity as the ocean, which is also a female symbol and whose waves are called teeth. In the ancient civilizations woman is not only regarded as giving life, but also as taking it.

The curved variant may also be interpreted as the crescent of the moon that is regarded as female, too. At any rate this sign contains magical power that was called 'me' by the Akkadians. To get the reading luḫ or something similar the main part of the sign can be related to the pictogram for the rising sun and the double yoke, whose equivalence is laḫ$_2$.[46] According to Deimel it means light, which recalls the Sanskrit root *ruc*, to shine.
If the second sign of the first line is read as a mouth, it can also mean to speak. Its Sanskrit equivalent is vac with the weak stem uc. This is contained in the second syllable of Meluḫḫa. Hence the first sign of this line must be read as the equivalence of mel. The only Vedic word that fulfils the necessary requirements in this connection is mr̥dhra (vāc) that we have mentioned already as denomination of the language of the Dasyus. Mr̥dhra means enemy. This means that it can be identical with the language of the Asuras that are the enemies of the gods in the later portions of the Veda. The first sign of this line could be read as Asura, if we identify it as the moon or the Soma who is several times called Asura in the Veda.[47] This would mean that it is used here like the related horse-sign . The first two signs of the upper line can hence be read as mr̥dhra-vāc, language of the Asura, or mr̥dhra ucyate, the language of the Asura is spoken (there).
The following stroke-sign of the first line is certainly a number-sign. Together with the triangle at the bottom that can be interpreted as a thumb we get the number five, pañca in Sanskrit. The penultimate sign can be read as river, the two additional strokes as water. Water is called ap in Sanskrit and Pañcāb means land with five rivers. This is still the name of the area at the river Indus. The last sign can be read as man directly. The whole line renders then *man from Pañcāb, (where) Mr̥dhrā (the language of the Asuras) is spoken.* This is equal to Akkadian Meluḫḫa. The last sign, another triangle, can be interpreted as the equivalent for lord, belu, which in Akkadian is used in relation to

[46] Op.cit. sign 684 and 700.

[47] Cf. R̥V IX.71.2, IX.74.7, IX.99.1. On the seal 9002 from Ur the sign occurs in an inscription that can be related to R̥V IX.71.2 (cf. sign-dictionary).

gods and distinguished men. Hence the logographic and phonetic value of the signs of the lower line would be *Meluḫḫa belu - distinguished man of Meluḫḫa.*[48]

The Akkadian name Meluḫḫa can also be related to Baluchistan, now the southern province of Pakistan. In the Veda, the land at the Indus river is called Sapta Sindhu, Seven-river-land. This denomination occurs only once, however. Like other peoples, the Āryans did not feel it necessary to designate the land, where they lived.

Apart from the reading mleccha that does not occur in the Veda, the Akkadian name could be derived from madhu-kṣā, land of honey, whose components occur in the Veda. This reading is suggested by the identical inscription  of the Indus seals 9102, found in the Mesopotamian town Kiš, and seal 2502 (M-228) found in Mohenjo Daro. Both seals have the motif of the unicorn. The first sign can be read as a bee called madhukara in Sanskrit.[49] Madhu, sweet or honey, is a name of the Soma. The pressing of the Soma-plant formed the centre of the Vedic sacrifice. The field-sign would render kṣā, place, abode, the cup-sign sthāna, standing, living. The three signs would then render Madhu-kṣā-sthāna, 'living in the land of honey'.[50] This would designate the owner of the seal. The unicorn of this seal and the bull of the Failaka seal may both be explained as an

---

[48] In the context of the R̥g-Veda, the inscription can be read according to V.63.4 addressed to the gods Mitra and Varuṇa: *You veil the sun through a cloud, through the rain at the sky, Parjanya, (now) your sweet drops burst forth!* Parjanya is a name of the rain-god. He is equal to the man-sign. The first sign can be read as a veil, the second as the sun, the third as the streams of rain falling from the sky, the accented cup-sign renders the drops of Parjanya.

[49] S.R. Rao reads the sign  as bee (Dawn and Devolution p. 258). All Indus pictogram have to be read, however, in a symbolic meaning. Therefore it must be found out, what the bee (or fly) stands for. In the Veda the fly is a symbol of the Dawn (cf. R̥V I.124.4).

[50] Affiliated to a Vedic hymn this incription could be read as: *The sweet Soma is purified on the sieve for the gods* (IX.61.9). The field-sign would render the sieve then, in which the Soma is purified, the cup-sign Indra. The reading of the fish-sign as Soma is confirmed by several similar inscriptions.

image of the Soma often compared with a bull in the Veda. Sweetness represents its female, the bull its male aspect.

The unicorn is the most frequent motif of the Indus seals. It has the body of a bull and the head of a goat or horse. The Vedic name of the goat is aja, whose second meaning unborn is equal to amr̥ta, immortal. The lines on its neck look like the cloth that domesticated horses often wear. Recent finds confirm that the horse was domesticated in the Indus civilization. In the Veda the unicorn is replaced by the horse, the deer or the bull. In R̥V IV.58.3 the bull of Soma is said to have four horns, three feet, two heads and seven hands or parts. It can be compared to the composite animal found on several Indus seals (cf. chapter IV). On seal 8630 this animal is associated with the standard normally found in front of the unicorn (cf. chapter I.7). The animal on seal 8630 has only one head, but there are seals with a unicorn bearing two additional heads.

Likewise, the single horn might have been attached to the unicorn from artistical reasons. This assumption is supported by Assyrian seals from the 8th century ante, where a winged unicorn with the body of a gazelle is depicted.[51] Some scholars believe that the unicorn is an urus that appears to have one horn only, because it is looked upon in profile as in the case of the bull on Sumerian seals of the Uruk period. Inspite of its one horn, the Sumerian animal is definitely a bull, however, whereas the unicorn is always a different animal, even when it has two horns, as it happens in a few cases.

The reading of the name Meluẖẖa^{ki} is also warranted by the square seal 9000 found in Ur.[52] It bears the three Akkadian signs ◁═⊟← separated from the bull-motif by a partly dotted line. The bull looks to the left in the impression, as on the Indus seals. The signs render, when read in the Akkadian way from left to right, the meaningless word sak-ku-ši. Read

---

[51] Cf. Frankfort, pl. XXXV. The unicorn appears as a composite animal in Europe, China and Japan. It has the elements of a horse, a bull and a deer. In Christian symbolism it is an image of Christ like the deer. Cf. K. Sälzle, Tier und Mensch, Gottheit und Dämon, München 1965, p. 294, 301.

[52] Cf. C.J Gadd, Seals of Ancient Indian Style found at Ur, London 1932, p. 194. A better photograph is given by A. Parpola (1994), p. 131.

in the direction of the Indus script from right to left, however, the first sign is equal to me_4 or ba_2,[53] the second to luḫ as on the Akkadian seal mentioned above. The last sign can be read as sak, head, or ka, mouth.[54] It could also be divided into two. The first half would then be equal to the fish, ḫa, the last half to land, ki.

We have got only the values of six signs through the reading of these two seals, but the cup-sign is the most frequent sign of the Indus script and the mouth-sign, the man-sign, the bee-sign and the field-sign are also quite frequent. Though the unaccented cup-sign invariably appears at the end of the inscriptions, it seems to be difficult to affiliate it to a word in the list arranged after the final letter in Grassmann's *Wörterbuch zum Rig-Veda.* This is in particular the case with the ending sthāna.

If we assume its reading as ha, because this is the last letter of the Sanskrit alphabet, we face the difficulty that this syllable has no word-meaning in Vedic Sanskrit as it has in Sumerian. There is, however, the related syllable hu meaning to pour in (the sacrificial draught). This meaning could be appropriate for the cup-sign. Besides, the form of the cup-sign is similar to that of the last letter of the Greek alphabet Ω, when turned upside down. In the Hittite script, this sign denotes without the strokes on the top the letter a and together with them the syllables hi and hu. Read from the right as a-(ha), it is identical to the first letter of the Sanskrit alphabet. Thus, it incorporates all letters and syllables like the chest incorporating the breath. By its form, the cup can have abstract and concrete meaning, it can represent male and female, subject and object, noun and verb, matter and spirit, as is obvious from the sign-dictionary.[55] Apart from the particular meaning in a

---

[53] Cf. Sumerisches Lexikon, sign 112.

[54] Cf. Sumerisches Lexikon, sign 894 and 15/194.

[55] The cup-sign is found in the 'priest alphabet' of the sunken continent of Mu and on a Maya tablet published by J. Churchward (Mu, Der versunkene Kontinent, Aitrang 1990, p. 41,184). Ch. explains the sign as hole, abyss (p. 185). This is certainly not the main meaning it has in the Indus script, because this would be in contradiction with its frequency. Though reading the signs in a symbolic way, Ch. did not take notice of their multivalence.

certain context the reading of the two signs shows that the Indus signs can be read logophonetical.

Nowadays a letter script is taken to be an advance to a word writing, but this judgement is entirely based on the values of an economic society without a religious background. The attempt to read the Indus signs as letters cannot be successful, as it does not take notice of the symbolic way in which the Indus priests thought, even if the words obtained in this way are found in the Ṛg-Veda or in the Atharva-Veda and the Nirukta. It is also contradictory to the structural analysis of the script.[56] There is no reason either to read the signs on the ground of the Old Semitic script, as Rao suggests,[57] since it is known that the first letter-script in India, the Brāhmī, was developed at least 700 years after the end of the Indus culture.

3. Short inscriptions (one to six signs)

The method applied in reading the Failaka-seal and the Kiš-seal on the ground of the Ṛg-Veda proved to be successful also in case of many other inscriptions. In the course of this study it was confirmed that not only the cup-sign, but also other signs with lesser frequency have several meanings. This cannot be otherwise in the case of a word script, it is even found with syllabic writings. Deimel mentions in the preface of his *Sumerian Dictionary* 26 signs for syllable 'ge', 12 for 'gi'. The ambivalence of the signs applies to a certain extent to sequences, too. On the other hand, their consistent meaning is a great help for the decipherment.

Which sign was taken for a certain word, was up to the writer, it seems, if it could only be justified by the pictographic meaning. Sanskrit offers many possibilities in regard to homophony and synonomy, that are far from infinite, however. The greatest difficulty is to find the most appropriate verse for a certain inscription in the bulk of the 1000 Vedic hymns. The Vedic reading of the Failaka-seal and the Kiš-seal (cf. note 48 and 50) were found out only at the end of a long study. Even with the help of the Veda not all inscriptions are readable. At least we need an 'indicator' to start with.

---

[56] Cf. I. Mahadevan, Recent Advances in the Study of the Indus Script, Purātattva 9.1973, p. 41.

[57] Cf. Dawn and Devolution, p. 214.

To illustrate that this method of reading the Indus inscriptions works and how it works we shall study at first several seals with one sign only. Apart from early Harappan graffiti and pot-marks where the script is still in a rudimentary stage, inscriptions with a single sign are rare.[58] It seems to be impossible to get more than a name from such an inscription, but we have to consider that the sign is a compound generally as in the case of the elephant-seal 2058 (M-1162)  and the five unicorn-seals 5131 , 1292 , 3089 , 4678 (H-481)  and 2704 (M-842) . On the tiger-seal 3246 (H-94) the man-sign is combined with a navel-sign .

The man-sign on the elephant-seal can be regarded as a symbol of the Puruṣa, the cosmic man. The man wears a girdle that indicates his female aspect, the hoofs stand for his animalic aspect. Thus he represents the principle of unity in diversity. This notion directs us to ṚV X.90.10:

Out of him (the Puruṣa) came forth the horses,
the animals with long teeth at both sides,
the cattle, the goats and the sheep.

The animal with long teeth on both sides can only be the elephant, because it is domesticated and lives on plants like cattle.

The principle of unity in diversity is also depicted in the compounds of the unicorn-seals. On seal 5131 it is rendered in a geometrical way, the upper bar can be explained as unity or oneness, the cross as diversity, the world with its four directions. This is contained in ṚV X.72.4c: *From Being came forth the universe.* The field-sign with additional strokes on seal 1292 can be read as puriṣa, humidity, which is a name of the cosmic father with many forms in ṚV I.164.12. The main sign on seal 3089 can be explained as a thigh. This leads us to ṚV X.72.4ab: *When it (the cosmic energy) spread apart its legs Being came forward.* The two oblique strokes that can be derived from the step-sign  are equal to spread apart. The whole compound renders the name of Uttānapad, (she, who) spreads the legs apart.

---

[58] The most frequent singularity is the tree-sign. On some seals it is inscribed on a gazelle or deer.

The cosmic energy is conceived as female in this hymn, whereas the unicorn is male, but its power can be regarded as female, too, in particular because it is a wondrous animal. On seal 4678 the Puruṣa is rendered by the man-sign with a staff indicating his age, the triangle or bag, that he draws behind him, can be read as the cosmic energy. It can be identified with Agni, the Vedic fire-god. The Christian Santa Claus has been modelled after this sign, it seems. A Vedic explanation of this compound is given in X.90.2: *The Puruṣa is the Lord (of the draught) of immortality, when he ascends through food beyond (food).* Food includes energy.

On seal 3246 the female aspect of the cosmic man is symbolized through the navel or bosom. His male and the female aspects are both mentioned in ṚV X.72.5 and X.90.5, where the female is born by his male and the male by his female aspect. The compound sign on seal 2704 can be interpreted as a plough or harrow and a hand at the back. This directs us to ṚV X.101.3: *Harness the ploughs/the harrows, put the yokes (on the oxen)!* In this hymn the creation of the universe is repeated ceremonially. The standard in front of the unicorn looks like a Soma-stalk on this seal.

The reading of all these inscriptions is based on the same cosmic principle: unity in diversity. This principle can be expressed in various ways. The Puruṣa can be represented by a bull or unicorn like the Soma. Like the Puruṣa the Soma is conceived as male and female in the Veda.

These two aspects of the cosmic man may also be represented in the early Harappan graffiti and on neolithic cave paintings. The cross-signs and the rhombus-signs which we find there can be interpreted as a symbol of the female organ and of the fire-place. The female organ is an aspect of Agni according to the Five-Fire-Doctrine of the Bṛhad Āraṇyaka Upaniṣad.[59]

On account of seal 4678 I have formerly affiliated the five unicorn-seals to the first verse of the Agni-hymn I.1. Obviously, the rule that different signs can have the same meaning can easily lead to a wrong interpretation. My former logographic interpretation of the compound of seal 2704 was also wrong though it led to an interpretation that agrees with X.101.3.

---

[59] For the neolithic signs in Indian and European caves cf. E.O.Tillner, Die Edakal Höhle im Ambukuthy Crack am Battery Rock, Jahrbuch der Gesellschaft für vergleichende Felsbildforschung, Graz 1981/82, p. 87. Cf. chapter II.

We shall now study the inscription  of markhor-seal 2606 (M-1179) as an example for two signs. The markhor is a goat with spiral horns. It lives until now in the Western Himalayas. Since the animal has a human face regularly, it may be a symbol of a god. For this reason, the two signs can be read as the streams of Soma running in the cup, the Soma being represented by the two curves. The Vedic name of the markhor is avika, derived from avi, wool. It is mentioned in ṚV I.126.7 as *a sheep of the Gandhārīs*. The verse records the words of a young girl addressed to the hundred years old seer Kakṣīvat, the author of the hymn, who obtained the girl together with horses and cows as a present from the king after having carried out a great sacrifice for him. It shows that such a donation is an old custom in India. A maiden together with cattle is given as a present to the sage Ṛṣyaśṛṅga, after he has procured rain for King Romapada as told in the Rāmāyāṇa and in other Indian literature. The words of the girl are rendered as:

upa_upa me parā mṛś   mā me dabhrānṇi
sarvāham asmi romaśā   gandhārīṇām iva_avikā
Come near and embrace me closely!
Do not believe that I have few (hairs);
I am full of hairs like a sheep of the Gandhārīs.

Romaśā, full of hairs, is also the name of the girl. The Gandhārīs are probably identical to the Gandhāras, after whom the Graeco-Buddhist style of art is named. The name of the king Romapada (hair-footed) is related to romaśā. The girl mentions her pubic hairs because it was forbidden in ancient India to have sexual intercourse with a girl, whose pubic hairs were not yet grown (cf. Geldner's note).

The seer Kakṣīvat is reported to have said to the girl in the previous verse I.126.6:

āgadhitā parigadhitā   yā kaśīkeva jaṅgahe
dadati mahyaṃ yādurī   yāśūnāṃ bhojyā śatā
Who holds tight, who embraces closely,
who hides like a female ichneumon (in the wood),
the voluptuous one gives me hundreds of joys.

The erotic frankness of the dialogue is not surprising for the Veda, where sexual allusions are frequent. It could have inherited this feature from the Indus tradition. With regard to his age, the author of this hymn may have expected a negative answer of the girl. Regrettably, his reaction to her love declaration has not been recorded. But from the stories of Ṛṣyaśṛṅga and of Agastya, with whom we shall deal in the next paragraph, we can deduce that he lived together with her for the rest of his life.

With regard to this hymn the cup-sign can be read as *hair of the pudenda*. The two curves would signify *embrace me closely*. It is also possible, however, to read the inscription in regard to the Soma. Then we can affiliate it to ṚV IX.74.9: *Mixed with water, purified Soma, your sap flows over the wool of the sheep (in the vat)*. The meaning is almost as erotical as in the other verse. Only the personal relation is missing here. Moreover, the two signs can be read as the name of the author of the hymn I.126, Kakṣīvat.

No wonder that there are a lot of inscriptions related to the same verse. The joy of the old man was unbounded to find a girl like Romaśā, who was to him like the Dawn to the Father of the sky (cf. chapter V). There is nothing to be upset about. The relation of God to the virgin Mary in the New Testament is of the same kind. The only problem is that men do not recognize the mythological character of these stories and try to be like God himself including using violence, and that many young women believe to have the right to seduce an old man like the Dawn.

That the dialogue had a spiritual dimension is also obvious from the human face of the markhor. Moreover, there is the related motif of a composite animal with human face that we shall discuss in chapter IV. On seal 2258 (M-301) we find the two signs 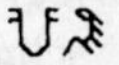 together with this motif that can be read in the same way as the inscription on seal 2606.

A long inscription ending with these two signs is found on seal 6115 (L-66) with a rather decrepit unicorn. The inscription on the obverse and five single signs on the borders read: 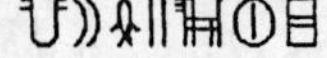 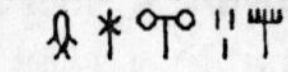. The five single signs can be related to I.126.5ab: *After the first donation I (the singer Kakṣīvat) obtained three yoked cars.*

The main inscription is equal to I.126.7. The first sign can be read as to hold tight (like two pressing boards), the second sign represents the embracing vulva, the third sign stands for the markhor, the two long strokes render the place of Gandhāra, the fish-sign represents the seer Kakṣīvat again, here in the sense of to believe. I am full of hairs is equal to the last two signs.

Three signs are found for example on the unicorn-seals 1038 (M-8) 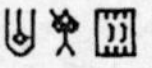 and 3042 (H-29) . The first two signs are identical. It can be inferred from the guardian-sign that the inscriptions have to do with Rudra. A name of Rudra is Vāstoṣpati, lord of the house or the homestead. This can be expressed by the initial field-sign. In R̥V VII.54.2 Vāstoṣpati is called Soma. This is a reading of the final sign in 1038. The Soma was used as a medicine. The last sign in seal 3042 can be regarded as an amulet that served for protecting the bearer like a medicine (cf. chapter I.1). Hence we can read the inscriptions as: *May Rudra protect our house and cattle* (I.43.6).

Another example of an inscription with three signs is found on the unicorn-seal 5030 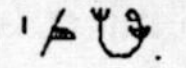. Its equivalence is found in verse 4 of R̥V X.129, the most famous cosmogonic hymn of the Veda, starting with the famous words *there was neither being nor non-being in the beginning*. The first half of verse 4 reads:

> *kāmas tad agre samavarta_adhi*
> *manaso retaḥ prathamaṃ yad āsīt*
> *In the beginning it felt desire, this was the first seed of thought.*

The initial compound can be explained as a flower and a hand or pillar, the second sign as a sprout which is equal to inclination or desire (cf. German Trieb, Antrieb). The flower is a female, the hand or pillar is a male symbol. The inclination of the male for the female was the first seed of thought rendered by the single stroke at the end.

Four signs are found in the inscription of the zebu-seal 1339 (M-1108): . In my former logographic reading I have affiliated them to the Viṣṇu-hymn R̥V I.155. This god is known for his three steps. He is identified with the cosmic man in the Brāhmaṇas and could be indicated by the third sign. The second sign does not represent Viṣṇu, however, but Rudra.

Rudra has to do with the number three only in later times, when he is replaced by Śiva. In the Veda, it is the bull Viśvārūpa, who has three faces according to III.56.3. This bull is an image of the creator-god, but not of Rudra, who is not the creator, but the liberator, the one who transcends creation. Besides, the cosmic man has three steps, and in his form as father of the sky he begets Rudra in the primordial incest with his daughter, the Dawn, according to ṚV X.61.7 (cf. chapter V). Rudra has a special affinity to the draught of immortality, the amṛta, according to ṚV X.136.6. The longest hymn directed to Rudra is II.33. In verse 9 of this hymn his asuraship is pointed out as never being lost:

īśānād asya bhuvanasya bhūre na vā u yoṣad rudrād asuryam
Never will Rudra, the lord of this great world,
be deprived of the dignity of his asuraship.

The three strokes can be read as the three worlds, replaced by great world in the hymn. The guardian-sign represents Rudra. The horned man-sign stands for lord, the cup-sign for asuraship that is illustrated on the seal by the majestic zebu. The same four signs are found on the unicorn-seal 1116, followed by the woman-sign. It shows that the asuraship has a female component like the Puruṣa. The word for Asura is used here in an abstract form as expressed by the English suffix -ship. The negation is not written on the seal, because it does not change the meaning of the sentence, if it is expressed in the affirmative voice.

The reading of the two seals is questioned by the inscription on the sealing 6170 (L-180) that has the same three signs as seal 1339, but two strokes instead of three in the beginning. The world can also be rendered by two strokes as idam (this), however. The strokes can also refer to Rudra's lordship and asuraship. In this case this world is omitted.

A similar sequence is found on the inscription of the buffalo-seal 2696 (M-1127), though the man-sign is replaced by a bird in brackets  written as  in the Finnish concordance. The inscription has the two additional signs  in a separate line. The compound sign can be interpreted as a bird in its nest. The bird is obviously of a bigger species, probably an eagle or falcon. If the first sign of this inscription is interpreted as the world, the second sign as demonstrative pronoun and the eagle in the nest as Asura, we arrive at the same Vedic verse.

These readings are further questioned by the inscription of the unicorn-seal 2632 with the same four signs as on seal 1339 at the end. In the beginning we find the three signs 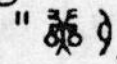, however. The moon-sign directs us to the first part of this verse of II.33.9:

sthirebhir aṇgair pururūpa ugro
babhruḥ śukrebhir pipiśe hiraṇyair
The reddish one, who has many forms and strong limbs,
the terrifying adorns himself with the golden ornament.

The reddish one is identical to the sign of the crescent of the moon. The moon has sometimes a reddish colour. The two strokes indicate the two possible readings of the water-carrier-sign: Having strong limbs and having many forms. Like the goddess of Dawn, otherwise written by this sign, Rudra wears a golden ornament and he has a terrifying aspect that is even more prominent with him than with the goddess.

Seals without motif are by no means less important than those with a motif. An example for this is the seal 2515 (M-1336). Its inscription 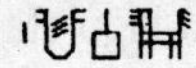 can be affiliated to verse 4 of the Soma-hymn IX.83:

As the Gandharva he (the Soma) guards his place.
The wondrous one guards the births of the gods.

This means that the Gandharva and the Soma are virtually identical, though they are different in their function. The Gandharva is written by the first sign that is modelled after the centaur whom we find on the seals 7038 and 7040 (cf. chapter III.2). Guarding his place corresponds to the second sign. Here the hand-sign that goes together with the field-sign generally has been omitted. The births of the god are rendered by the cup-sign here, the number three is equal to thirty or thirty three which is the number of the gods given in later time. For the wondrous one we get the single stroke as place-holder representing the drop of Soma.

In concluding this paragraph we shall study the round seal 1309 (M-416) with five signs and the unicorn-seal 3006 (H-6) with six signs. Round seals are very seldom in the Indus Valley. Therefore we can interfere that the inscription of seal 1309  has a cosmic connotation. Its equivalence can be expected hence in the cosmogonic hymn I.164. This hymn contains a lot of numbers in relation to the year and its parts, months, weeks and days. The second half of verse 5 of this hymn reads:

On the one-year-old calf the seers drew up
the seven threads to weave with them.

The six strokes and the single stroke render the seven threads, to draw up is written by the hand-sign. The horse-sign can be read as the calf that is equal to the year, the last sign is equal to a loom or something similar.

Seal 3006 has the signs 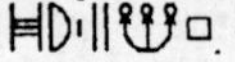. The second sign is certainly depicting a plant or tree, it appears together with the leaf-sign on seal 3862, but there is no sufficient reason to explain is as the banyan tree as I formerly did induced by Parpola.[60] Since the sign follows twice a square-sign and since the crab-sign is often placed in the middle of it and because of the form of the 'berries', it can represent the vibhītaka tree, whose fruits were used as dice. The flower-cup of these trees is nearly identical to this sign, only the number of the pistils have been reduced from five to three. By cross-checking it was corroborated that most of the inscriptions with this sign can be affiliated to the die-hymn, ṚV X.34 (cf. sign-dictionary).

The inscription of seal 3006 can be read according to X.34.1:

The trembling ones from the high (tree) born by the storms
intoxicate me, when they roll on the dice-board excavation;
like a draught of Soma from the hill of Muñjavan
the Vibhītaka nuts that keep awake appear to me.

The first sign stands for the trembling dice, the second for the vibhītaka tree, the two long strokes render the storms, the small stroke stands for me, the bow-sign for the intoxicating womb and dice-board excavation, the last sign renders to keep awake (like a hard bed). The single stroke can also represent the number one of the die that designated the worst throw (X.34.2). The Vedic dice were oblong and had only four numbers. The dice that have been found in Mohenjo Dharo (called Muñjavan here) are square, have five or six numbers and are made from ceramic, a material which was not to be had in later Vedic times (cf. chapter IX).

---

[60] Op. cit. (1994), p. 240-246. Cf. Interpreting the Indus Script, Helsinki 1974, p.14.

4. Narrative motifs

The motif of a seal or tablet can be of great help for the decipherment of the inscription. This will be illustrated in detail in the following chapters, but to demonstrate how far it will take us we shall study here the four-sided tablet 2719 (M-1431). The fourth side is almost totally worn, but probably a unicorn with the standard and two human beings, one standing and the other one sitting like those on tablet 3304, are on the left of this side. At the right could be a three-headed animal like that on tablet 2734 or a man and an animal in cohabitation as on tablet 1574. In the middle of the third side two persons are engaged in pressing Soma, a branch of an acacia growing over their heads. At the left two goats eat from a pipal tree, at the right a person seems to dance in front of a Soma-vessel. On the second side a file of three animals (unicorn, elephant and rhino) with two birds and a crocodile above them is found. On the first side four signs can be distinguished that are followed by the motif of the deity on a tree and the tiger. The signs, rather worn, can be restored as 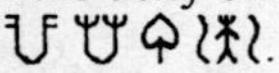.

The Soma pressing on the third side and the two lines enclosing the first sign make it likely that this tablet illustrates the same dual principle that we have come across on the previous seals. The Sanskrit word for the dual or for both is ubha. This leads us to R̥V III.3.11cd:

> *ubhā pitarā mahayann ajāyata_*
> *agnir dyāvāpr̥thivī bhūri retasā*
> *Raising both parents, heaven and earth,*
> *that are rich in seed, Agni was born.*

Ubhā pitarā mahayan, raising both parents, corresponds to the first sign. Agni ajāyata, Agni is born, is written by the leaf-sign, because Agni is generated in the wood. Bhūri retasā, rich in seed, is equal to the womb-sign and the cup-sign referring to mother and father.

We do not find any explanation for the motif of the tablet in this verse or in other verses of this hymn. For this purpose it is necessary to study the two-sided tablet 2761 (M-1400). On the obverse it is inscribed with the last three signs of tablet 2719 together with a markhor, on the reverse with the signs 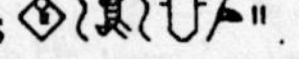. The first sign of the inscription on the obverse may have been damaged, but we can take the markhor instead of it and read it like the first compound on tablet 2719.

The sign between the brackets is again almost unreadable, but on account of its shape it is most probably the horse-sign that can represent the Soma or his magic power.[61] The two strokes at the beginning of this line seem to confirm the affiliation to R̥V III.3.11, but there is another Vedic verse similarly starting with ubhau: R̥V I.179.6c. In this hymn the relation between the famous seer Agastya and his wife Lopāmudrā is described. In verse 6, the last verse, the poet says:

Agastyaḥ khanamānaḥ khanitraih
prajām apatyaṃ balam icchamānaḥ
ubhau varṇāv r̥ṣir ugraḥ pupoṣa
satyā deveṣva_āśiṣo jagāma
Agastya, digging with (wooden) pegs,
desired children, descendants and power;
both colours the mighty seer let bloom,
with the gods his desires became true.

If the second half of the verse agrees with the inscription on the reverse, that on the obverse must be affiliated to the first half. The man-sign can obviously be identified with Agastya. The horns are a symbol of divinity suitable for a Vedic seer. The curved lines that can be regarded as furrows are equal to khanamāna, digging. The leaf-sign can stand for the pegs, because their material was taken from a tree. The penultimate sign can be regarded as a compound of two hand-signs that form a womb. Therefore it can be read as to ask (as a beggar does) or to desire. The cup-sign renders children, descendants and power. The second sign of the second line is a nose or beak obviously. Hence it can be read as varṇa, colour or caste. The caste depends for a great deal on the nose. The cup-sign can be read as mighty, the horse-sign in brackets as making furrows by magic power. The last compound, whose parts are ◇ and , can be read as a vulva also called flower, puṣpa, whose verbal form is pupoṣa, he lets bloom (the two colours or aspects of being).

[61] In Parpola's transcription (1994,. p. 70) the sign looks like the head of a bear. Franke-Vogt (op. cit. plate 31) transforms it into a fish upside down. Both renderings are quite unlikely.

On the ground of this hymn the motifs of tablet 2719 become understandable now. The tiger on the first side can be explained now as a symbol of Agastya, the person on the tree as Lopāmudrā. She is a substitute of the goddess of wisdom, Vāc. The file of animals on side two can be a symbol of descendancy, the crocodile and the birds of initiation (cf. chapter XI). The person at the right of side three in front of the Soma-vessel is Agastya again. Lopāmudrā is the gazelle or goat eating from the tree at the left, whereas the tree is Agastya, whose name literally means be (asti) [like] a tree or hill (from aga - not moving).
Both aspects are combined in the remaining initial compound sign  on the broken Kalibangan seal 7077 (K-53). The Soma pressing illustrated in the motif of the third side of tablet 2719 is a simile of cohabitation (cf. ṚV I.28). It is also referred to by the motif at the right corner of side 4. The two persons in the middle are Agastya and Lopāmudrā, too, the unicorn at the left is Agastya again, who is called a *restrained bull* by Lopāmudrā in I.179.4, the standard is a symbol of androgyny here. This means that we have restored even the almost totally obliterated motif of the fourth side with the help of the Veda.
Some 'narrative' seals are without an inscription. Their motif is often identical to the name of Meluẖẖa. This is also the case with the cylinder seal 9006. Here a scorpion follows a bull that is standing before a date tree. The scorpion can be read as mala, explained in Monier-William's dictionary as the 'tip of the scorpion's tail', the bull as ukṣa and the tree as sthāna. Together we get malukṣasthāna. On Akkadian seals the scorpion is an attribute of Ištar who can be identified with the female figure in the upper register of seal 9006. With her legs stretched apart she is giving birth to a tree. At the same time she is beating the bull with a stick. Bull and scorpion are also connected astrologically, Scorpio is opposite of Taurus in the zodiac, where the spring equinox took place in about 2500 ante. This means that the motif states the date of the Indus civilization.[62]

[62] The "astral character" of this seal was hinted at already by C.J. Gadd, op. cit. p. 209. For further discussion cf. chapter VII.1.

5. Long inscriptions

If we do not find an adequate Vedic verse for an inscription, the translation is confined to a pictographic approximation. The longer the inscription, the greater the chance to find an indicator for such a verse. Still there remains a certain amount of ambiguity. It is reduced in proportion to the signs whose pictorial meaning is known already from other inscriptions. The difference between a syllabic and a logographic reading is enlarged, of course, the longer the inscription is. The longest inscriptions that were found so far are on the motifless tablet 2757 (M-495) and on the unicorn-seal 2405 (M-326). On the tablet three sides are inscribed. Since it is rubbed at the corner, a cup-sign was added at the end of the third line:

With regard to the seven strokes I formerly affiliated the inscription to R̥V X.82.2, where the Seven Seers are mentioned, but since it contains many pictograms for Indra, it is preferable to read it according to R̥V I.32. The first line can be read as I.32.3:

vr̥ṣayamāṇo 'vr̥ṇīta somaṃ
trikadrukeṣv_apibat sutasya
ā sāyakaṃ maghavavā_adatta vajram
ahann enaṃ prathamajām ahinam
Filled with desire he [Indra] choose the Soma
and drank three vessels of the pressed one;
the generous one seized the missile, the thunderbolt,
and killed the first-born of the snakes.

The hand-sign in a circle is a symbol for Indra as Vr̥trahan, the killer of Vr̥tra, the first-born of the snakes, represented by the third sign that can be explained as the hood of a cobra. The crab-sign can be read as to seize or to kill. The cup-sign can be read as vr̥ṣayamāṇo, filled with ardent desire. The water-carrier, who is a symbol for Varuṇa and the Dawn normally, can be read as the generous one here. The hand-sign at the end renders to drink here. The three simple cup-signs stand for Soma-vessels. The line can be read literally then as: *Indra, the killer of Vr̥tra, the first-born of the snakes, the generous one, drank, filled with ardent desire, three vessels of the pressed Soma.*

The second line is contained in I.32.12:

> *aśvyo vāro abhavas tad indra*
> *sṛke yat tvā pratyahan deva ekaḥ*
> *ajayo gā ajayo śūra somam*
> *avāsṛjas sartave sapta sindhūn*
> *You became a hair of a horse-tail,*
> *when he struck you back at the tooth, you, the only god;*
> *you won the cows, you won the Soma, o hero,*
> *you set the seven streams free to run.*

The accented cup-sign stands for the hair of a horse-tail and for Indra, the only god, here, the second sign can be read as a tooth in a mouth. The king-sign renders hero. The long strokes surrounding it can be explained as the streams of Soma and also as the cows, Indra has won. The seven strokes and the two curved lines are equal to the seven streams. The banner-sign stands for Indra's thunderbolt, by which he let the (canalized) streams free from the clouds after having drilled them up, as is said in I.32.1. The horned man-sign and the cup-sign are both representatives of Indra.

The third line agrees with I.32.14:

> *aher yātāraṃ kam apaśya indra*
> *hṛdi yat te jaghnuṣo bhīr agacchat*
> *nava ca yan navatiṃ sravantīḥ*
> *śyeno na bhīto ataro rajāṃsi*
> *Whom did you see, Indra, as an avenger of the snake,*
> *that you felt afraid in your heart after having killed him?*
> *You who crossed the ninety-nine rivers*
> *are (now) like an eagle in the air full of fear.*

The first sign, a feathered cross, may stand for revenge, the following long stroke can be read as snake, here. The accented cup-sign stands again for Indra, the stroke can be read as an eye here for to see. The man-sign with arms stemmed up can be read as avenger here. The bird in brackets is equal to eagle in the nest, the nest being a reference to fear here. The ninety-nine rivers are a metaphor for heaven and earth rendered by the following intersected circles. The two long strokes can be read as to cross, the cup-sign stands for Indra again.

The inscription of the unicorn-seal 2405 starting with the three lines written on the borders and followed by the two lines written on the back is:

There is some evidence that this inscription belongs to a Soma-hymn, for the first sign can be read as the teeth of the pressing boards, the single sign as drops of Soma. The two car-signs in the penultimate line can be read as a ship (cf. chapter VII.2). It has often to do with the Aśvins, but in R̥V IX.73.1 the ships are mentioned together with the Soma. Therefore this verse renders a better reading than R̥V X.85.14 that I selected in the former editions induced by a wrong interpretation of the car-signs. The verse reads:

srakve drapsasya dhamataḥ samasvarann
r̥tasya yonā samaranta nābhayaḥ
trin sma mūrdhno asuras cakre ārabhe
satyasya nāvaḥ sukr̥tam apīparam
In the teeth rushed together (the streams) of the bubbling drops,
in the womb of thē (Soma)-ritual the tribes united;
three heads the Asura created to seize (him),
the ships of the truth have brought across the pious.

If the teeth of the first sign are a metaphor for the pressing boards, samasvaran, rush together, can be rendered by the intersected circles. The third line starts with the sign for womb, the tribes are written by the man-sign and a simple cup-sign of smaller size for the vessel in which the Soma was collected. The (former) tribes are called the navels, because the following depend on them. To unite has been rendered by the hand-sign, which means to press at the same time.

The three heads are written by three strokes and the field-sign. The Asura who is also a king, is equal to the king-sign. To seize is rendered by the cross-sign. The Asura has caught the Soma in the whim, the Āryans have learnt to press the Soma from the Asuras that lived in the Indus cities.

The ships of the truth, being a metaphor for the whim, bring the participants of the ritual beyond the dangers of life and beyond the world to immortality. The ship is written by a sign that can be read as the wheels and the post of a car, but for the Vedic seer a ship is a car for the water.

The streams of water are rendered by the long strokes. The oblique stroke stands for to cross. There is no sign for the pious, because it is self-evident that they are the owners of the ships.

The inscription on the obverse of the seal corresponds to IX.73.9ab:

> *ṛtasya tantur vitataḥ pavitra ā*
> *jihvāyā agre varuṇasya māyayā*
> *The thread of the (Soma-)ritual has been stretched over the sieve,*
> *on the top of the tongue, through Varuṇa's creative power.*

The sign of the crescent of the moon has been rendered poetically as the stretched thread of the Soma-ritual, the moon and the Soma being interchangeable. The stroke-sign is used as an indicator of comparison. The cup-sign can be read as sieve here, the additional stroke stands for the drop of Soma. On the top of the tongue is written by the two curves, Varuṇa by the fish-sign with a triangle on the top. For his creative power we get another cup-sign.

Among the long inscriptions a large wooden board with 10 signs excavated recently in Dholavira deserves special attention, one sign is about 40 cm high. Since the inscription is not included in the manuals yet, I give it the number 8352*: 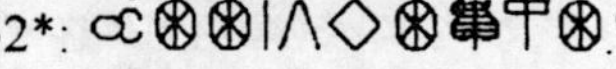.[63] The 'indicator' is the wheel-sign here, because it is repeated four times. It can be supposed that at least one of them refers to Indra, the king of the gods and the god of the monsoon-rain. This would also agree with the size and the place of the board at the entrance of the town. In ṚV I.32.15, the last verse of the hymn, Indra is described in the following way:

> *indro yāto 'avasitasya rājā śamasya ca śṛṅīṇo vajrabāhuḥ*
> *sedu rājā kṣayati carṣīnām arān na nemiḥ pari tā babhūva*
> *Indra is the king of the moving and the standing the resting,*
> *of the animals with and without horn, he who bears the vajra;*
> *indeed, he rules as the king over the peoples,*
> *like the rim the spokes, he encloses them.*

Here we meet with an exact explanation of the wheel-sign and that it is used to designate the king, because he encloses his people like the

---

[63] For an illustration cf. S.R. Rao, Dawn and Devolution,pl. LIV-C. A better photograph has been published by A. Parpola (1994), p. 113.

spokes enclose the rim. The vajra, the thunderbolt, is identical to the second sign. Indra's weapon is also called hammer (ghana; khedrā) in the Veda as it is depicted on the Dholavira board. The standing and the moving are rendered by the tree-sign, the moving aspect is found in the leaves, the standing in the trunk. The next wheel-sign can be read as to rule. The rhombus-sign stands for the earth or the peoples on earth. The step-sign that can be read as a horn and the long stroke render the animals with and without horn. The next two signs have been explained already. The last sign renders to enclose here, which agrees indeed with the pictogram.

The sequence 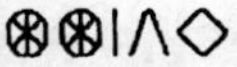 of the Dholavira board occurs also on the two daggers 2798 and 2796 and on the zebu-seal 2119, all from Mohenjo Daro. In front of it are the two signs 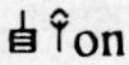 on the daggers as well as on the seal. All inscriptions have a different second line. On seal 2119 it is , on the dagger 2798  and on the dagger 2796 

The zebu can certainly be a symbol of Indra on account of its majesty, the weapons can be related to Indra, too.

The initial compound is equal to a post and the step-sign and renders to stand and to move. The following field-sign replacing the wheel-sign in the Dholavira-board can be explained as an amulet or breast ornament of the king and renders to rule (the peoples).

The three signs of the zebu-seal can be affiliated to ṚV I.32.3a that we have come across already in discussing seal 2757: *Greedy like a bull he chose the Soma.* The nose-sign can stand for greedy, since it can be looked upon as a phallus. The nose is also the sense-organ that plays the most important role among the senses to incite greediness. The step-sign with additional lines can stand for to choose, because Indra runs to the cups of Soma with great speed. The Soma is written by the mortar-sign.

The two additional lines on the weapons can also be affiliated to this hymn. The short strokes can be explained as the pieces into which the snake-demon Vṛtra is crushed by Indra (I.32.7).

The last sign of the dagger 2798 can be regarded as the vertebrae of a snake that are strewn all over the earth like the members of Vṛtra's body. On the dagger 2796 it has been replaced by a single curve. The remaining two signs of the second weapon can both be explained as epithets of Indra that are most frequently used. As explained before, the hand (or phallus) in the circle can be read as Vr̥trahan, killer of Vr̥tra, whose name literally means 'encloser'. The water-carrier can be read as Maghavat, bringing goods or being generous. Here Indra has been invested with the attributes of the Dawn, who is the goddess of luck, too. On the ground of a syllabic reading, I have formerly affiliated these inscriptions to the Soma-hymn IV.27, where Indra plays an important role, but in this case the tree-sign has no pictorial equivalence.

6. Inscriptions of the Late Harappa phase

One of the most important inscriptions belonging to this time is the already mentioned graffito on a jar found in the sea near Dwārkā and brought to the surface by S. R. Rao. The inscription is redrawn by him in the following way:[64]

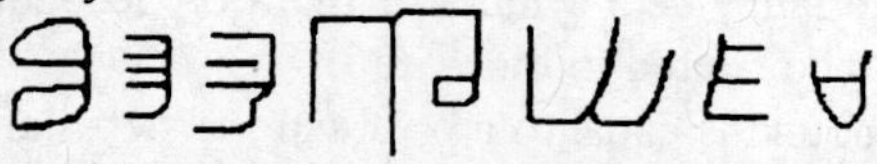

The signs can be explained as an early form of Brāhmī corresponding to the characters 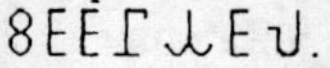. This is equal to ma-ja-ja-nā-ya ja-lam, water for ablution. Transcribed into the signs of the Indus script we obtain 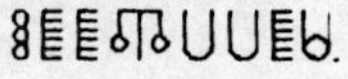. Directed by the root majj we can affiliate these signs to R̥V IX.64.21:

abhi venā anūṣata_ eyakṣanti pracetasaḥ
majjanty_avicetasaḥ
The yearning cry after him (the Soma),
the wise strife for him,
the foolish are drowned.

The first sign representing a phallus can be read as yearning, the woman-sign renders to cry, the two womb-signs represent the Soma, for the wise we get a sign that can be explained as a balance. The following two woman-signs render foolish. The last sign can be read as drowned, since it can be explained as an image of the bubbles made by a person under water.

64 Cf. Dawn and Devolution, pl. XLIX.

Rao believes that the inscription reflects Agni's concealment in the water described in ṚV X.51,[65] but this assumption is neither corroborated by the Brāhmī reading nor by the signs of the Indus script.
Rao's transcriptions of seal 8351 (Rakhigarhi-2) and of the clay tag 0831 (M-1384), which was formerly regarded as coming from Djoka (Umma),[66] are rather misshapen. This is evident from the photographs in CISI I and from the transcriptions of the signs in the concordances. The inscription of seal 8351 given there as 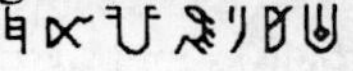 agrees most with ṚV V.85.5:

im amū ṣvāsurasya śrutasya
mahīṃ māyāṃ varuṇasya pra vocam
māneneva tasthivām antarikṣe
vi yo mame pṛithivīṃ sūryena
I will sing now of Varuṇa's,
the far-known Asura's, great magical power:
Taken it as measuring line, standing between heaven and earth,
he has measured out by it the earth through the sun.

The mortar-sign can be a symbol of Varuṇa, because by the vessel turned upside down he has poured out the three worlds (cf. V.85.3). The bow-sign can be read as Asura, the stroke-sign as foremost or far-known. The snake-sign and the cup-sign can be read as magical power. The triangle-sign with an additional stroke is equal to measure out by the sun. The field-sign renders the earth as being measured out. Standing between heaven and earth is omitted here.
The clay tag 0831 has the inscription 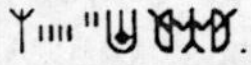. The most prominent gods that carry bow and arrow are Indra and Rudra. On account of the other signs the inscription can be affiliated to ṚV II.33.14cd:

ava sthirā maghavatbhyas tanuṣva
mīḍhvas tokāya tanayāya mṛḷa
May Rudra loosen the tough bow for our generous patrons,
may he be gracious to our children and grandchildren.

---

[65] Ibid, p. 281.

[66] Cf. Vergessene Städte am Indus, fig. 95.

The mortar-sign represents the generous patrons, who prepare Soma in the mortar and offer it to the gods. The next two strokes can be read as the personal pronoun, the children and grandchildren are equal to the four strokes. The hand-sign renders to be gracious.

The Daimabad pottery referred to by Rao as intermediary link[67] is not to be found in the concordances. His intention to prove by these examples that the Indus script became *cursive* at the end of the Indus civilization is only partially supported by the inscriptions. It is true, that the number of the signs and especially of the pictograms is considerably reduced on the copper tablets and on the sealings on clay excavated for the greatest part in Lothal, but the distribution of the signs does not support the assumption that they form an alphabet.

The peculiarity of the copper tablets, that have only been found in Mohenjo Daro, is that inscription and motif are in a fixed relation. But this does not mean that they served for a purpose different from the seals and earthen tablets. The main line of the copper tablet 2815 (M-1452)  for example with the motif of a deer agrees with V.85.5 like tablet 8351: The hand in a circle can be read as measure out the earth, the fish-sign as Varuṇa, the snake-sign and the cup-sign as magical power. The three signs 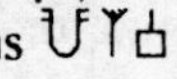 added in a separate line can be read as *The gods are the guardians of the truth*. This is said of Mitra and Varuṇa in ṚV V.63.1 and elsewhere.

It is obvious that the sealings on clay found in a ware-house at Lothal had an economic purpose. But that does not mean that the inscriptions have a secular character, too. Apart from the clay tag just mentioned, there have been found only two more sealings in Mohenjo Daro, 0261 (M-425) and 2725. As an example for the Lothal sealings we shall study now 6092 (L-190), that consists in several cases of the three lines 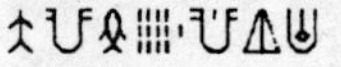 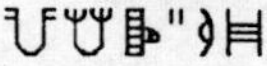 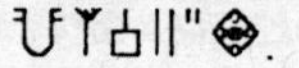. Sometimes the line 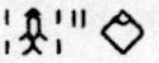 is added to the first line instead of the two other.[68] All lines can

---

[67] Ibid, p. 272.

[68] For the regularities in the sealings from Lothal cf. A. Parpola (1994) p. 114.

be affiliated to verses of the marriage-hymn ṚV X.85, which shows that one of the most important reasons to send goods was a marriage.
The first line agrees with X.85.1:

satyena uttabhitā bhūmiḥ śūryena uttabhitā dhyauḥ
ṛtena ādityās tiṣṭhanti divi somo adhi śritaḥ
By the truth the earth is hold up, by the sun the sky is hold up,
by the (Soma-)ritual the Ādityas exist, is the Soma set at the sky.

The first sign can be read as the first line. The Ādityas, the sons of the earth-goddess Aditi, are rendered by the field-sign, the Soma is rendered by the long strokes representing the pressing boards, to exist or stand is written by the hand-sign, by the ritual is rendered by the cup-sign. The two short strokes are equal to above or the sky. The two padas have been exchanged in the hymn.
The second inscription corresponds to X.85.4:

ācchadvidhānair gupito bārhatair soma rakṣitaḥ
grāvṇām icchaṇvan tiṣṭhasi na te aśnāti pārthivaḥ
Secured by safety devices,
guarded by mightiful powers you are, Soma,
hearing only on the pressing stones.
No mortal ever enjoys you.

The first sign can be read as the safety devices, the second renders the moon or the Soma, the mightiful powers are equal to the wall-sign, the short strokes stand for the two guarding powers. The last two signs correspond to the last line rendered as positive statement: only the gods enjoy the Soma. The pressing stones are omitted.
The third and longest line agrees with X.85.5:

yat tvā deva prabibanti tat ā pyāyase punaḥ
vāyuḥ somasya rakṣitā samānām māsa ākṛtiḥ
When the gods, o god, are drinking you,
you afterwards increase again;
Vāyu is the guardian of the Soma -
the months form the years.

Soma as a god and the moon is rendered by the mortar-sign, the gods are equal to the fire-sign, because they drink from the fire, into which the Soma is offered. To increase is written by the cup-sign with an eye, that can be explained as a fecundated womb. The twelve months that form the year are equal to the respective number-signs. Vāyu, the god of the air, is written by the fish-sign as representative of the stars. Guardian of the Soma is equal to the man-sign and the cup-sign.

The shortest line agrees with X.85.2:

somena ādityā balinaḥ somena pṛthivī mahī
atho nakṣatrāṇām eṣām upasthe soma āhitaḥ
Through the Soma the gods are strong,
through the Soma the earth is wide;
that is why the Soma is set
in the womb of all those stars.

The first sign can be read as heaven (the place of the gods) and earth, the two possibilities are indicated by the short strokes. The Soma as the moon sits like a king in the womb of the stars rendered by the short strokes around the crowned fish-sign.

Sealing 0261 consists of three lines written above each other:

The last sign of line 1 and 3 has been supplemented. The three last signs of the first line obtained in this way are found at the end of 25 other inscriptions, the four signs of the third line occur even in about 50 inscriptions.

The second line directs us again to ṚV V.85.1: *Varuṇa has separated the earth and stretched it out like a hide under the sun.* For separate we get the crab-sign, for Varuṇa the fish-sign, for to stretch the triangle-sign, for the hide the field-sign. The rest is obliterated.

The first line can be affiliated to V.85.4b-d:

yadā dughdaṃ varuṇo vaṣṭyādit
sam abhreṇa vasata parvatāsas
taviṣīyantaḥ śrathayanta vīrāḥ
When Varuṇa wants the sky to be milked the hills clothe in a cloud
and the vigorous men, the winds, rise up.

The line is read from left to right. Varuṇa is equal to the water-carrier-sign, to milk the sky can be written by the hand in a circle. The following compound is equal to the hills clad in a cloud. The man with upraised hand represents the rising winds, whose weapon is the lance.[69] The winds are also rendered by the long strokes. The mortar-sign representing the Soma is equal to vigorous. The vigour of the winds is obtained from drinking Soma.

The remaining inscription of the third line starts with the number-sign for six that corresponds to the three heavens and the three earths. In relation to this hymn it refers to Varuṇa who is said to stand between heaven and earth in V.85.5. The horse-sign can be read as the sun that is often compared with this animal in the Veda. The stroke-sign renders to measure out, the earth is equal to the crossing-sign representing a regularly built town. The cup-sign represents Varuṇa's magic power.

The sequence of the three line does not agree with the sequence of the verses in the Vedic hymn. Obviously the hymn starts again with verse 5 that was perhaps the first verse once.

Varuṇa belongs to the oldest gods of the Veda. He is related to Indra like Cronus to Jupiter. His seats are in the water. Varuṇa is also the god of the ships as is obvious from ṚV X.24.7. Therefore it is not to be wondered at that he plays a prominent role in the inscriptions and that he is referred to in a sealing that probably was carried out on the packing of a merchandise that came by ship.

On the sealing 2725 the sign for the standard (or mortar) is found in the middle of the three repeated remaining signs . The two lines can be affiliated to ṚV IV.58.1, one to two padas each:

samudrād ūrmir madhumān ud arad
upāṃśunā sam amṛtatvam ānaṭ
ghṛtasya nāma guhyaṃ yad asti
jihvā devānām amṛtasya nābhiḥ

[69] On Indian memorial stones a person with upraised hand represents the sati, the women that has let herself burn up on the pyre with her dead husband. The same sign is used for a man that has sacrificed himself for the community. He is called sattā. The upraised hand signifies to rise up to heaven. Sati and sattā are regarded as deified by their deed. Cf. U. Thakar, The History of Suicide in India, Delhi 163. p. 126-160.

From the ocean the sweet wave has come up,
together with the Soma-stalk it has obtained immortality.
That is the secret name of the melted butter,
the tongue of the gods, the navel of immortality.

The net-sign is equal to ocean and melted butter, the mortar-sign to Soma-stalk and tongue of the gods, the inscribed field-sign renders immortality gained by the script. A sign for wave and secret name is missing.

7. The unicorn-standard and the Soma-plant

A standard whose function is unknown is regularly placed in front of the unicorn. Its prototype is found together with a bull on a sherd from Mehi in Baluchistan (Mode, fig. 5). The contrivance has roots here like a tree or plant and the bull is fastened to it. The upper part of the standard has often the form of a net, the lower part looks like a vessel. A small ivory sculpture of the standard, that has recently been excavated in Harappa, shows that it had a round form and holes in the lower part.[70] On account of these features it could be an image of a fire-drill, a mortar or a whim. When regarded as a whim the upper part could be a wind-blast.

On the Mehi sherd we simply find the frame. Obviously, the whim was set in motion by the ox fastened to it. A pipal tree stands behind the standard here. The pipal (ficus religiosa) has been venerated in India until today as the cosmic tree, though it suffocates other trees. Its fruits have berry-form and are sweet like dates. The standard could have been used for pressing these berries to get the sweet Soma juice or madhu. A standard is also found on many Failaka seals.[71] Here the net is at the bottom: .

Mahadevan suggests, that the net represents a filter for the purification of the Soma.[72] In the Sumerian script the net-sign is used as a determinative

---

[70] Cf. Meadow/Kenoyer, Harappa Excavations 1993: The city wall and inscribed materials, in: South Asian Archaeology II, Helsinki 1994, p. 467.

[71] Cf. P. Kjærum, op. cit. fig. 139-148.

[72] Cf. The Sacred Filter Standard Facing the Unicorn, in: South Asian Archaeology I, Helsinki 1994, p. 435. The hairs that are to be seen on the top of the lower part in some cases are explained by him as "the splash of the liquid" (p. 437).

for plants (Deimel sign 593), particularly for a medicinal plant (Akkadian šammu). Since the standard has the form of the crescent of the moon on the Failaka seals we can translate the whole symbol as 'moon-plant'. This is identical to the Soma-plant, for Soma is a name of the moon. The 'hairs' issuing sometimes from the lower part can then be interpreted as the rays of the moon or the stalks of the plant. On several Failaka seals the net-sign appears together with a plant that has pinnate leaves, on others with a temple-door giving it a sacred purpose. The motif of a "tree in a railing", sometimes together with a swastika, is found on several north Indian coins from the time of 300 to 100 B.C.[73] Like the standard it can be explained as a symbol of the cosmic tree (cf. chapter XI). This could be the reason, why the standard has roots on the Mehi sherd. That on the Indus seal the 'net' is placed on top agrees with the normal direction of reading of the Indus inscriptions with several lines, which is from bottom to top, whereas it is from top to bottom on Akkadian seals. When the 'net' is interpreted as a pressing board or stone, we get 'Soma press' for the contrivance.

The whim may also be regarded as a car (cf. note 82). In this way it is described in the marriage-hymn ṚV X.85 and in the Yama-hymn X.135. The ox that drew the whim was supervised by a boy. It was the ox, that did not see, not the boy, as is said in X.135.3.[74] Of the wind-blast a reminiscence is retained in ṚV I.28.6.

If the standard is regarded as a symbol of a fire-vessel, the hairs issuing from the lower part would be the flames. The fire would be generated by moving the upper part in the lower or through the wind-blast. In later Vedic times it was generated by the friction of two sticks, the method of making fire in a vessel was forgotten. We may call that the Gandharvic method, since a fire-vessel was given to Purūravas for a sacrifice, by which he could enter the world of the Gandharvas (cf. chapter VI). Mortars, stands and strainers have been found in fire-

---

[73] Cf. E.J. Rapson, Indian Coins, Straßburg 1897, pl. I.16; III.8-15.

[74] We would arrive at this meaning by changing the nominative apaśyan (from apaśyat) into the accusative apaśyam (from apaśya).

temples in Bactria.[75] In Lothal and Kalibangan fire-altars with vessels in or beside them were excavated.[76]
In the Agni-hymn ṚV VI.7.1,2 the fire, in which the Soma is poured, is compared to a vessel for the gods:

In Agni's mouth the gods made themselves a vessel (pātra);
in the navel of the sacrifice, to the seat of wealth,
in the great vessel (āhāva) they roared together.

In the Vasukra-hymn ṚV X.27.15 the vessel is called sthivi, stand (from the root sthā). It is said that nine seers brought it with them from the west. This could mean that the fire-cult was brought from Persia or Bactria to the Indus Valley. In the same verse seers coming from the three other directions are mentioned. This indicates that the Indus Valley was inhabited by clans coming from different countries and belonging to different races. A description of the standard is contained in the Ṛbhu-hymn ṚV I.110.5:

Like a field (kṣetra) the Ṛbhus measured out
the single yawning vessel with the rod (tejana).

The *field* resembles the upper part of the standard, the *rod* the staff in the middle. *Yawning vessel* can be referred to the lower part. The standard the Ṛbhus constructed is fourfold because it consists of four parts: The 'field' with the upper part of the rod and the vessel with the lower part of it. The standard can also be compared to the monogram of the fire-altar on Kuṣān and Sassanide coins,[77] its lower part resembles the dish-on-stand (Aachen, fig. 185) and the cup-sign.
The tree on tablet 2719c, where the Soma pressing is illustrated looks like a butea frondosa. This tree belongs to the family of the acacias called śami in India. The acacias have generally pinnate leaves. In the Indian concordance the acacia is called kino tree. The kino is a gum-

[75] Cf. V. Sarianidi, Recent Archaeological Discoveries and the Aryan Problem, in: South Asian Archaeology, Stuttgart 1993, p. 252.

[76] Cf. S.R. Rao, Dawn and Devolution, p. 287,289. Rao explains the standard as a fire-altar with flames as the upper part.

[77] R. Göbl, op. cit. KS 1,3,4,7; E 53,71,108,145,160; Marshall pl. CLXIV, 18,19; E.J. Rapson, op. cit. pl. II.12.

like, mostly red, sometimes amber-coloured resin exuding from these trees after the incision of their bark mentioned as 'milking of the Soma' in the Veda. The resin of the acacia delivered probably the astringent variant of the Soma.
The resin of these acacias was called 'gum arabicum' in the West, because it reached Europe via Arabian harbours. The word gum is Egyptian. The Egyptians imported it from India via Eritrea. Mixed with water they used it as ink for their papyri.[78] The Akkadian šammu and the Egyptian gum can both be derived from śami. It is also related to Arabian kimiya, out of which the words alchemy and chemistry developed. What the alchemists searched for, the stone of the wise, i.e. something that could give, if not immortality, at least a long and healthy life, was there already in the form of the Soma. The juice of an acacia tree is chewed in India today together with the betel-nut. It is said that it is refreshing like chewing gum. Surely Soma had an intoxicating effect, too, but it would hardly have it on modern man, since he has become insensible for such simple drugs. The Soma can be compared to cannabis that is produced from the resin of a plant, too.[79] Like cannabis the Soma-plant may have been used for making mats and ropes. This would be another reason for representing it by a net.
In ṚV X.89.5 the Soma is called śimīvat. In the context it should be translated as feathered, literally it means 'like a śimī or śamī'. The śamī is often hostess of the aśvattha, the tree for the fire-sticks. The pinnate leaves of the śamī that are also found on the Failaka seals, look like a feather or like the teeth-sign symbolizing woman, but the resin is regarded as male like the seed. The feather in relation to the Soma-plant is mentioned in ṚV IV.27.4 In ṚV X.89.5 we read: Soma is all shrubs and trees. This agrees with his name vanaspati and vīrudhāṃ pati, king of the trees and plants.

---

[78] Cf. W. Wolf, Die Welt der Ägypter, Stuttgart 1954, p. 29,38.

[79] Cf. J. Herer, Hanf, Frankfurt 1993.

Geldner believes that the Soma-plant belongs to the ephedra-family.[80] Residues of ephedra, poppy and cannabis have been found recently in vessels and mortars in the Zoroastrian temples in Bactria,[81] but this does not mean that the Soma-plant is identical with one of these plants. It seems more likely that these are only the herbs, with which the Soma was flavoured. Moreover, these herbs have neither to do with the fig-tree nor with the acacias which we find on the seals.

The motif of the Mehi-sherd (see below) may also be interpreted as an illustration of the deed of the Vedic king Purūravas, who brought the fire from heaven to the earth in a standing vessel. The bull can be an image of Purūravas, the vessel represents the standard, the tree stands for the forest, where Purūravas forgot the vessel, as told in the Śathapatha Brāhmaṇa. The triangle between the horns of the animal is a symbol of the sun and of the fire-sticks. There are found a number of small drawings together with the main motif that later became signs of the Indus script. One is the comb-sign standing for woman, the second is a wavy line that can be read as water. Water is generally used in the plural in Vedic and later Sanskrit. Together with the comb-sign they render water-woman or Apsaras, whose most prominent in the Veda is Urvaśī. There is another sign on the back of the first bull which can be read as the head of a fish. It is an image of both, Purūravas and Urvaśī, but here it stands for Purūṛavas addressing the water-woman. The five gazelles under the bull can represent Urvaśī's companions. The triangular eye between the horns of the bulls may represent the Venus replaced by Rohiṇī or Uṣas in the Veda. Inside the stomach of the bull some leaves are depicted which the bull has eaten before. The rumination of this animal is a symbol of resurrection like the whim for drawing up water referred to in ṚV X.135.

---

[80] Op. cit. p. 284. An ephedra has also been identified with the Soma-plant by E. D. Caspers (1993, 80,82) on the ground of H. Falk, Soma I and II, London 1989. That ephedras do not appear on Indus seals is explained by her as "sorcery"

[81] V. Sarianidi, op. cit. p. 252, 253)

On a jar from Nindowari (Aachen, fig. 44) the bull is fastened to the trunk of a tree, too. Beside it are twigs, one with leaves of the pipal, the other with leaves of the śamī. There are many teeth-signs and eyes above and under the animal, a meander is painted on its back and a lot of lines are drawn on its belly. The meander can be read as water, the eyes are a female symbol like the teeth. Pipal leaves and eyes are also found on painted urns at the Harappa cemetery (Aachen, fig. 181). Its main motif is the peacock whose tail sometimes looks like a foot. Pad, foot, is homophonous with pati, bird. The peacock is the vehicle of the soul after death. Obviously, the Harappans believed in rebirth.

A śamī tree with two birds sitting in its crown carrying a fruit in their beaks is depicted on a jar from Lothal.[82] This motif can be related to ṚV I.164.20, where the two ways after death, the way to the sun and the way to the moon, are referred to. The tree is an image of the cosmic tree (cf. chapter III.4):

> *Two birds, closely befriended,*
> *sit together on the same tree,*
> *one of them eats the sweet berries (pipal),*
> *the other looks on them without eating them.*

The way of the moon leads to reincarnation. The cosmic tree is an aspect of the cosmic man. The reincarnating entity, the soul, is a spark of him. Therefore both are called puruṣa in Indian philosophy later.

A stylized pipal tree with the heads of two unicorns attached to its trunk is found on seal 1387 (M-296). At the place, where the heads meet the trunk has the form of a round sieve recalling the round lower part of the standard. Under the sieve 'lamellas' are depicted that could represent the flow

---

[82] For the illustration cf. S.R. Rao, Dawn and Devolution, fig. 31,1.

Soma juice. That the heads of the unicorns are attached to the tree shows that it could be regarded as a car.[83] The sun-daughter is brought in a car to her bridegrooms, the Aśvins. It is described as *all-shaped* in the marriage-hymn R̥V X.85.20. This agrees with the first sign of the inscription of the seal 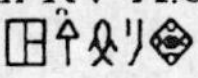 that can be read according to X.85.13 quoted before already:

> *sūryāyā vahatuḥ prāgāt savitr̥ yam avasr̥jat*
> *aghāsu hanyante gāvo 'r̥junyoḥ paryuhyate*
> *The wedding procession went ahead*
> *which was dismissed by Savitr̥ (the father);*
> *in the lunar mansion Aghā the bulls are killed (sacrificed),*
> *in the lunar mansion Phalgunī she (the bride) is brought home.*

The second sign can be read as prāgāt, it went ahead, the fish-sign as Savitr̥ (the sun-god is also a seer), the lance-sign corresponds to avasr̥jat, dismiss. The field-sign that is also found on seal 2279 with the motif of a bull-sacrifice renders the lunar mansions that are mentioned in the second half of the verse. The marriage of the sun-daughter took place in the time of maturity, whereas human marriages nowadays are preferably arranged in spring-time, the seed-time (cf. chapter I.1). This has to do with the extraordinary value we attach to the virginity of the bride. Only in recent time this custom has changed in the West. Everywhere in the world a great feast takes place together with marriage. In ancient India a lot of bulls had to be killed to provide the food for the retinue and relatives of the bridegroom and the bride. The name of the lunar mansion Aghā, when the bulls were killed, can be derived from the weak stem gha of the root han, to kill. Agha means not killed, how-

---

[83] The nave of the wheel, the mortar and the fire-sticks are all constructed after the same principle that is also found in the piston motor. The car of the Aśvins is not moved by oil or steam, however, but through the hymns of the poets (R̥V X.114.6). Its hidden wheel" (R̥V X.85.16) is the rotation of the earth. It is the reason why the gods come every morning to the sacrifice. The car of the Aśvins is often compared to a ship, but it has nothing to do with the modern space-ships, moved by rockets, or with UFOs. Its astral counterpart in the zodiac are the constellations of Gemini and Libra. The visions of the Vedic seers were always in tune with the laws of nature, not against them as the behaviour of the UFOs is according to the reports of people who pretend to have seen them.

ever, because the bulls that were sacrificed, were not killed in our sense of the word, but sent to heaven. They became immortal. In later time the mansion was called Maghā, enjoyment, rendered by the feast. The 'lamellas' in the motif of seal 1387 can also be regarded as the blood dripping from the head of the sacrificed bull or unicorn. The *bloody forms* of the sun-daughter are mentioned in X.85.35. This verse is contained in the inscription of tablet 3320 (H-742) 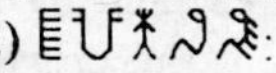:

> *śasanaṃ viśasanam   atho adhivikartanam*
> *sūryāyaḥ paśya rūpāṇi   tāni brahmā tu śundhati*
> *Cutting, dissecting, crushing into pieces -*
> *behold the forms of the sun-daughter! But the brahmin purifies them.*

The different forms of sacrificing a victim are rendered by the first two signs that can be explained as thread here related to the root kṛt, to cut, to spin. The horned man-sign renders the daughter of the sun, the cup-sign and the teeth-sign stand for her divine and dangerous aspects here. The brahmin is not mentioned, but according to ṚV VIII.93.19 he can be identified with the woman-sign (cf. chapters II and VII).

The tree of the motif has nine leaves, five pointing upwards, four pointing downwards. This agrees with the triangles of the Śrī yantra and the enneagram. Both are symbols of luck that is wished especially for marriage.

In verse 6 of the apocryphal hymn to the goddess Śrī (ṚV V.88) her tree, the wood-apple (bilva), is asked to drive away by its fruits all sorceries and ill-luck inwardly and outwardly. The first pada reads:

> *O sun-coloured one (āditya-varṇe),*
> *from heat your tree has been preborn (adhi jātaḥ).*

Sun-coloured can be a reading of the first sign of seal 1387. Vanaspati, literally king of the trees, is a name of the Soma, but here it refers to the tree of the goddess Śrī, the bilva or wood-apple. Tapas, heat, is a creation principle in ṚV X.190. The first and the last sign can also be identified with the place of Yama, the king of the dead, in ṚV X.135.1.

There are several seals and tablets with the standard as the sole motif. On seal 3256 (H-98) it is followed by the signs 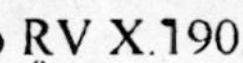 written in two lines. The inscription can be read according to ṚV X.190.3:

sūryacandramasau dhātā yathāpūrvam akalpayata
divaṃ ca pṛthivīṃ ca antarikṣam atho svaḥ
Sun and moon the creator has made as before,
and heaven and earth, the intermediate space
and the effulgence of the sky.

Heaven and earth are represented by three strokes each. The fish-sign and the lance-sign represent the creator and to create. Sun and moon are equal to the two signs of the second line, the rhombus-sign can also be read as the effulgence of the sky.

In the inscription of the two Harappa tablets 3309 (H-196) and 3322 (H-227), we find the sign  as the equivalence of the standard. On tablet 3309 it is carried by a man as on many Failaka seals. The inscription written over both sides of the seal is 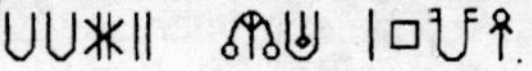. It agrees with ṚV IX.74.2:

divo yaḥ skambho dharuṇaḥ svātata
apūrṇo aṃśuḥ paryeti viśvataḥ
sa ime mahī rodasī yakṣad āvṛtā
samīcīne dādhāra samiṣaḥ kaviḥ
Who is the pillar, the well-erected support,
who as the full stalk encircles everything,
who sacrifices to the great world-halves turned to him,
he holds together the conjoined (halves) and all draughts, the seer.

The pillar of the sky is rendered by the first two signs of the first line, the stalk by the long stroke, everything by the square-sign. The world-halves turned to the Soma are equal to the second line. To hold together the conjoined halves is equal to the first two signs of the third line, all draughts to the two simple cup-signs. The kavi or seer is the person in the motif, who carries the standard.

On the reverse of tablet 3322 the standard is depicted three times together with 3 x 4 small circles in a vertical line that can be related to the year. The inscription on the obverse corresponds to ṚV IX.74.6cd:

Four naves, fixed downwards at the sky,
bear the immortal juice, dripping with butter.

Four naves fixed downwards (at the whim) is equal to the first sign, at the sky is rendered by the two curves. To bear the immortal juice is equal to the water-carrier-sign, dripping with butter (ghṛta) to the woman-sign. Butter is like fat a synonym of fertility.

The inscription of tablet 3321 written on both sides 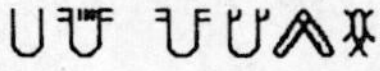 corresponds to the first half of ṚV X.125.2:

I carry the swelling Soma,
I carry Tvaṣṭṛ, Pūṣan, Bhaga.

The bee-sign stands for the goddess, the step-sign for to go, the womb-sign and the cup-sign are equal to the swelling Soma. The womb-sign on the reverse renders I carry, the cup-sign with three additional strokes is equal to the three gods Tvaṣṭṛ, Pūṣan and Bhaga.

In the inscription of the tablet 3440 (H-291) we find the fish-sign with a triangle in the beginning that can be read as Varuṇa: 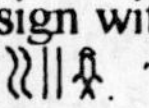. The Soma is mentioned in connection with Varuṇa in ṚV IX.90.2cd:

vanā vasāno varuṇo na sindhūn
vi ratnadhā dayate vāryāṇi
Dressing in wood like Varuṇa in the streams
the giver of treasures distributes the things desired for.

The wood is equal to the long strokes, the streams to the curved lines, the giver of treasures to the cup-sign, the things desired for to the woman-sign.

In the inscription of tablet 3665 we meet the king-sign: 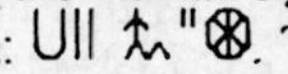. The Soma is compared to a king in various verses. The one coming nearest to this inscription seems to be contained in IX.90.6ab:

evā rāja_iva kratumān amena
viśva ghanighnat duritā pavasva
So purify yourself with vigour like a wise king
warding off all difficulties.

With vigour is rendered by the two short strokes here, because they represent the vigorous seed. For warding off all difficulties we get a man-sign with an additional triangle. Purify yourself is equal to the simple cup-sign with two long strokes for the pressing boards.

There are two inscriptions with this motif consisting of only two signs. They are found on the tablets 3443 (H-292) and 4561 (H-197). The two signs of tablet 3443 can be read as womb and seed. This is contained in ṚV IX.74.5c: *The Soma puts the seed in the womb of Aditi*. The other two signs render IX.92.3d: *The wise makes the five tribes his retinue.*

The lower part of the standard carried in procession with a unicorn or bull on a pedestal appears on tablet 1568 (M-491) as illustrated at the left (Franke-Vogt 257). The signs engraved on the reverse can be read according to I.164.6cd as:

Who is the one in the form of the unborn,
who has stemmed apart the six worlds?

The intersected circles and the six strokes render the six worlds, the hand in the circle can be read as to stem apart, the two strokes indicate the two possibilities of being born or not. The guardian-sign representing Rudra generally and the rhombus-sign are equal to the form of the unborn, the additional stroke in the rhombus-sign stands for one. The procession may have been done in reverence to Rudra, who was one of the main gods of the Indus civilization as he still is in Bali.

The upper part of the standard that is a sign of the Indus script, too, is mostly written in duplicate. The two signs appear in the inscription of the bull-seal 2423 (M-252) The signs are . They agree with the frog-hymn ṚV VII.103.9ab:

devahitiṃ jugupur dvādaśasya ṛtuṃ
naro na pra minante ete
They kept the divine rule of the twelfth month,
the men (the frogs) never forget the right season.

For the field-signs we get ṛtu or ṛta, sacred action, homophonous with kṛt, to spin. The two strokes render divine. The first man-sign is identical to jugupur with the root gup, to guard, the second renders man directly. The 12 strokes refer to the twelfth month. The first sign, the black (or red) fish, stands for the frogs, since they are a metaphor for the seer.

The tree on the Indus seals and tablets, be it a pipal or a śamī, is often flanked by one or two gazelles as on tablet 2719c. The same motif is found on seals from Uruk (Frankfort IVj) and Susa, where the tree is replaced by a pipal leaf.[84] On the round Dilmun seal 6057 (L-123) found in Lothal the tree between the two gazelles has been replaced by a snake looking like the pinnate leaves of a kino tree (Aachen, fig. 101). The snake can be regarded as the Kuṇḍalinī, the two gazelles as Iḍā and Piṅgalā (cf. chapter VIII).

On tablet 3314 the standard is found in front of a goat and the signs . The signs on the reverse 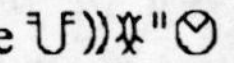 lead to ṚV X.5.2:

samānaṃ nīḷaṃ vṛṣaṇo vasānāḥ saṃ jagmire mahiṣā arvatibhiḥ
ṛtasya padaṃ kavayo ni pānti guhā nāmāni dadhire parāṇi
Wrapped up in the common nest
the ardent bulls united with the mares;
the seers guard the trace of the truth,
they keep secret the highest names.

The first half of the verse agrees with the two signs on the obverse. The common nest is the Soma-vessel, the bulls and the mares represented by the strokes are the male and the female energies, who unite on a higher level. Therefore the cows have been replaced by mares. The trace of the truth is rendered by the two signs on the reverse, the fish-sign stands for the seers, the two curves that can be interpreted as a double wall are equal to keep secret. The highest names are represented by the cup-sign.

The smile cup-sign and one or more strokes are found on many tiny seals from Harappa. Apart from their meaning in the context with the main line, they can be read as Hariyūpiyā, the Vedic form of Harappa. The literal meaning of Hariyūpiyā is 'golden post (yūpa)'. Hari, the golden or yellow one, is a name of the Soma. It is rendered by the strokes that can be identified with the streams of Soma. The cup-sign can be read as the bed of a river. A post can be compared with it, because its branches are like tributaries. The name of the river Ravi, on whose bank Harappa is situated, can be derived from hari. If there are more than two strokes, the sequence can also be translated as Sapta

[84] For the Susa-seal cf. E. Paroda, Alt-Iran, Baden-Baden 1962, p. 26.

Sindhu, (land of) seven rivers, as the Indus land is called in ṚV VIII.24.27. Sapta means also many.

On tablet 4645 (H-801) the cup-sign has an additional stroke at the bottom, which can be interpreted as seed or fertility. The inscription is 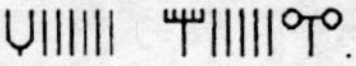. Starting from the second line it can be affiliated to ṚV IX.70.10ac:

> *hito na saptir abhi vājam arṣa*
> *nāvā na sindhum ati parṣi vidvān*
> *Run like hit joined horses to the price of victory;*
> *like a ship take us skilfully beyond.*

The price of victory that is equal to fertility is rendered by the womb-sign, the joined horses by the six strokes. The first sign of the first line corresponds to a car or a ship, the five strokes to the streams and the banner-sign to skilful.

On the unicorn-seal 2316 the standard is replaced by a dancer with a tail. The inscription 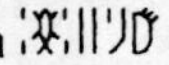 agrees with ṚV X.94.4c:

> *saṃrabhyā dhīrāḥ svasṛbhir nartaṣur*
> *Being seized the wise danced with the sister-like (fingers).*

The first sign can be read as a hand with fingers, the second as like, the third as the pressing boards, the fish-sign renders the wise, the Soma, the four short strokes around it may be interpreted as to dance (like sparks).

On seals from Akkad and Elam two gazelles are illustrated drawn up at their hind-legs by a god. This can be a simile of his power or of the inversion of creation called pratisarga by Patañjali in sūtra II.10 and explained as the aim of Yoga. On a Greek vase the lady of the beasts stands between two hares, holding up one of them at their hind-leg. Here compassion and power, the two aspects of the goddess, may be represented. We shall deal with the lord of the beasts and the lady of the beasts as aspects of the cosmic man in the following chapter.

II. THE LORD OF THE BEASTS AND THE DEITY IN THE TREE

We have seen in the first chapter that there are similarities between the pictograms of the Sumerian and the Indus script. Another way to compare these two cultures is rendered by the motifs of the seals. The most suitable for this purpose are the Indus seals 2420 (M-304) and 2430 ((M-1186) called *lord of the beasts* or *Proto-Śiva* and *deity in the tree* by J. Marshall.[1]

The motifs of the two Indus seals have been studied separately by various authors,[2] the motif of the lord of the beasts, with which we shall start our investigation, was studied in comparison with a similar motif on a Celtic caldron (cf. page 92) by F.O. Schrader,[3] H. Mode[4] and K. Sälzle.[5]

---

[1] Op. cit. p. 52-54 and 63-65. The photographs have been taken from Mode, plate 66 and Aachen C 85.

[2] Cf. A. Hiltebeitel, The Indus Valley Proto-Śiva, Anthropos 73,1978; D. Srinivasan, The so-called Proto-Śiva Seal from Mohenjo Daro, Archives of Asian Art 29, 1975. P.V. Pathak, The Lady of Beasts or the Lord of Beasts, Purātattva 21, 1990-91, p. 57-64; Sh. Artre, The Lady of Beast - The Harappan Goddess, Purātattva 16, 1986.

[3] Cf. Indische Beziehungen eines nordischen Fundes, ZDMG 13, p. 185.

[4] Op. cit. p. 67.

[5] Cf. Tier und Mensch, Gottheit und Dämon, München 1965. The illustration has been taken from this volume, p. 149.

The latter two referred also to a relief found in the Hittite town Kargamiš.[6] The same motif appears as a written testimony in the figure of Enkidu in the first tablet of the Gilgameš epic. Moreover, a seal from Tepe Yahya in Kerman/Iran depicts a man sitting in a cross-legged position like the central figure of the Celtic caldron.[7] The Celtic caldron was found in 1891 in a moor near Gundestrup in Denmark. It is supposed that it has been manufactured between 200 ante and 200 post our era.[8] With regard to its motif it could be related to the legendary Celtic grail that was searched for by the knights of Artus who is said to have lived in the 6th century.

The Kargamiš relief is dated between 1050 and 850,[9] the Kerman seal between 2200-1800 BC. Since the Indus civilization flourished between 3000 and 1600 ante, there are more than 2500 years between the first and the last find and nearly 1000 years between the intermediate links.

The New Babylonian version of the Gilgameš epic was written about 1200 ante. It goes back to an Old Babylonian version from the 19th century and Sumerian myths from the 21st century. Since the erection of the great wall of Uruk by Gilgameš is dated between 2750 and 2600,[10] it is historically possible that at least the Babylonian tales of Enkidu and Gilgameš were influenced by the Indus civilization.

The distance of time and space is only of secondary importance for a symbolic comparison of motifs. From this point of view, the motif that is called 'lord of the beasts' or 'animal trainer' has to be regarded as an aspect of the cosmic man or macroanthropos called Puruṣa in the Ṛg-Veda. The idea of the macroanthropos is common to the whole archaic world and can also be

---

[6] Cf. M. Riemschneider, Die Welt der Hethiter, Stuttgart 1954; pl. 55. The drawing has been taken from Mode, fig. 39.

[7] Cf. A. Parpola (1994), p. 250. The figure has no animals around it.

[8] Cf. J. Moreau, op. cit. p. 258,259.

[9] Cf. L. Woolley, Mesopotamien und Vorderasien,Baden-Baden 1965, p. 133.

[10] Cf. Schott/Von Soden, Das Gilgamesch-Epos, Stuttgart 1980, p. 4.

found in the Jewish and the Christian religion. In the mythology of the Germans he is known as the giant Ymir. It had a central position with the Celts, too, as can be inferred from the motifs of the caldron.

Though the basic conception of the cosmic man is everywhere the same, different attributes are attached to it, which may have been adopted either from another culture or developed in one culture only. Thus, on the Syrian relief the sitting figure has no horns, whereas on the Celtic caldron it has the horns of a deer, on the Indian seal the horns of a buffalo and the surrounding animals vary in number and species. It does not prove a cultural dependence either, that one of the animals in all images looks in the opposite direction. This may have been caused by artistic reasons or it may have been a general means of expressing a circular movement in ancient times that could indicate a fertility dance as the motif of a horned flute-playing deer-man surrounded by animals in the cave of Trois Frère suggests.[11]

Schrader points out, that the Celtic as well as the Indian figure is sitting cross-legged, that both wear a belt round their belly, and that the animals at their right side have the same horns as the main figure.[12] Though he refers to the original and not to the impression of the seal, his observation could be correct, if the motif is read like the script from right to left. It must also be noticed that the Indian way of sitting is not only more complicated than that of the Celtic, but also than the normal yoga seat. In Yoga treatises this posture is called yoni-āsana, because the feet form a female organ called yoni in Sanskrit. In the R̥g-Veda this posture could be related to the deity of lightning called Ekapad, the one-footed.[13] The female symbolism of the position of the feet would then have become male, however.[14]

---

[11] Sälzle (op.cit. p. 151) thinks that the deer-man dances, but he may stand still like the flute-player Kr̥ṣṇa standing in front of the cows on Indian miniature-paintings, who has likewise placed one leg over the other.

[12] Cf. op. cit. p. 112

[13] Cf. A.A. Macdonell, op. cit. p. 74.

[14] During-Caspers (op.cit. p. 71) interprets this position as *squatting or dancing*. The gods are compared with dancers in R̥V X.72.6, but they do not dance on a pedestal., but in the ocean.

The female outlook of the main figure is increased by the bangles and his upper garment consisting of seven lines formed like a female triangle. The animals surrounding it can also be regarded as female, since they are part of nature. On the other hand, the ends of its belt can be interpreted as ithyphallus, as was done already by Marshall.[15] Thus we get an image of an androgyn related to the gods Śiva and Viṣṇu in later Indian tradition.[16]
Female features are also found with the central figure of the Kargamiš relief, especially in the hair-do. The long hair and the animals around it are part of the description of Enkidu in Gilgameš epic I.ii.34-41:[17]

Aruru washed her hands, she pinched off clay and threw it down,
Enkidu she made, the hero, a son born from the glory of Ninurta.
The body was covered all over with hairs,
his curly hair grew heavily like that of Nišaba.
He knows neither men nor country, he is clad like Šumukan.[18]
He eats with the gazelles from the herbs,
with the animals he throngs in the watering place,
in their crowd his heart rejoices in the water.

The Hittites were acquainted with Enkidu through their own version of the epic. Perhaps the relief is a copy of Enkidu's image that Gilgameš ordered to be made after the premature death of his friend (Gilg. epic VIII.ii.26). Enkidu is brought into the city of Uruk by a temple prostitute. This motif is related to the Indian story of the young sage Ṛṣyaśṛṅga, who is brought by a prostitute to the city of Romapada.[19]

---

[15] Op. cit. p. 52. It can also be compared to the liṅga at the end of the spinal cord, the abode of the Kuṇḍalinī snake in Tantric literature (cf. chapter VIII).

[16] Since the Puruṣa is male and female, the central person cannot be a goddess, as Sh. Atre maintains (op.cit. p. 9).

[17] Translated from the Akkadian edition published by R.C. Thompson, The Epic of Gilgamesh, Oxford 1930.

[18] Aruru is a name of the mother-goddess, Ninurta is the god of war, Nišaba the goddess of grain, Šumukan the lord of the beasts.

[19] In other versions it is the daughter of the king, who seduces him. The story is recorded in India for the first time in the Rāmāyaṇa. For a comparison of the Mesopotamian and the Indian stories cf. D. Schlingloff, Die Einhorn-Legende, Christiana Albertina AF 1970/71.

Life in the forest is an ancient institution of the Indian society. It is quite likely that it was already invented by the sages of the Indus cities. The Indian seers were also called yati, magicians. Their name has survived in the word yeti for a sort of ogre who is said to live in the Himalayas. In Mesopotamia such men appear very seldom. In the Gilgameš epic there is only the ogre Ḫuwawa who lives in the forest like Enkidu. The name Enkidu can be explained as 'made from Enki'. Enki is the Sumerian god of wisdom, the Akkadian Ea. The god Ninurta may be regarded as one of his aspects. Enkidu is hence a sage like R̥ṣyaśr̥ṅga. Perhaps he and Ḫuwawa were related to the people that founded the Indus civilization called Meluḫḫa by the Akkadians.
Because of his friendly behaviour, Enkidu is fit for being a translator or ambassador of Meluḫḫa. This function is mentioned in the inscription of the Akkadian seal XLVII,557 (catalogued by Böhmer):[20]

Its complete reading is šu-ì-lí-śu, eme-bal me-luḫ-ḫa^{ki} - Šuiliśu, interpreter of Meluḫḫa.[21] With regard to similar motifs, the horned person in the middle of this seal, who carries a smaller figure on its lap, can be the goddess Ištar. There are several other seals where she is carrying a child

[20] The illustration has been taken from Parpola (1994), p. 132.

[21] Cf. D.O. Edzard, op.cit. (1968/69). The phonetic value of Šuiliśu is 'he of his god'. If read logographically, Šuìlíśu would mean 'bearded (śu) [man protected by] the hands (šu) of the god or goddess (ilí).' Perhaps the owner of the seal wanted to increase his fame by using scenes from the life of Enkidu. Similar motifs ooccur on three more seals bearing the name of Šuilíśu.

on her lap. They are classified by Boehmer (pl. XLVII,555-560) under the headline goddess with child. The crescent of the moon used as a 'filling motif' on many Akkadian seals is placed on the head of the smaller person in such a way, that it looks like two horns. This recalls the bull-man found on many Akkadian seals. They can be compared to the centaur-motif on the Indus seals. The centaur is called Gandharva in the Veda (cf. chapter III.4). The horns are an emblem of divinity, but in Greek mythology the centaur has lost the divine character he had in the Veda and probably in the Indus civilization.

Two persons are standing in front of the 'goddess' on the Akkadian seal, a bearded man with a turban and a woman, either his wife or a disciple.[22] The first person carries a goat on his shoulder, the other one has a pot in the hand. With regard to the inscription, they could be visitors from Meluḫḫa, though their coat is Akkadian. In the left corner of the seal a man is sitting behind a vessel holding a stick in his hand. He could be engaged in taking something out of the vessel. Above him are two other vessels of the same kind. All these vessels are probably butter-tubs.[23] The butter is equally sacred in the Veda as the Soma (cf. ṚV IV.58). The person sitting on the lap of the goddess, one of the persons in front of him and the man behind the vessel have raised one hand for saluting each other.

The Italian archaeologist M. Tosi thinks that the person sitting on the lap of the 'goddess', whom he regards as a king, is the interpreter,[24] but it was surely not customary in Akkad that interpreters sit on the lap of the king. Except for the children this was the place for the lover or the wife. A child is out of discussion here, however, as the figure has a beard. A child with a beard is mentioned in Akkadian word-lists only as an abortion. But perhaps the man on the lap of the goddess wanted to indicate that he is under her protection in a special way. We can identify the 'goddess' then with Gilgameš, since as the king he is her representative on earth. In this way,

---

[22] A similar motif is found on a seal from Failaka. Cf. P. Kjærum, op.cit. fig. 369. The person on the lap of the goddess is missing here, however.

[23] Cf. Boehmer, op. cit. p. 122.

[24] Op. cit. p. 119.

Tosi's interpretation could be justified. As they are friends, Enkidu can even sit on the lap of Gilgameš.

We read about the two in II.iv.12,13 of the epic:

They took the hands of each other,
they held their hands like lovers.

Moreover, we hear the sun-god saying to Enkidu in VII.iii.40-44:

Now, friend, Gilgameš is thy favourite brother.
He lets thee rest on a kingly bed,
in a well-prepared bed he lets rest thee.
He lets sit thee in peace on a seat at his left,
the kings of the world he lets kiss thy feet.

Enkidu can be called 'interpreter of Meluḫḫa' not only because his life in the steppe is similar to that of the yatis, but because it can be compared to that of the wandering ecstatics or *muni* who live according to R̥V X.136.6 together with the wild beasts and the Gandharvas (cf. chapter IV). Through his life in the steppe, Enkidu is not only an interpreter, but also a representative of the sages of Meluḫḫa. Like R̥ṣyaśr̥ṅga in Indian mythology, Enkidu is born from a gazelle (tablet VIII.i.3). According to tablet VIII.i.4 Enkidu's father was a wild ass. Hence he can be regarded as a Gandharva, too.[25]

Contrarily to the Indian and the Mesopotamian lord of the beasts, the central figure on the Celtic caldron has no female features, but on one of its plates a goddess to be recognized by her bosom is depicted between a pair of horses and elephants and a tiger in front (for the illustration cf. p. 92).

Schrader compares this motif with the Indian Elephant-Lakṣmī, without being aware of the fact that the goddess with the tiger appears as a motif on several Indus seals. We may compare her with the Greek lady of the beasts, Artemis.[26]

---

[25] G. Dumézil records king Midas, who is said to have had the ears of an ass, among the centaurs. Cf. Le Problème des Centaurs, Paris 1929, p. 242.

[26] For the lady of the beasts in relation to this goddess cf. K. Sälzle, op. cit. p. 57. On a torso from Italy (Sälzle, p. 63) she stands in the middle of two lions drawing them up with their hind-legs.

The lord of the beasts is a minor god in the Akkadian pantheon. Enkidu, however, who is compared to the lord of the beasts in the epic, is otherwise regarded as a god like Gilgameš. This is expressed by fixing the determinative for god to their names. In the Ṛg-Veda the name Paśupati, lord of the beasts, is not mentioned at all, it occurs only in the hymn II.34 of the Atharva-Veda. However, the animals that live in the air, in the forest and in the village are made from the Puruṣa according to ṚV X.90.8. Moreover, there is the god Vāstoṣpati, the lord of the village, a cognate of Rudra, the Vedic Śiva, created by the gods from the seed of the father of the sky (cf. chapter V).[27]

The Indus seal is of similar importance. Marshall has recognized this by calling the central person 'Proto-Śiva'. The sign above its head is an internal proof of the importance of this figure, as it appears as a singularity on the Harappa tablet 3005 with the motif of a horned man carrying a club on his shoulder.

The central figure of the Celtic caldron is obviously the deer-god Cernunnos who is regarded as the most important god of the Celts. According to the description given by Lengjel, he is closely related to the Vedic Viśvakarman.[28] This corresponds to the role Mercury played with the Romans. On a sculpture in the cave of Trois-Frère Cernunnos is pictured together with Apollo and Mercury.[29] This means that he was on a par with these gods.

Ṛṣyaśṛṅga, who may be regarded as the lord of the beasts in later Indian tradition, is an important personality, too. It is he who officiates over the sacrifice of king Daśaratha leading to the birth of Rāma, one of the ten major incarnations of god Viṣṇu. Ṛṣyaśṛṅga, meaning literally 'having the horn of a gazelle', is described in Indian stories and depicted on Buddhist cave paintings with a horn on his head. It is explained by his birth from a gazelle in a mythical way. He is begotten in a lake,

---

[27] The Paśupati of the Atharva-Veda must hence be understood in a larger sense than Pathak did (cf. op. cit. p. 62,63).

[28] Cf. L. Lengjel. Das geheime Wissen der Kelten. Freiburg ²1981.p. 223.

[29] Cf. Lengjel. op. cit. p. 222.

which can be identified with the Great Bath of Mohenjo Daro. The gazelle, his mother, is an Apsaras, the Vedic name of a hierodule. This relates her to Enkidu's seductrice.[30] In the Buddhist version of the story, the name of Ṛṣyaśṛṅga is changed into Ekaśṛṅga, meaning unicorn. This animal is the most frequent motif on the Indus seals, but it does not appear elsewhere in later Indian literature and art.

A man like Ṛṣyaśṛṅga with a horn in twig-form on his head kneeling in front of a deity with horns standing in a pipal tree is found on seal 2430 (M-1186). Behind him we see a ewe or markhor with helical horns and a human face. It can be identified with the goat sacrificed before the bull in Vedic sacrifices. Both are representatives of the Puruṣa. In a similar way the fallow-deer standing behind the kneeling Enkidu on the Kargamiš relief can be explained as a sacrificial animal. Enkidu has no horn on his head, but the bull he holds at its horn with his right hand looks as if it had only this horn. With the other hand Enkidu grasps the leg of a lion, but he does not draw the animal up, as the hero standing between two goats or lions on several Akkadian seals does. The Hittites cannot have taken these traits from the Indian Ṛṣyaśṛṅga-stories, as they lived at an earlier time, but it is possible that they knew it from the Indus Valley. This would mean that the Enkidu-story was not a forerunner of the Ṛṣyaśṛṅga-story, as Schlingloff contends,[31] but that both have their origin in the Indus civilization. In a Hittite treaty from 1350 ante, the first testimony of the Vedic gods Mitra, Varuṇa, Indra and the Nāsatyas is found.[32] Nāsatya is an older name of the Aśvins, the divine twins.[33]

In the Gilgameš epic, Enkidu is avoided by the animals after he has had sexual intercourse with the hierodule. The wise Indian hermits and

---

[30] The goddess Lakṣmī or Śrī is said to be hariṇī, yellow-brown (like a gazelle) in RV V.87.1.

[31] Op. cit. p. 52.

[32] Cf. F. Wilhelm. Indien. Fischer 17, Frankfurt 1967, p. 26.

[33] The older name recalls a relation of the twins to boats (nau: nāva), whereas aśvin is related to horse (aśva) as it is found with the twins Castor and Pollux in Greek mythology. Cf. chapter III.7.

munis live until today in the company of animals, as it is described in a hymn of the Sufi poet Galāladdin Rūmi. A similar trait is found in the images of Orpheus. Enkidu, though he is called a god and wise by the hierodule in I.iv.34 of the epic, does not behave as such, when he is on the verge to die.[34] Likewise Gilgameš, though a god, has to go in search for the truth. The place, where he eventually arrives, the 'mouth of the streams', could be the river Indus (cf. chapter VII). Meluḫḫa was the land of wisdom for the Akkadians as Egypt became it later.

We can take up now the investigation of the animals surrounding the main figure. Many explanations have been given on this aspect of the motif.[35] If the main figure is simply the lord of the beasts, the surrounding animals have no meaning of their own, their selection and arrangement are accidental. If we interpret the main figure as the cosmic man, however, the animals càn be explained as the four castes that are mentioned in X.90.12 of the Puruṣa-hymn. The elephant known for its memory would correspond to the brahmins, that it looks in the opposite direction may illustrate their dignity. The aggressive tiger is a representative of the kings, the rhino of the vaiśyas, the land-owners, on account of its plumpness and irascibility, the humble water-buffalo corresponds to the śudras, the servants. The gazelles under the pedestal would represent the tribal population. There were no slaves in this on the whole peaceful community.

We have already mentioned ṚV X.90.8, where the animals of the air, of the forest and of the village are said to have been made from the Puruṣa. The rhino and the tiger of seal 2420 live in the open field and in the forest, elephant and water-buffalo live in the forest and in the village. There are no birds on the seal, but the two gazelles under the pedestal live in the heights of the mountain. In ṚV X.90.10 horses, cattle, goats and sheep and animals that have teeth on both sides of the mouth are mentioned. The latter can be identified with the elephant.

---

[34] Thompson's reading 'damqata' in I.iv.34 is confirmed now by a fragment from Ḫattuša (cf. G. Wilhelm, Neue Akkadische Gilgameš-Fragmente aus Ḫattuša, ZA 78, p. 104). Its literal meaning is not wise, but benevolent. Enkidu appears like a god to the hierodule because of his benevolence.

[35] Cf. A. Hiltebeitel, op. cit. (1978), p. 767.

The animals around the deity can also be related to the seasons, only three of them, however, are mentioned in X.90.6. It is possible that in the Indus Valley five seasons were known as they are enumerated in other Vedic scriptures. They animals can then be classified in the following way:

water-buffalo - spring - Venus (Uṣas);
tiger - summer - Mars (Rudra-Śiva);
elephant - rainy season - Jupiter (Indra or Varuṇa);
rhino - autumn - Saturn (Puṣan or Parjanya);
gazelles - winter - Mercury (Viṣṇu or the Aśvins).

Mercury is known to be connected with the constellation of the Twins. If they represent the Aśvins, the gazelles can be regarded as a symbol of day and night.[36] The moon can be affiliated to the horns of the lord of the beasts, the earth to the pedestal.

Not regarding the gazelles the animals can also be affiliated to the four cardinal points, for which Hiltebeitel offers a lot of arguments.[37] According to ṚV X.90.14, which Hiltebeitel does not pay any heed to, the directions emanate from the ears of the Puruṣa. This can be easily understood, if they are identified with the faces of the horned god. If there are only three they can be related to the three worlds. The faces of the deity have similarity with that of a bull.[38] Three faces of the bull Viśvarūpa are mentioned in ṚV III.56.3, who is said to be the seed-giver of all beings. These beings may also be identified with the animals around the deity, whose function as a seed-giver is expressed by the erected phallus. On the other hand, the girdle is a symbol of austerity. Both qualities relate him again to Śiva who is known for his austerity (tapas) and his passionate desire (kāma).

In several hymns of the Ṛg-Veda addressed to the gods Viśvakarman, Varuṇa, Indra and Viṣṇu the creative work of these gods is said to consist mainly in stemming heaven and earth apart. This aspect is more evident from the seals with a man holding two tigers apart. On the Akkadian seals we find two lions instead of the tigers. In the epic of Gilgameš the hero tells

---

[36] Day and night is one of the affiliations of the Aśvins given by Yaska. Cf. A. Hillebrandt, Vedische Mythologie, Hildesheim 1965, p. 56.

[37] Op. cit. (1978), p. 776.

[38] This was pointed out by D. Srinivasan, op.cit. p. 51.

his mother of a dream, in which he tried to stem up the firmament, that fell down on him with all the stars. This is an exact description of the position of the Puruṣa between heaven and earth. The king is his representative. The stars can be identified with the planets placed at the sky by Marduk according to Enûma eliš VI.30-35. They are not only physical entities, but gods themselves like heaven and earth and the air.

A cosmic explanation can also be given for the Kargamiš relief. The fallow-deer standing between the lion and the bull can represent the air, identified with Mummu, the god of wisdom, in the Enûma eliš.[39] The big lion can represent heaven, the bull the earth, the two small lions day and night or activity and leisure, as the paw of one of them rests on Enkidu's knee and the other one is stretched out to the lion lying asleep at his feet.

On the plate with a goddess on the Celtic caldron the divine duality is expressed by the two elephants and two winged horses that can be interpreted as the light and the dark half of the year and as day and night, the tiger underneath the goddess would then represent the moon or the soul wandering through the year, being reborn again and again. This is also illustrated on another plate of the caldron where the year is depicted as a horizontal tree. Under it a file of warriors wanders in the direction of a big caldron, into which they are dived down over-head. Above them a file of horsemen, the reborn or initiated, moves in the opposite direction.[40]

On the plate with the god Cernunnos, the duality is expressed by the two fighting or playing lions at his left. The relation of day and night can be regarded as a play or as a fight. The duality becomes a trinity by the bull behind the lions. If the lions represent day and night as the Aśvins in Indian mythology, the bull would be the sacrifice. Through this sacrifice the movement of the earth is preserved in the same way as by the bull that draws the whim. The symbol of wisdom necessary for this work would be the dolphin in the background with a man riding on it. The dolphin is also found in the inscription of the Indus seals.

---

[39] Cf. Enûma eliš tablet I, line 20 and A. Heidel, The Meaning of Mummu in Akkadian literature, JNES VII, 1948.

[40] For the explanation of this motif cf. J. Moreau, op. cit. p. 114.

The surrounding animals can be affiliated to the seasons and the planets as in the case of the Indus seal, but in a different sequence:

deer - spring - Mercury;
bull - summer - Jupiter;
tiger - autumn - Mars;
wolf - winter - Saturn.

The animal remaining for the Venus would be the snake with the head of a ram the god holds in his left hand. The snake is also a symbol of the year, starting with the sign of the ram (Aries), and of rebirth. The moon corresponds to the ring called torque held by the god in his right hand. A similar circle is formed by the tail of the big lion on the Kargamiš relief. The four seasons in their crosswise sequence going round the central figure form together the rune with the significance of man: ᛗ. A sign can also be formed by the figures on the Kargamiš relief. It is the ligature 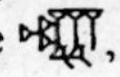, meaning ilu + en, the determinative and beginning of Enkidu.

Although the classifications of the animals agree with astrological and alchemist symbolism, they look somewhat arbitrary. This impression will last, even if they are made as reasonable as possible. It is a characteristic of archaic cosmology to explain the origin of the world by a divine will and person, and to handle the elements of creation in an associative manner, whereas modern science explains the origin as accidental, but try to be very exact in describing how one element developed from another.

The ambivalence or multivalence pertains to the inscriptions of the Indus seals too. Seal 2420 carries the signs 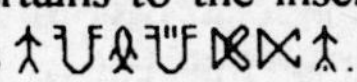. On the presumption that the additional stroke of the man-sign represents a phallus, it can be read as the creator-god Dakṣa, whose name means potency literally. The inscription can then be affiliated to R̥V X.72.4c,5c:

aditer dakṣo ajāyata dakṣād aditiḥ pari
tāṃ devā anvajāyanta bhadrā amr̥tabandhavaḥ
From Aditi Dakṣa was born, from Dakṣa Aditi;
then the beneficial gods were born,
the friends of the draught of immortality.

The sequence of the first two signs has been changed in the Vedic hymn. The two triangle-signs may represent the mother-goddess Aditi called Uttānapad in X.72.3 and 4, she, who spreads her legs apart (for giving birth).[41] The triangle-sign is used in neolithic Indian cave-paintings for depicting human beings or gods.[42] The cup-sign with two additional strokes can be read as Dakṣa again. The strokes represent his seed. The fish-sign can be read as the gods, the penultimate cup-sign as the draught of immortality, the Soma, the last man-sign as the friends.

Aditi is identified with the earth in Atharva-Veda XII.1. That means that Dakṣa is born from the earth. In a similar way, Enkidu is formed by the mother-goddess Aruru from a lump of earth. In the Old Testament, this work has been carried out by the Jewish god himself. The name of Adam means earth literally. The rune for man is almost identical with the sign for the mother-goddess in the Indus script. Probably its original meaning denoted the androgyn cosmic man.

The inscription can also be read according to ṚV X.81.1, where the creator-god Viśvakarman, literally all-maker, introduces himself as the seer, the priest and the father. This sequence corresponds to the last three signs. The first sign can be interpreted as 'father of the eye' then, as Viśvakarman is called in the beginning of the verse. Therefore I formerly affiliated the whole inscription to this verse.

The Celtic and the Indian mythology are closely related. This is also transparent from the image of the dolphin on the Celtic caldron. Like the dolphin the human figure riding on it can be regarded as a symbol of wisdom. The most famous representative of wisdom in the Celtic mythology is the old magician Merlin. Quite similar to an Indian hermit he goes into the forest at the end of his life. There he meets the nymph Viviane who is born from his own imagination. He is seduced by her like an Indian hermit by the water-women and the creator Brahmā by his daughter Uṣas, the Dawn (cf. chapter V). The responsibility for violating the law against incest and the transgression of the limits set to old age is solely laid on Brahmā. Rudra, the son born from this union, even punishes his father with decapitation, which really means castra-

[41] The motif of a woman with legs spread apart occurs also on an Etruscan bronze tablet as lady of the beasts. Cf. K. Sälzle, op. cit., p. 63. For the uttānapad-motif cf. also H.P.M. Janssen, op. cit. p. 457.

[42] Cf. Brooks/Wakankar, Stone Age Painting in India, New Haven 1976, p. 13.

tion. The Greeks have similar myths. No son is born to Merlin and Viviane, but Merlin is punished by being imprisoned in a tower. This is done by Viviane with the help of the magic power she has got from him. Hence Merlin is sacrificed like Brahmā.

In the case of Ṛṣyaśṛṅga the son takes over the responsibility for his father by following the hierodule or in another version the daughter of the king into the city. First he is the sacrifice, later he becomes the priest. This is expressed by the horn of the gazelle on his head. The gazelle is a symbol of the ancient goddess, who was both, virgin and prostitute.

Likewise, Enkidu sacrifices himself or is sacrificed to appease the anger of the goddess Ištar after he has killed the bull of heaven together with Gilgameš. In Pauline Christianity it is the son again who is sacrificed to reconcile humanity with the eternal father. Indeed, an idea so subtle and so far from the historical events, that nobody would have believed in the beginning that it would attract many followers.

The difference of the two ways of thought lies in the fact that in the archaic cultures the creator is not outside the universe as in the Jewish and Christian religion. As the cosmic man he is himself the universe, and it is unimportant, whether he is the father or the son. In both cases it is his sacrifice, through which the universe is created and overcome.

In all the myths it is the male part of the cosmic man that is sacrificed or sacrifices himself. The male does not violate the female, on the contrary, he is brought under her control. Even the great Lord Śiva cannot evade this fate: The goddess Kālī dances on his corpse with protruding tongue, a symbol of shame according to Indian tradition, but more probable of her male aspect.

Enkidu becomes a sacrifice of slandering. Inspite of his benevolence, he is called a rogue and a murderer in I.iv.7 of the Gilgameš epic, though on account of his benevolent nature the hierodule had no difficulties in seducing him and bringing him into the city. He follows her not for his own profit, but in order to fight with Gilgameš. Likewise Ṛṣyaśṛṅga and Merlin act for the welfare of the community.

Seal 2430 is not furnished with the same extensive possibilities of comparison as they exist for seal 2420. There is, however, a neolithic wall painting discovered in the Edakal cave in South India showing seven male figures with rays issuing from their heads.[43] Moreover, seal 2430 can be compared like seal 2420 to similar motifs on other Indus seals and tablets (cf. chapter III). Mahadevan gives the following description of the motif of seal 2430 in the Indian concordance (from the right):

A horned personage standing between the branches of a pipal tree; a low pedestal with some offerings; a horned personage kneeling in adoration; a ram; a row of seven robed figures in the lower register.

That the two seals are related to each other, is also indicated by their inscriptions that are very much the same. This is getting clearer, when they are written under each other:

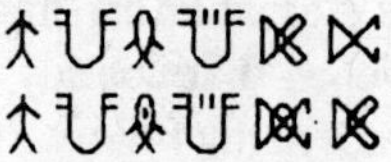

The first man-sign is missing in 2430, but it can be supplemented by compound  found in the motif. The field-sign  which we have come across already in the inscription of seal 1387 is written much apart from the other signs under the tree at the right side of the seal. In the concordances it is therefore written at the end. The deity in the tree is probably an image of the mother-goddess as was suggested by Marshall, this can also be inferred from the triangle-signs, as we have found out in connection with the inscription of seal 2420 already. On this account we can try to affiliate the inscription of seal 2430 to the same hymn. A suitable verse is found in X.72.5:

aditir hyajaniṣṭha dakṣa yā duhitā tava
tāṃ devā anvajāyanta bhadrā amṛtabandhavaḥ
For Aditi was born as your daughter, Dakṣa!
Then the beneficial gods were born,
the friends of the nectar of immortality.

---

[43] Cf. E.O. Tillner, op. cit., p. 89.

The first sign can be read as Aditi again, the second as to be born as the daughter, the fish-sign with additional stroke renders the beneficial gods, the cup-sign and the man-sign the friends of the draught of immortality. The field-sign has the same meaning, since it represents the standard or whim, in which the Soma was pressed.

The circle in the second triangle-sign on seal 2430 can also be explained as the cosmic egg, that is an attribute of the mother-goddess. It is called the 'golden egg' in the famous creation-hymn R̥V X.121. Moreover, the female principle can be called 'navel of the unborn', into which the male cosmic principle is set according to R̥V X.82.6cd:

In the navel of the unborn is set the One,
on whom all creatures are established.

The dotted fish-sign is interpreted as referring to the goddess by Parpola recently, formerly he has equated it with Br̥haspati, however, the husband of the goddess Vāc, another name of the mother-goddess.[44] Both identifications are possible, because the goddess can also appear as male. This is due to the androgyn nature of the cosmic man, but in the inscription of these two seals the fish-signs with and without dot both stand for the gods.

The seven persons in the lower register of seal 2430 are referred to in X.72.8 as the seven sons of Aditi with whom she went to the gods. They may be equal to the seven stars of the Great Bear that are called seers and priests in the Veda. Aditi has an eighth son who is called Mārtāṇḍa, dying egg, whom she sets apart. This son is equal to the moon, not to the sun as it is stated in the dictionaries. It is represented by the sign set apart on the seal.

The rectangular figure in the middle of the seal is explained by Kosambi as a head on a dais.[45] A. Parpola, giving the same explanation, suggests that the two circles on the back of the head are depicting the hair-do of a *divided bun*, that is worn by several persons on other seals, too, no-

[44] Cf. 1994. p. 261 and 1969, p. 13.

[45] Cf. Ancient India, New York 1965, note to fig. 46.

tably by the two warriors on seal 7038 (K-65).[46] A similar dais is found on tablet 2756 (M-481), where a snake is lying on it with its head (cf. chapter III.1).
The head is identical to the tower-sign  and the head-sign  that often occur together with the number seven. In the cosmogonic hymn X.125.7 addressed to the goddess of Language, Vāc, she declares: *I give birth to the father in the head of this (world)*. The head is equal to the sky here. Besides, it is a simile of the virile member. The sacrifice of the head is equal to the sacrifice of the male potency. It was replaced by ūrdhvaretas, drawing the semen upwards, in later times. This process together with prāṇāyāma, the controlling of the breath, and certain positions of the body like standing on the head, are said to be the basis of yoga in the Tantric Saṃhitas. It the Veda we only find a temporary austerity called tapas, heat. The sexual activities can be resumed, as the story of Agastya reveals, only the dissipation of the semen especially in day-time is prevented (cf. Praśna Upaniṣad I.13). The Soma as a liquid is the substitute of the semen.
The same idea is illustrated by the long plaits that are worn by the seven figures. They can be regarded as a female hair-do, but here they indicate priests, who prefer to appear as female (cf. ṚV VIII.33.19). In the cult of the goddess Kybele in the Near East ūrdhvaretas is replaced by the castration of the priest who were eunuchs in the literal sense. The Greek word eunuch can be derived from Sanskrit Vena, the lovely, the final chi would correspond to the Sanskrit nominative ending ha. The general etymological explanation as to guard (echein) the bed (eune) is insufficient. To guard the bed was not the original task of the eunuch. The Vedic Vena is equal to the rainbow and the centaur. It is not a symbol of castration, but of immortality (cf. chapter III.2).
It is not impossible that ūrdhvaretas was derived from the custom of circumcision and that it was replaced by castration in the Near East. St. Paul, who speaks of the circumcision of the heart in 2.29 of his letter to the Romans, certainly not only knew the circumcision of his own people, but also the rite of castration done in the name of the goddess

46 Cf. The Sky Garment, Helsinki 1985, p. 120. He has repeated his arguments 1994 in Deciphering the Indus Script, p. 260.

Kybele, and wanted to replace both of them. Anyhow, a sacrifice of this sort had to precede the permission of entering the Christian community, too. A reference to ūrdhvaretas could also be contained in the warning given by Urvaśī to Purūravas, when he wanted to have sexual intercourse with her (cf. chapter VI).

In R̥V X.82.2 seven seers are mentioned who are equal to the seven stars of the Great Bear. Bear, Sanskrit r̥kṣa, is homophonous with r̥ṣi, seer. Because of their rays, the seven figures of the neolithic cave-painting could be identical to them.

A prototype of the eunuch is the demon-king Vr̥tra called vadhri, castrated, in I.32.7. Vadhri and Vr̥tra have homophonous consonants. Vr̥tra is often called a snake, ahi, in the Veda. In R̥V VIII.17.15 the lord of the house, Vāstoṣpati, is called pr̥dāku-sānu, he whose back is speckled. The lexicographers explain pr̥dāku either as snake or tiger. In the first case it would correspond to the snake on tablet 2756, in the second to the motif of the hero between two tigers (cf. chapter III.5).

Hence there are several reasons to suppose that the kneeling figure in the middle of seal 2430 is the leading priest engaged in sacrificing his vital energy, standing it like a tree or head on the wood (of a dais), as it is called in X.101.11. One could even see a phallus on his knee, but this is only a scratch in the material.

If the kneeling person is the main priest, the markhor with human face behind him can be regarded as the sacrificial animal whose Vedic counterpart is the horse Dadhikrā 'giving curd' according to R̥V X.101.1. It can also be identified with the bull of Soma. Though curd is obtained from cows and goats normally, it stands for the vital male energy. X.101 is addressed to the sacrificial priests. Their number is given as seven generally in the Veda. Austerity seems awful in our eyes, but after studying this hymn, we realize that the Vedic priest is a happy man. He draws from a well with *inexhaustible water* (X.101.6) which he has sunk *without digging* (X.101.11).

In the archaic conception of the world there is no fixation on a god outside the universe. This Jewish and Christian conception has caused a lot of suffering in the course of time. If ever, it can only be removed by meditation on the nature of the cosmic man. Herein the Celtic figure of

Merlin can be of equal help as that of Ṛṣyaśṛṅga and of the Indian practice of ūrdhvaretas. This practice would liberate us from the scientific dichotomy of taking the destructible world as real, too. The ancient conception of the cosmic man is not to be compared with the associative way of imagination in modern art. Being a child of the modern way of thought the modern artist is not able to imagine the cosmic man as a real entity. The archaic way of thought is associative, but it rests on the idea of the wholeness of the universe imagined as the cosmic man. When the universe, though maya, is imagined in a personal form it is much easier to transcend it. As long as we do not recognize the universe in its personal form, we cannot hope to understand what archaic thought and art really means. The signs and the motifs of the Indian seals and tablets have been created to express this conception.

Two plates of the Celtic caldron (from Sälzle, p. 149)

III. SEALS AND TABLETS WITH ANTHROPOMORPHIC MOTIFS

1. Compound motifs

Under this headline motifs with several inseparable anthropomorphic and theriomorphic elements are classified. The most interesting compound motifs are found on seal 2420 (M-304) and 2430 (M-1186) that we have both discussed in the previous chapter. We have seen there that the man in yoga posture on seal 2420 represents Dakṣa, who is an aspect of Viśvakarman. There are seals with a similar horned being in the middle and human beings and snakes at both sides which we shall study in detail in chapter III.4. The snakes are part of the mythology of Śiva, who wears some of them round his neck and who is called lord of the snakes. Under the name of Krivi, whose literal meaning is 'leather-bag', i.e. a rendering of the cup-sign, Rudra, the Vedic substitute of Śiva, is fought by Indra like Vr̥tra (cf. R̥V II.17.6; II.22.2; VIII.51.8). In the Veda Indra was the victor, but in the long run he has almost been forgotten, whereas Rudra under his name Śiva is one of the main Hindu gods now. This seems to have been anticipated by the poet in R̥V I.32.14:

Whom did you see, Indra, as an avenger of the snake,
that you felt afraid in your heart after having killed him?
You who crossed the ninety-nine rivers
are (now) like an eagle in the air full of fear.

An account of its three faces that are similar to the face of a bull the deity on seal 2420 can also be related to the bull Viśvarūpa, but then we do not consider his female aspect. The most prominent female deity in the Veda is the goddess of Dawn, Uṣas, whose car is drawn by a crocodile according to R̥V I.116.18. Because of its long teeth that are similar to the woman-sign the crocodile can be regarded as an image of this goddess. But it can also be related to Varuṇa who is the god of water in the Veda.

There are the broken seal 1376 (M-294) and the tablets 2742 (M-1395) and 0526/2783 (M-439/40) with the motif of a crocodile in the middle surrounded by other animals that could be related to this goddess. On the broken seal 1376 only half of the crocodile flanked by an elephant and a unicorn has remained. The fish-sign of the inscription of seal 1376 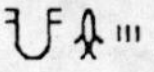 can be read as Varuṇa who is said in ṚV V.85.3 to have poured out from his vessel turned downwards heaven and earth and the intermediate space. The three strokes represent the three worlds then, the cup-sign the vessel (for the vessel turned downwards cf. sign 328 in the sign-dictionary).

The inscription of tablet 8545 (B-23) 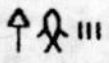 is almost identical to that of seal 1376, only the cup-sign at the end has been replaced by the lance-sign. On this tablet a man, whose profession of a teacher can be inferred from his upraised finger, stands in front of a unicorn and a markhor. The signs are written vertically as on Akkadian seals and the lance-sign looks like a cuneiform wedge here. This inscription can be related to ṚV I.154.2cd: *In Viṣṇu's three far-reaching steps all beings have found shelter*. The three strokes and the lance-sign are equal to the three far-reaching steps, the fish-sign can be read as Viṣṇu here. All beings are illustrated in the motif.

On the signless tablets 0526/2783 the crocodile is surrounded by five animals: two bulls at each side on the top, a rhino and an elephant at the left and another bull at the right. Elephant and bull are led by a man. Most interesting is another figure on the back of the bull at the right side of the motif. It looks like a child with the beak of a bird. Mackay has explained it as a monkey.[1] This could be correct, since the monkey Vṛṣākapi is the substitute of Indra in the carnivalistic hymn ṚV X.86, but a human figure with the beak of a bird is also found on tablet 8545 and on other tablets. A Vedic rendering of this motif is found in the Dawn-hymn ṚV I.49:

[1] Cf. Further Excavations, p. 358.

O Dawn, come down with your benevolence
from the realm of the sky;
the red-looking (bulls) shall take you
to the house of the Soma-offerer.
With the adorned easy-going car,
that you have mounted,
with that (car) be graceful to the man
of good reputation, daughter of the sky!
The beautifully winged birds
and the two-footed and the four-footed beings,
white Dawn, have come forward
in agreement with the rites from all directions of the sky.
For in flashing up you fill
the whole sky with light.
You the Kaṇvas desiring property
have saluted with hymns.

If the crocodile represents the Dawn, the two bulls at the top would be the animals that draw her car. The two-footed and the four-footed beings are the rhino, the elephant and the bull drawn by men. The human figure with a beak is the Soma-sacrificer. The twig he holds in his left hand, would be a twig of the Soma-plant, of which he removes the bark with the stone he holds in his upraised right hand.

The hymn has been composed by a member of the Kaṇva family. Therefore we can suppose that the inscription of tablet 2742 that has a similar motif belongs to a hymn of the same family. Here the crocodile is surrounded by four animals: Two bulls on the top, a rhino and a tiger. The human figures are missing, instead a bird is flying over one or both bulls. On the reverse we find three tigers in a whirl pressing their back against each other and the signs ʹUJ|| "◇. The motifs and the inscription can be related to R̥V I.48.5-6:

Like a beautiful young woman
the Dawn appears giving enjoyment;
she awakes all the beings that have feet,
she makes the birds fly up.

She who causes fight and promotes business,
sprinkles the path of men like a voluptuous girl;
the birds that flew up in the morning light
do not sit down again, beneficent goddess!

The four signs can referred to I.48.6b. The rhombus-sign stands for the Dawn, the two short strokes are equal to her dew with which she refreshes the path of the seer like a voluptuous girl, the two long strokes render the path, the simple cup-sign can symbolize the male organ. The three tigers are a symbol of war, but also of activity and business.

Tigers in a whirl are also depicted on seal 1386 (M-295), which has the inscription 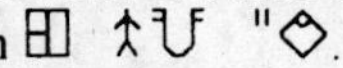. It can be affiliated to the same verse. Activity (in the form of the ritual) is rendered by the field-sign. A whirl-pool (śūghanya) is mentioned in ṚV IV.58.7.[2]

A yogi on a pedestal similar to the personage we have come across on seal 2420 is depicted on the reverse of the two-sided tablet 3303 (H-176). At his left we find the goddess in the tree together with the tiger, at his right near his pedestal a gazelle and another tiger separated from the gazelle by a wall. On the obverse a reed-house can be imagined that recalls the house that is mentioned in the Akkadian story of the Great Flood as the place where the god Ea speaks to Utnapištim (cf. chapter VII.2). One part of the house is separated by a curtain. At the entrance seems to be a fish-sign. At the left a priest with a pig-tail and a trident is standing behind a bull.[3] At the right the three signs 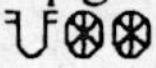 are inscribed.

On account of the two wheel-signs that can also mean king the inscription and the motifs can be affiliated to ṚV VII.33.11-13, where the birth of the seers Agastya and Vasiṣṭha is related. Both were born from a pot into which the seed of the gods Mitra and Varuṇa fell after they had been incited by the nymph Urvaśī during a long sacrifice. Urvaśī is also known as the wife of Purūravas (cf. chapter VI). The pot is equal to the cup-sign and the two wheel-signs represent Mitra and Varuṇa, both

---

[2] P. Thieme (Kleine Schriften, p. 52) explains the word as killing (han) cattle (paśu)'. This is suitable for a whirlpool as for the tigers. Both kill and swallow. This they have in common with the crocodile on the obverse.

[3] For the trident cf. chapter I.1.

being known as kings in the Veda. The two tigers on the tablet can be related to Agastya and Vasiṣṭha, the gazelle and the deity in the tree to Urvaśī. The bull-sacrifice depicted on the tablet is an image of the great sacrifice mentioned in the hymn.

A bull-sacrifice is also illustrated on the tablets 2734 and 2746. Tablet 2734 will be discussed in chapter IV. The inscription on tablet 2746 has several signs in common with that of the three-sided tablets 2752/2753 (M-493/M-1428). On one side of the tablets we find a crocodile and a tortoise above it following two fishes (cf. Franke-Vogt, fig. 234), on the other two probably female persons are standing beside an amphora (Franke-Vogt fig. 242). We shall study the inscription of tablet 2753 that is better readable: . It agrees with R̥V IV.27.1c,2d, where the eagle is described that robbed the Soma:

Hundred iron castles guarded him.
Nevertheless he escaped the guarding women,
having got strength through the Soma he conquered the winds.

The hand-sign can be read as to guard. The house-sign and the rhombus-sign are equal to an iron castle. The rhombus represents the strong walls that were made of bricks, not of iron, of course. In addition, there is a second hand-sign in the middle of the rhombus. Hundred is the same as one for the Vedic poet. To escape is written by the step-sign, the single stroke is equal to the winds, the guarding women (seven of them) and the Soma are equal to the last two pictograms. The guarding women are also illustrated by the two female persons beside the amphora, in which the Soma was kept.

The inscription of tablet 2746 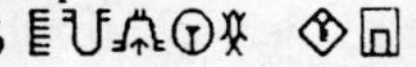 agrees with the same two verses, but here the first half of IV.27.2 is found, where the Soma is speaking:

The eagle did not carry me away through his own will,
I superseded him in strength and resoluteness.

The fish-sign stands for the eagle, the hand-sign in a circle for to carry away, to supersede is written by the head-sign. The cup-sign and the teeth-sign render strength and resoluteness.

The first line of tablet 2778 (M-483) is identical to that of tablet 2746. The additional line 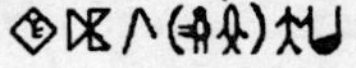 agrees with ṚV IV.27.1:

garbhe nu sann anveṣām avedam
ahaṃ devānāṃ janimāni viśvā
śataṃ mā pura āyasīr arakṣann
adha śyeno javasā niradīyam
When I was still in the egg-shell,
I perceived already the births of the gods;
hundred iron castles guarded me,
but I escaped through my speed.

To recognize the births of the gods is equal to the man with the vessel, that can also be read as a womb. The additional lines are representing a measure. To measure and to perceive are synonyms. The fish-sign and the bird-sign in brackets are equal to the first line. The step-sign renders to evade, the triangle-sign is equal to speed here, as it can be regarded as the wings of a wind-mill. The womb-sign with a hand stands for the iron castle.

The name of Agastya is rendered by the two signs of the three-sided tablet 2734 (M-1430): . The leaf-sign can be read as a tree, aga-stya means literally to stand without moving (like a tree), the cup-sign recalls Agastya's birth in a pot (cf. ṚV VII.33.13). The composite animal on the third side of this tablet represents Agastya's wife Lopāmudrā. According to later mythology Agastya formed her out of parts of all animals. The two foot-prints at the right side pointing in opposite directions are a symbol of cohabitation. The three human beings on the first side are equal to Agastya, Lopāmudrā and their son, the following tree can be Agastya or the wishing tree. The bull and the priest, by whom the bull is sacrificed, are both images of Agastya (cf. Bhagavadgītā 4.24).

On side two Lopāmudrā represented by the gazelle eats from a tree that is a symbol of Agastya as on tablet 2719. The following bull with two additional heads represents the two colours Agastya let bloom, the man standing on his head on the back of the bull illustrates Agastya's yogic power. By standing on the head for three hours daily death is overcome according to Śiva Saṃhita IV.63.

There are several tablets with the motif of a deity in a tree and an adorer in front as on seal 2430. The motif of the signless seal 1561 (M-442) is almost identical with that of seal 2430. The two registers have been exchanged, however, and there are six figures with pig-tails instead of seven, but they amount to seven, when the officiating priest is included.[4] Parpola suggests that the figures on seal 1561 are the Kr̥ttikās (the Indian name of the Pleiades),[5] who are regarded as the wives of the Seven Seers in later Indian mythology. In this case, the figures on seal 2430 would be male, on seal 1561 female, which is quite unlikely.

On tablet 2717 (M-488) and 3316 (H-177) the seven figures in the foreground are missing, on tablet 2756 (M-481) the markhor is missing, too. On seal 3251 (H-97) we find the seven figures without any other motif. The inscription of tablet 2717 will be studied in chapter XI. The inscription on the two-sided tablet 2756 is given in the Finnish concordance as 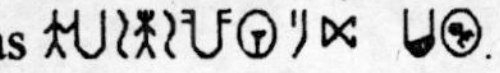. The compound in the beginning leads us to R̥V I.43.9 directed to Soma:

yās te prajā amr̥tasya parasmin dhāman r̥tasya
mūrdhā nābhā soma vena ābhūṣantīḥ somaḥ veda
On the children of immortality
at the highest place of the truth,
on them look, Soma, like the head on the navel
and know that they are adorned.

The children of immortality at the highest place of the truth are illustrated in the motif as the snake resting with its head on a dais. In the compound on the obverse the woman-sign is equal to a head, because the strokes can be explained as hairs, the wheel-sign with a nave renders the navel. The Soma is illustrated in the motif as a tree. To be adorned is equal to the second sign that can be regarded as a breast ornament. The inscription on the reverse agrees with I.43.8:

---

[4] Contrarily to Sh. Artre, who takes the figures to be female, I do not think that the exchange of the two registers makes any difference. Cf. Lady of Beast - The Harappan Goddess, Purātattva 16,1986, p. 11.

[5] Op. cit. (1985), p. 136.

mā naḥ soma paribādho mā_arātayo juhuranto
ā na indo vāje bhaja
Obstacles and guardians shall not obstruct us, Soma!
Give us a share of the trophy, drop!

The hand in a circle can be read as the guardians here, the cup-sign renders the share. The horned man-sign represents the deity, the man with a vessel the leading priest and speaker of the words of the last line. Obstacle is equal to the first sign. The second sign can be read as like. The obstacle is personified in an obstinate woman otherwise rendered by the first sign.

The inscription on tablet 3316 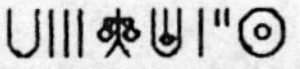 corresponds to ṚV III.33.12, where the crossing of two rivers by the Bharatas under the guidance of the sage Viśvāmitra is described:

atāriṣur bharatā gavyavaḥ
samabhakta vipraḥ sumatim nadīnām
pra pinvadhvam iṣayantīḥ surādhā
ā vakṣaṇāḥ pṛṇadhvam yāta śīvam
The Bharatas looking for cows have crossed over,
the wise (poet) has enjoyed the favour of the streams;
swell again, refreshing ones, gracious ones,
fill your breasts and flow quickly along!

The eye-sign stands for the wise poet, the two short strokes and the long stroke are equal to the two rivers, enjoy their favour is rendered by the mortar-sign, the Bharatas are written by the water-carrier-sign. The simple cup-sign and the long strokes represent the rivers as quickly running in their bed.

Seal 3251 reading 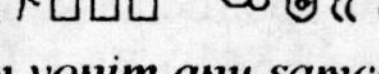 corresponds to ṚV X.17.11cd:

samānaṃ yonim anu saṃcarantàṃ
drapsaṃ juhomy anu sapta hotrāḥ
The drop that runs for the common womb
I sacrifice for each of the seven priests.

The running drop is equal to the first sign, the common womb to the mortar-sign, the mortar is in every house, the crab-sign can be read as to sacrifice. The three field-signs, that denote the threefold sacrifice, are

the place-holders for the seven priests. They are equal to the three parts of the sign ⊞. The stroke-sign can be read as to be occupied with.
It is evident from this investigation that the inscriptions with compound motifs either deal with cosmogonic or with ritual topics. This implies the birth of the seers Agastya and Vasiṣṭha. The main subject of these motifs is the idea of the sacrifice of the male energy symbolized by the phallus-sign U. Soma is another reading of this sign, as it was collected in a vat and drunken from a cup. In the centaur the compound motif has taken the form of a composite being, consisting of a human upper and an animalic lower part. We shall deal this motif in the next paragraph.

2. The centaur

The Vedic name for the centaur is gandharva. In R̥V X.123 he is identified with the rainbow called Vena, the lovely. Since the nature of the centaur is both, human and divine, he is able to connect the two worlds like the fire-god Agni. According to Greek mythology the centaur is born from a cloud.[6] The same is said in X.123.2 of the Vena. He is the most beloved of the Apsaras, who smiles at him (X.123.5). Gandharva is also a name of the sun. Grassmann says in respect to gandharva in his dictionary: "Die Ableitung ist ungewiß, Zusammenhang mit den Zentauren unwahrscheinlich." (The derivation is uncertain, a relation to the centaurs is unlikely). Yet he refers to a stem gandhāra with the female form gandhārī. According to R̥V I.126.7 Gandhāra is the native place of a sheep called avika. We have identified it in chapter I.2 with the markhor, the goat with spiral horns. These horns are also found with the centaur of the Indus seals 2347 (M-311), 7038 (K-65), 7040 (K-50) and 7711 (Nausharo-9).
It is quite possible hence that the Vedic name gandhāra has survived in the Greek kentaur.[7] With reference to the winter-solstice as the time when the centaurs appear on earth, G. Dumézil mentions a former

---

[6] Cf. R. Ranke-Graves, op. cit., p. 187. The cloud Nephele, out of which the centaur was born, is a substitute of Hera.

[7] Both can be derived from the root gadh, to cohabit (cf. chapter VI).

Polish custom celebrated at Christmas. On this occasion children go from house to house disguised as wolf, bear or turoń.[8] A similar custom is practised in Bavaria.

On seal 7038 the centaur stands beside a tree. In front of him we find the tree-sign and three short strokes. On seal 7040 four short strokes are written together with the tree-sign. The tree-sign can be read as to guard, because the tree has the form of a hand, the strokes are equal to the Soma-drops. This is contained in R̥V IX.83.5 that we have come across already in connection with the centaur-sign: *As the Gandharva he guards his place*.

The guarding of the Soma that is also described in R̥V IV.27.2,3 and X.85.4 is depicted in the motif on the left side of seal 7038, where two warriors hold their lance crosswise in front of a smaller womanlike person. The cross is a symbol of tabu and prohibition. The Soma is guarded like a woman.

The centaur consists mainly of four parts: The human upper part, the undulated horns of a markhor, the feet of a bull and the body of a tiger. Horns and feet can also be regarded as parts of one and the same animal. Man, tiger and bull form a coincidentia in oppositorum and are a simile of the cosmic man. As the rainbow the Gandharva reaches the sky. From there the truth enters the earth and the mind of the seer (X.123.2). The Gandharvas in the plural and the wind are the companions of the ascetic (the muni) in R̥V X.136.3. On the other hand, the Gandharvas are said to be fond of women.

This is reflected too in the inscription of seal 2347, where we find the woman-sign twice: 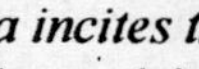. It agrees with R̥V X.123.1ab:

> *ayaṃ venaḥ codayat pr̥śnigarbhā*
>
> *This Vena incites those pregnant with the speckled one.*

The first sign can be explained as a pictogram for the rainbow or Vena. The nose-sign that can also be read as a phallus is equal to codayat, incite. The two short strokes render the two (heaven and earth), the

---

[8] Le Problème des Centaurs, Paris 1929, p. 12. The turoń is an animal with a horn (cf. T. Pierwszy, Słownik Języka Polskiego, Warszawa 1978).

two woman-signs stand for garbha, to be pregnant. The speckled one is the Vena or centaur illustrated in the motif.

The centaur on seal 2347 illustrated at the left (Franke-Vogt 225) is depicted in analogy to the 12 main nakṣatras or moon-houses of the zodiac.[9] The short horns correspond to Taurus ~ ♉, the nose is equal to Capricorn ~ ♑, the fore-part to Gemini || ~ ♊, the hair-clip of the pig-tail to Cancer ~ ♋, the tail to Leo (originally a tiger) ~ ♌ (the Sanskrit equivalence śravana - [time of] hearing - refers to the rainy season, too), the belly is equal to Virgin ~ ♍, the fore-finger as a symbol of equivalence corresponds to Balance ~ ♎, the snake on the head to Scorpio ~ ♏. The centaur as a whole who probably holds a bow in his hand is equal to Sagittarius ~ ♐, the undulated horns correspond to Aquarius ~ ♒, the skirt to Pisces ~ ♓, the invisible male organ is equal to Aries U ~ ♈.

Most of the letters of the Greek alphabet can be derived from the pictograms of the zodiac. The sign for Taurus corresponds to A, the sign for Gemini to B, the sign for Cancer to Γ (from graphein, to write), the sign for Leo to Δ, the sign for Virgin to E, the sign for Balance to T, the sign for Capricorn to H (with an additional long stroke at the right), the sign for Sagittarius to I and K (the string has been placed at the end of the inverted sign), the sign for Aquarius to Λ (it can be interpreted as a symbol of a wave), the sign for Pisces to M (the sign has the form of a wave, too, the element of the fish), the sign for Aries to Y (as vowel = U). Likewise the other letters of the Greek alphabet can be derived from Indus signs. Z that has been placed at a wrong position there is similar to ∫, O to O, P to ⍑, Φ to ⓣ, Ψ to the tree-sign, X corresponds to ✕, Θ to ◉, Ω to the inverted cup-sign. The rest are variants of other signs or simply strokes. It is said that the Greek took the al-

[9] For the symbolism of the zodiac cf. H. Frankfort, op. cit. p. 156; A. Scherer, Gestirnnamen bei den indogermanischen Völkern, Heidelberg 1953; P. Jensen, Die Kosmogonie der Babylonier, Berlin 1890.

phabet from the Phoenicians,[10] but obviously there is an older relation to the Indus signs probably established through the agency of astrology. It is not surprising hence that the symbols of the planets can also be derived from Indus signs: For Mercury ☿ we get 8, the caduceus, for Venus ♀ the flower-sign (the Egyptian sign for vital energy (ank) ☥, for Mars ♂ the lance ↑, for Jupiter ♃ the hammer ⊤ or the cross for the directions, for Saturn ♄ the tower-sign ⊓.
The inscription of seal 7711  recalls again the sexual appetite of the gandharvas, here it has been imbodied in the ape Vṛṣākapi. Like the gandharva, the ape is half human, half animal. The inscription agrees with X.86.5, where Indrāṇī, Indra's wife, says:

> *priyā tuṣṭāni me kapir vyaktā vyadūduṣat*
> *śiro nvasya rāviṣaṃ na sugaṃ duṣkṛte bhuvam*
> *viśvamad indra uttaraḥ*
> *The ape has polluted my painted things/my pots,*
> *I shall tear off his head,*
> *the wicked shall not come to me;*
> *Indra is higher than everything.*

The two strokes can be read as a sign for pollution (by the seed), for woman we find the flower-sign. The ape-sign is the geometric form of the sitting ape 卐 depicted on seal 5076.[11] The following sign can be read as a painted pot, the triangle-sign renders wicked, because it can be explained as to assault, to assail (to run fast), the circle-sign stands for the womb, the additional triangle indicates that it is forbidden to come near to it. To tear off the head is omitted here.
The second line corresponds to the refrain *Indra is higher than everything*: The man with the staff can be read as Indra, the stroke-sign as higher and the cup-sign as everything.

---

[10] Cf. H. Haarmann, op. cit. p. 284.

[11] The sitting ape is one of the few pictograms correctly read by N. Jha. Cf. Vedic Glossary on Indus Seals, Varanasi 1996, p. 34.

3. Standing horned person ± arch

The horn of the person indicates that it is a deity, it can be male or female, but normally it is male, as on seal 1227 (M-1224) and on the tablets 3305, 3307 (H-179), 3317 (H-242), 3318 (H-178), 3319 (H-175) and 4117 (H-363). On tablet 3317 and 3319 the deity stands under an arch of flames. Seal 1227 is inscribed on both sides and has the motif of a unicorn on its reverse.

The two lines are 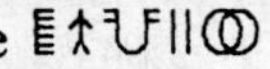 . The first line can be read according to R̥V X.101.11ab:

> *ubhe durau vahnir āpibdamāno*
> *'antaryoneva carati dvijāni*
> *Between the two shafts the drawing animal*
> *goes treading firmly like a man with two women in bed.*

The first sign that can be explained as a star with rays or the sun is equal to the drawing animal, the six strokes represent the six worlds that are compared with two shafts here. The hand-sign represents the man, the two comb-signs the two women.

The second line is equal to X.101.10cd:

> *pari ṣvajadhvaṃ daśa kakṣābhir*
> *ubhe dhurau prati vahnim yunakta*
> *Harness the drawing animal to the two shafts,*
> *fasten it with ten belts!*

The intersected circles represent heaven and earth again, the long strokes are equal to harness the two shafts, the cup-sign renders the drawing animal, the ten belts are equal to the woman-sign, to fasten to the man-sign. Both, the horned person and the unicorn, that corresponds to the drawing animal, represent the sun.

The tablets with a horned deity have all been found in Harappa, on two of them the deity is standing under an arch, on two not. The two tablets with an arch have inscriptions of three signs only: 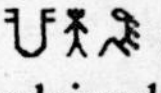 (3307) and 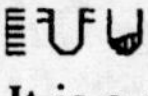 (3318). The first sign of tablet 3307 can be explained as a snake. It is a symbol for the magic power of the gods like the Kuṇḍalinī. If the motif is again interpreted as the sun, the inscription can be read according to R̥V X.72.7:

yat devā yatayo yathā bhuvanāni apinvata
atrā samudra ā gūḷham ā sūryam ajabhartana
When you gods like magicians let swell the worlds,
you brought forth the sun that was hidden in the ocean.

The snake-sign can be read as magician, the horned man-sign as the gods, the cup-sign as the sun.

The first sign of tablet 3318 renders to measure out, the woman-sign is equal to the earth, the cup-sign to Varuṇa. This agrees with V.85.5: *Varuṇa measured out the earth by the sun.* The sun is found in the motif.

On the round tablet 3317 the signs have been arranged around a swastika, therefore we shall discuss it in chapter XI. The inscription of tablet 3319 is . It corresponds to ṚV IX.74.1:

śiśur na jāto 'va cakradad vane
svar yad vājy_aruṣaḥ siṣāsati
divo retasā sacate payovṛdhā
tam īmahe sūmatī śarma sapráthaḥ
Like a new-born child he bellows into the wood,
when the tawny runner tries to reach the sun;
he who unites with the seed of heaven full of milk,
him we ask for his far-reaching protection.

The first two signs are equal to like a new-born child, the child being the Soma or the moon. The wood or vat, into which the drop runs is rendered by the cup-sign with additional stroke. The short strokes and the phallus-sign are equal to the seed of heaven, to unite, referring to the process of pressing, is written by the mortar-sign. The last sign can be read as far-reaching protection, because it represents the circle of the sun or the sky with sun and moon that are also mentioned in line b.

The inscription on the three-sided tablet 3305 consists of the sign  only. On one side a deity with a club on his arm is depicted that looks like the guardian-sign . The person on the third side seems to be female. The single sign is repeated on all sides. The deity can represent Rudra or Indra, who is known for his thunderbolt similar to the club held by the deity. Indra is also very fond of Soma, which could be hinted at by the cup-sign, and he is called the manliest god. This could be indicated by the big phallus of the deity on the second side.

The inscription of the four-sided tablet 4117 is written on three of its rectangular sides: 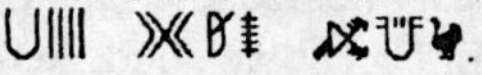. It agrees with ṚV X.177.1,3:

pataṇgam aktam asurasya māyayā
apaśyaṃ gopām anipadyamānam
ā ca parā ca paṭhibhiś carantam
ā varīvarti bhuvaneṣvantaḥ
The bird anointed with the magical power of the Asura,
the restless guardian I saw
going to and fro on his(two) ways;
he moves up and down in the beings.

The three signs of the first line are equal to X.177.1a. The cup-sign with two additional strokes stands for Asura, the triangle-sign with a hand at the end is equal to anoint (the hand) with magical power. The first sign of the second line renders restless, not sitting down on a roost, the bow-sign is equal to the guardian, the man-sign has to be supplemented here, crossing-sign can be explained as going up and down on two ways. The phallus-sign and the four strokes render to move up and down in the beings (like the pestle in the mortar for preparing Soma). The bird is an image of the sun that is also depicted in the motif of the tablet.

The archer on eight copper-tablets, starting with 1606 (M-588), could also be a form of Rudra or Indra. Since he looks more like a hunter than a king, it can be supposed that he represents Rudra For the inscription 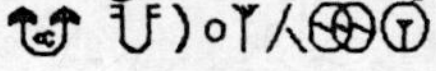 we find indeed the corresponding verse in ṚV I.71.5:

mahe yat pitra īm rasaṃ dive kar
avatsarat pṛśanyaḥ cikitvān
srjad astā dhṛṣtā didyum asmai
svāyāṃ devo duhitari tviṣiṃ dhāt
After having created seed for the great father, the sky,
and having noticed his desire, he crept near (like a hunter);
boldly the bowman shot the arrow at him,
(since) the god approached the own daughter impetuously.

The hand in a circle corresponds to he created, the seed and the sky are contained in the sign of the intersected circles. The step-sign renders to creep near, the hand-sign, the circle and the curve can be read as to draw the arrow for a certain aim, the cup-sign is equal to the father of the sky.

The single compound  corresponds to the last line, since its main part can be interpreted as a womb or flower-bud, here representing the daughter, the crab-sign is equal to approach impetuously, to violate. R̥V I.71.5 refers to the relation of the father of the sky to his daughter, the Dawn, that is described in X.61.5-8 in plain sexual metaphors. We shall study these verses in relation to the horse-sacrifice in chapter V.

4. Man in yoga-posture on a pedestal ± snakes or crocodiles

There are only two seals with a man in yoga-posture as a single motif. They have the numbers 2222 (M-1181) and 2235 (M-305). The inscription of seal 2222  agrees with R̥V X.125.3:

ahaṃ rāṣṭrī saṃgamanī vasūnām
cikītuṣī prathamā yajñiyānām
I am the queen, the collectrice of riches,
I am the knowing one, the first of those deserving sacrifice.

The town-sign stands for the queen, because the town is the place, where she rules. Collectrice of riches is equal to the two snakelike lines. The snakes are a symbol of riches, vasu, which they guard like the dragon of the German mythology. Vāsuki is the name of a king of these snakes. I am the first is rendered by the stroke-sign, the dotted fish-sign can be read as the knowing one. Deserving sacrifice, an attribute of the gods in general, is equal to the cup-sign. Two snakes are found on either side of the deity in the motif of the tablets 2826, that we shall discuss later on, and on and tablet 2774 that we shall discuss in chapter VIII. They indicate that the deity is a lord of riches like a king or queen.

The inscription of the broken seal 2235 consists of two lines, but only two signs are readable on each of the lines. In addition, there is a long oblique stroke that seems to belong to the second line. The signs are written on both sides of the motif. They can be rendered as 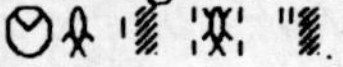. The fish-signs can be identified with the two birds of R̥V I.164.20:

dvā suparṇā sayujā sakhāyā samānaṃ vr̥kṣaṃ pari ṣasvajāte
tayor anyaḥ pippalaṃ svādv abhyanaśann anyo cākaśīti

Two beautifully winged birds, connected in friendship,
sit on the selfsame tree;
one eats the sweet berries,
the other looks on without eating.

The two remaining signs of the first line render the two beautifully winged birds. The one that eats the sweet berries is indicated by the single stroke. The other that looks on without eating is equal to the fish-sign and the mouth-sign that can also symbolize the sun. That one that eats the sweet berries is equal to the moon being born again and again as is said in X.85.18. The tree is the cosmic tree. It is represented by the deity. The way to the moon leading to rebirth and to the sun leading to immortality are known from the teaching of the Upaniṣads and the Bhagavadgītā. The two birds are also mentioned in X.114.3. The stars in the horns of the crown of the deity are probably the Venus as morning and evening star. The Venus not only leads the skipper over the ocean, but also the speaker of the truth to immortality like the Dawn.

The inscription of tablet 2826  corresponds to R̥V X.5.3 addressed to Agni:

r̥tāyinī māyinī saṃ dadhāte
mitvā śiśuṃ jajñatur vardhayantī
viśvasya nābhīṃ carato dhruvasya
kaveścit tantuṃ manasā viyantaḥ
The two devoted to the ritual, with magic power united,
formed and created the child and fostered it,
the navel of all that moves and stands fixed,
cutting even the thread of the seer in the mind.

The two are the father of the sky and the Dawn rendered by the second and the third sign. The ritual is their sexual union (cf. chapter V) repeated in the pressing of Soma represented in the first sign. The child born from this union is Rudra depicted in the fourth sign. The last sign represents the Puruṣa, who is the navel of all which moves and stands.

The last line is contained in the signs of the first side: The snake is a synonym of the thread or the energy of life. The seer is rendered by the fish-sign as usual, to cut by the mouth of the crocodile. In other hymns of the Veda, it is the Dawn who is criticised for shortening even the life of the seer, here it is the moon, whose sign has an additional stroke therefore. The reduplication of the symbols refers to the reflection of the creation in the mind.

The same idea is contained in the motifs of the tablet 9910* found in the Near East described by A. Parpola as follows:[12]

> One of the two anthropomorphic figures carved on this seal wears a crown of water buffalo horns with the leafed branch of a fig and sits on a throne with hoofed legs, surrounded by a pair of horned snakes, a pair of fishes and a pair of water buffaloes. The other figure stands, fighting two tigers, and surrounded by trees, a markhor goat and a vulture above a rhinoceros.

Parpola has omitted the ring between the water-buffaloes that can be interpreted as a bucket. The Indian concordance renders as inscription two fish-signs and the tree-sign, but the second fish-sign is only a reflection like the tree and the snake. The inscription would then simply be . It is not sure that the bird on the rhino is a vulture. Even if it is, it cannot do harm to it, as long as it is alive. The two water-buffaloes with the bucket between them need not be an image of enmity either. Though creation is composed out of antagonistic powers, it is held in equilibrium by them. The same is true for life and death, and the complain of the seer to the Dawn is not rectified, though understandable, because nobody wants to die.

According to IX.83.4 the Soma that is represented by the bucket is guarded by the Gandharva or centaur. The centaur is the figure with hoofed legs and the person fighting with the two tigers. Its written equivalence are the fish-sign and the hand-sign. The latter indicates his guarding function. If the hand-sign is read as tree-sign it represents the Soma, who is often called a seer in the Veda. This is the general meaning of the fish-sign.

A fish and a twig written as Y are also found on the cylinder seal 9007 from Ur together with a unicorn in front of another fish, replacing the standard, and a large kino-tree in front of both. The kino-tree represents the plant, from which the Soma was obtained (cf. chapter I.7). The meaning of the two signs is identical to those on tablet 9910*.

---

[12] Deciphering the Indus Script, p. 186. Here an illustration is given, too.

On tablet 1579, whose motif is hardly to be recognized, a yogi sits on a pedestal before an adorer who stretches out his hands to him (cf. Franke-Vogt, fig. 247). The inscription of the last four signs is identical with that of the unicorn-seal 3005 (H-12) 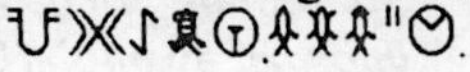. It can be read on the ground of R̥V V.85.5,6:

> *Nobody reaches Varuṇa's magical power,*
> *With it as measuring line he has*
> *measured out the earth through the sun.*

Varuṇa's magical power is the sun at the sky, as is said in R̥V V.63.4. This is equal to the first two signs. For Varuṇa himself we get the crowned fish-sign. The following two fish-signs represent other gods. That they do not reach Varuṇa's magical power is rendered by the hand in the circle. The rest of the signs is already known to us.

There are the broken tablets 2777 and 0298 (M-456) with the same motif. The inscription, that is partly broken off, is different, however. On tablet 2777 the three signs 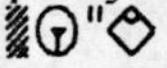 are preserved, on tablet 0298 the two signs 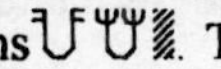. The signs of tablet 2777 can be read as (Varuṇa) has placed the sun at the sky (V.85.2). The two signs of tablet 0298 agree with R̥V IX.12.1, where the womb of the truth is mentioned (cf. seal 2238 in the sign-dictionary).

5. Deity between two tigers

There are four seals and two tablets with the motif of a deity between two tigers. It is certainly related to the motif of seal 2420, where the second tiger is replaced by a buffalo. The seals have the numbers 2075 (M-308), 2086 (M-306), 2122 (M-307) and 2454 (M-1183), the tablets 0512 (M-1182) and 3308 (H-181). An ithyphallic man is depicted on seal 2075 and 2454. This seal and tablet 3308 have no inscription. The two tigers can symbolize the two worlds giving way to the creator as melted butter or ghr̥ta according to R̥V X.82.1. Ghr̥ta is phonetically related to r̥ta and to the first participles of gra(b)h, to seize, and gr̥̄, to swallow. Therefore it can be rendered by a tiger or a snake that represent the cruel aspect of Nature. The deity between the animals has also a guarding function as pointed in the discussion of tablet 9910*

The inscription of seal 2075 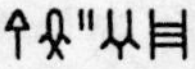 can be related to X.85.4ab:

ācchadvidhānair gupito bārhatair soma rakṣitaḥ
Secured by safety devices,
guarded by mightiful powers you are, Soma.

The first sign can be read as safety devices, i.e. something like a veil or cover, the last two signs render the mightiful powers. The second sign that can be explained as a vessel with fluids trickling down, is an image of the Soma. The two strokes refer to the two guarding arrangements, the safety devices and the mightiful powers.

The inscription of seal 2122 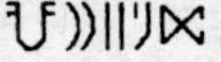 can be related to ṚV X.125.8ab:

aham eva vāta iva pra vāmi_ ārabhamāṇā bhuvanāni viśvā
I blow like the wind seizing all the worlds.

The first two signs can be read as I seize, all the worlds is equal to the curved lines and the cup-sign, the long strokes render to blow like the wind. The deity between the tigers can also be regarded as female. The inscription of seal 2086 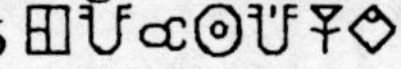 can therefore be related to ṚV I.92.4ab addressed to the Dawn:

adhi peśāṃsi vapati nṛtūr iva aporṇute vakṣa usrā iva barjaham
She puts on bright ornaments like a dancing girl,
she uncovers her breast as a cow her swollen udder.

The first sign can be read as a breast ornament, the second, written as the flower-sign  in the Finnish concordance, is equal to the dancing girl. The dotted cup-sign can be read as vapati, she puts on, because the root vap means to sow. The fourth sign renders to uncover the breast, the crab-sign the cow, because the scissors can be interpreted as horns. The second cup-sign and the field-sign are equal to a swollen udder, which is obtained by bringing the cows to the meadow being equal to the last sign.

Tablet 0512 was probably inscribed with the four signs 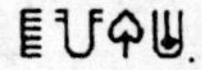. They can be read as I.179.4cd:

lopāmudrā vṛṣaṇaṃ nī riṇāti dhīram adhīrā dhayati śvasantam
Lopāmudrā milks the strong man,
the unwise squeezes out the panting wise.

The mortar-sign can be read as to squeeze, the leaf-sign and the cup-sign are equal to Agastya, the comb-sign to Lopāmudrā. Here the man between the two tigers has been overwhelmed by them, as it were.
On tablet 3308 the deity between the tigers stands on an elephant. The same motif is depicted on tablet 4750* that was recently excavated.[13] Here the wheel-sign ⊛ that can also represent the sun is written on top of the deity that must be female on account of its bosom. Hence the sign can stand for the sun-daughter, whose marriage is described in R̥V X.85. On the reverse of tablet 3308 we find the motif of the deity in the tree with the tiger in front, on tablet 4750* a man in yoga-posture is depicted watching the sacrifice of a bull. This can be affiliated to R̥V X.85.35, where the colours of the sun-daughter are explained as cutting up, dissecting and cutting asunder. The elephant that carries the world in later Indian mythology can be identified with the car of the sun-daughter, the two tigers with day and night.

6. The tiger and the goddess in a kino tree

There are about 15 seals and tablets with this motif. On four tablets, 2717, 2719, 2828 and 3308, it occurs together with other motifs. Four seals with this motif have no inscription, two inscriptions are broken off. On tablet 3308 the motif of the deity between two tigers is depicted on the reverse.
On seal 5018 from Chanhu Daro the deity is sitting under the tree. On tablet 3306 (H-182) the tiger is looking back to the goddess who carries a drum. Instead of the tree we find five swastikas on the reverse, three turning right, two left. Several inscriptions affiliated to this motif agree with verses of R̥V X.125 directed to Language, Vāc. That the deity is female is also indicated by the pinnate leaves of the tree similar to the woman-sign.
The equivalence of the inscription of seal 1355 (M-310)  is found in X.27.16ab:

[13] Cf. J. M. Kenoyer, Around the Indus in 90 Slides, www.harappa.com/indus/90.html, Harappa 1996.

The one, who equals ten, the reddish one (kapila),
they incite to a helpful sacrifice;
the mother holds the beautiful child to her breast
and nurses it, though it does not want to drink.

The reddish one who equals ten is Agni. He is written by the single stroke and the step-sign that can be read as the fire-sticks. The first sign renders to incite, the cup-sign and the field-sign are equal to a helpful sacrifice. The second half of the verse gives a description of the motif. The mother is the deity in the tree, Agni is the tiger that does not want to listen to her (or to drink her milk) as indicated by his reluctant behaviour.

The inscription of seal 2522 (M-309) 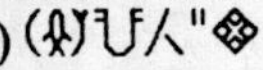 agrees with X.125.3cd:

Me the gods have divided into different parts,
me, who dwells at different places and has various forms.

The two short strokes can be read as me, the town-sign is equal to dwell at different places, the step-sign can be read as to divide. The cup-sign stands for the gods and the fish-sign with two curves for having various forms.

Tablet 4204 (H-715) has the inscription 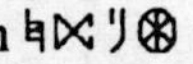 that is equal to IX.83.5c: *As a king you take the food.* The second sign stands for as, the first for king, the third for to take, and the last sign for food.

Seal 5018 with the goddess squatting on the ground underneath the tree has the four signs . The separate sign is found on many seals from Chanhu Daro. The inscription is contained in ṚV X.125.8b:

I move like the wind carrying all beings (all worlds).

For moving like the wind (in the tree) we get the tree-sign, because the trees are moved by the wind and they are believed to create the wind vice versa. For carrying we get the water-carrier, for all beings the crossing-sign and the three strokes.

The inscription of seal 7024 (K-49)  agrees with ṚV X.72.9a, where the goddess is called Aditi:

With seven sons Aditi went up (beyond the three worlds).

For the inscription of tablet 3306  cf. chapter XI.

7. The sacred marriage

The sacred marriage belongs to the must important motifs of the Indus seals. In the Veda it is celebrated between the father Sky and the daughter Dawn, Uṣas, or between the Aśvins, the twin-gods, and Uṣas. The second form is preferred by the poets in later time, perhaps because it avoids the trap of an incestuous relation. The Veda does not state the natural equivalence of the Aśvins, but they are always described as extremely beautiful. From their name it can be inferred that they were horse-drivers. Their horses were not natural beings, however, because they had wings. They look like the unicorns on Assyrian seals (cf. chapter I,2). According to R̥V X.85.10 their car was drawn by oxen, not by horses. This implies that the origin of the Aśvins is older than that of the horse-driving Āryans. Their car is miraculous, too, because it could be driven over the ocean. It was not the first amphibian, however, but a ship (cf. chapter VII.2). Through their ownership of sea-going ships the Aśvins are linked to the Indus civilization. Their zodiacal houses are Gemini and Libra and these two houses form also the beginning and the end of their daily voyage with the Dawn, who is identical to the Mesopotamian goddess Ištar and the Venus-star, as we have pointed out already. During the Indus civilization, Gemini was the morning constellation and the Venus was standing exactly between its two stars.[14] In the evening it was standing in Virgin, the house of the marriage-night.

The car of the Aśvins remained unyoked during the night and was yoked in the morning, especially in spring-time, to bring the Dawn to the earth. When unyoked, its place is at the firmament, when yoked, it moves through the sky. According to R̥V X.85.14,16 it had three wheels, one of which was hidden. It can be explained as the axis mundi or the wheel of the earth, whose movement is not seen except by the wise (cf. R̥V I.30.19). This statement makes it likely that the rotation of the earth and its movement around the sun was known to the Vedic seers and their ancestors in the Indus Valley as well as to the Mesopotamian priests.

---

[14] Cf. the map given by Parpola (1994, p. 202).

In Greek mythology the Aśvins have become warriors, in the Veda they are called kings, but they have no martial attributes, their main characteristic is their healing power. They are said to have been born at different places, i.e. in heaven and on earth, but there is not the least enmity between them. This trait has been retained in Greek mythology. As the Aśvins have to do with day and night, they can also be affiliated to life and death. The name 'Aśvin' is probably of a younger date. Nāsatya seems to be their older name. Grassmann explains it in his dictionary as na asatya, not untruthful, but it is more likely that it is derived from nausatya, having ships. In later mythology this name is explained by the way of their birth. They are said to have been born through the nose, nāsa, of their mother, who had taken the form of a mare. Indeed, the Aśvins can be compared to the two nostrils of the Venus, when looked at the sky in the era of the Indus civilization. As husbands of the Dawn or Venus, the Aśvins are similar to the centaur.

Several seals whose motif is related to the sacred marriage have been found in Ur. On the Failaka seal 9014 that belongs to the seals published by Gadd two ithyphallic bull-men adore the goddess Ištar sitting between them on a chair. Both carry a moon-standard of the form discussed in chapter I.7. The right one is touched by the goddess, too. If we regard the goddess as the sun-daughter and the bull-men as the Aśvins, we can affiliate the motif to ṚV X.85.9ab:

> *somo vadhūyur abhavat aśvinā āstām ubhe varā*
> *Soma was the bridegroom,*
> *the two Aśvins were the suitors (of the sun-daughter).*

An inscription related to the scenery of this seal seems to be contained in the probably motifless damaged seal 9003 also found in Ur: 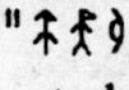.
The first sign represents the moon, the second sign can be interpreted as a man with long hairs, i.e. a woman, but here it could denote the bridegroom, who is decorated like a woman. Bridegroom, vadhūyu, can be derived from vadhu, woman. The next sign is a variant of the man-sign. It can be read as vara, suitor. The two short strokes may represent the Aśvins here. The rest is obliterated.

The sun-daughter as the Venus star and the Soma-standard are depicted on the round seal 9703* from Failaka (Aachen, fig. 29).[15] The standard has been placed on a net, to which two oxen have been attached, of which only the heads and a leg are visible. This recalls the motif of seal 1387. On either side of the net a man is standing holding a stick or lance in his hand. Like the two men on seal 7038 they can be identified with the Aśvins guarding the sun-daughter and the Soma. One, who could be regarded as the immortal, has picked up a fish with his stick, the other, who could be the mortal, touches the net with his stick or lance of which the probably brazen head is visible. There is an eye in front of him indicating his guarding function. Underneath the net a bull is depicted like that on seal 9014. The eye and the fish can be regarded as representing the verses that go together with the Aśvins according to R̥V X.85.11ab:

r̥k sāmābhyām abhihitaṃ gāvau te sāmanāv itaḥ
Yoked with the verse of the R̥g and the Sāmān
your bulls go smoothly together.

The motif is described in verse X.85.8cd:

sūryāyā aśvinā varā agniḥ āsīt purogavaḥ
The two Aśvins were the bridegrooms
of the daughter of the sun, Agni was going ahead.

The daughter of the sun is equal to the Venus-star, Agni as going ahead, purogava, is represented by the two bulls, the net is equal to the place of sacrifice, where the daughter of the sun is going to be married with the Aśvins and where the bulls were killed or sacrificed (cf. X.85.13). The Aśvin at the right may partake in the killing with his iron-pointed lance.

The water-carrier on seal 9012 can also be regarded as a symbol of the sun-daughter or the Dawn in her aspect of a hierodule or Apsaras. The water is carried in bags that have fish-form. A third bag stands at the right side of the deity, a centaur at the left side, whose close relation with the Apsaras is known from X.123. A star is placed on either sides of the head of the central figure that can be explained as the Venus in her aspect of the morning and the evening star as on seal 2235.

---

[15] For a better photograph cf. P. Kjærum, op. cit. fig. 174.

The whole motif is put in brackets that can be interpreted as egg-shells or as the womb of the goddess. All these motifs can be related to the Vāc-hymn ṚV X.125.2:

ahaṃ somam āhanasaṃ bibharmi
ahaṃ tvaṣṭāram uta puṣanaṃ bhagam
I carry (in my womb) the swelling Soma,
I Tvaṣṭṛ, Pūṣan and Bhaga.

The three bags in fish-form correspond to the three gods Tvaṣṭṛ, Pūṣan and Bhaga, the centaur represents the swelling Soma. The two stars can also be explained as lotus-flowers. A lotus forms the head of the Lajjā Gaurī in later mythology.[16]

It is not surprising that several Indus seals found in Ur refer to the sacred marriage, because spirituality and religion form an equally important link between the two cultures as economical connections. It is also referred to in the inscription on seal 9902 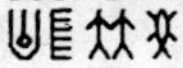, whose motif depicts the mating of a bull and a cow. It can be related to the Aśvins on account of the two man-signs, as was suggested by Gadd.[17] If the first sign is read as a bee, a corresponding verse is found in X.40.6cd, where the maiden Ghoṣā, who is in search of a suitable husband, says to the Aśvins:

yuvor ha makṣā pary_aśvinā madhva
āsā bharata niṣkṛtaṃ nā yoṣaṇā
To you the bee has brought with the mouth the honey
like the girl who informs (the lover) of the meeting-place.

The literal translation would be: The bee has brought the honey to the Aśvins like a girl that presses the Soma in the mortar.

In an ironical way the sacred marriage is dealt with in the Soma-hymn IX.112. Verse 4cd of this hymn contains the famous words:

śepo romaṇvantau bhedau
vār in maṇḍūka icchati indrāya indo pari srava

---

[21] Cf. F.H.P. Janssen, On the Origin and Development of the so-called Lajjā Gaurī, in: South Asian Archaeology, Stuttgart 1993, p. 457. The word 'lajjā gaurī' means shameful woman, but it stands for a shameless woman.

[17] Cf. Seals of Ancient Indian Style at Ur, p. 209.

The tail looks for the hairy slot, the frog desires water;
for Indra, drop, run around.

This agrees with the inscription of the tiger-seal 2045, that bears a frog and a crocodile on two of its edges. Its inscription is 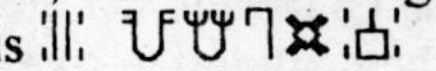 The first sign can be read as a phallus with seed, the second as hairy slot, the third sign represents the frog, because this animal was regarded as bringing coolness and refreshment (cf. R̥V X.16.14) like a shadoof does. The womb-sign can be read as well, its water is called vār, enclosed water, the cup-sign renders Indra. The last pada is equal to the compound written separately. Frog and well are also related in a western fairy-tale that deals with the sacred marriage. The frog is a seer also, as is known from R̥V VII.103. It is conceived as male in the inscription, and this is also implied in the Vedic verse. When looking for water the frog is often caught by a crocodile in it. Though both sexes have a mutual desire for each other, for the writer of the Indus seal it is the male that has to suffer for the illusion of getting happiness through sexuality.

The motif of the sacred marriage is also depicted on the third side of the signless tablet 1574 (M-489), which we shall discuss in chapter V, and on tablet 2740 (M-1406). Considering the sacrificial post at the right of its obverse as a pestle, this tablet can be affiliated to R̥V I.28. The author of this hymn, Śunaḥśepa, was bound to such a post. After composing several hymns, he was released. He could be identical to the right man standing near the post and to the dog-like figure lying over a prostrated person in the middle of the tablet. This is corroborated by his name, because Śunaḥśepa means dog-tail. In the left corner of the lower register a man beats a long drum from both sides. This sort of drum is still found in India today. Near the head of the prostrated person is sitting a fourth person, apparently holding two boards in his hands, probably a musical instrument, too. The rest of the tablet is broken off.

In I.28 the woman is compared to the mortar, the drum is mentioned in I.28.5. The pestle is a simile of the sacrificial post and the male organ. Mortar and pestle represent the inverted tree, too, described in R̥V I.24.7. The mortar resembles the crown, the pestle the stem.

On the obverse of tablet 2728 a man sacrifices a cup of Soma, that has the same form as a phallus, to a kino tree, then follows the inscription and a design. On the reverse at the left a jar with a lid and the motif of the deity in the tree together with a tiger is depicted, at the right hand three persons are occupied in uprooting a kino tree. It could be an image of the eternal aśvattha tree, that should be uprooted in order to obtain true knowledge according to Bhagavadgītā 15.3. A similar motif is found on the signless tablet 5069, where two men are carrying a branch of an aśvattha tree between them.
The inscription of tablet 2728 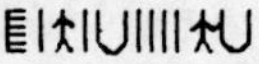 agrees with R̥V X.101.12ab:

kapr̥n nara kapr̥tham uddadhātana
codayata khudata vājasātaye
The phallus, men, erect the phallus,
move it and insert it to win the prize.

For the first compound that is also part of the motif, we get kapr̥n, phallus, and nara, man. Uddadhātana kapr̥th, erect the phallus, is equal to the four strokes, that are used onomatopoetical here, and the second phallus-sign. For codayata, move, and khudata, insert, we get the man-sign and the two strokes. The woman-sign stands for the womb that must be supplemented here. Vāja, the prize, is equal to the jar with a lid and the design.
A man holding a ring in the left hand and a sickle in the right is depicted on the obverse of the two-sided tablet 3304. He stands in front of a sitting person, who on account of its long hairs is most probably female. The arms are turned upwards as if to pray. At the left of the reverse two tigers stand on their hind-legs and touch each other with their paws, a woman lies at the right with her legs spread apart, a plant or leaf coming out of her womb.[18]
These motifs suggest a relation to the cosmogonic conceptions of the Veda. This is confirmed by the inscription 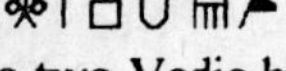 written alike on both sides of the tablet. It can be affiliated to two Vedic hymns. The first reading agrees with R̥V X.129.5 and 7. The last half of X.129.5 reads:

There were seed-givers, their were (antogonistic) powers,
and the impulse was at the bottom and the granting above.

---

[18] Mahadevan explains this object as a crab, Franke-Vogt as a tortoise, but both these animals have no tail, for this reason it must be a plant or leave.

The nose-sign that can also depict a phallus or sprout can be read as seed-giver. The wall-sign renders the antogonistic powers. The dotted cup-sign is equal to the last line of the verse. The second half of the inscription is contained in X.129.7, though in a different way. It reads:

This creation, from where it came,
whether it was created or not,
the guardian in the highest heaven,
he alone knows it - or perhaps he does not know it?

The field-sign can be read as creation, the hand-sign as guardian, the sign of the water-carrier as carrying the world in the womb. This would render the affirmation: He is the guardian of creation that was born from the womb of the mother-goddess.

The female part in creation that was mentioned in verse 5, has been omitted in verse 7. The last line testifies for the tolerance of the Vedic seers that is also found in the ambiguity of the signs of the Indus script. The Vedic conception of creation is much ahead of the linear theory of a Big Bang of modern science.

It is also possible to read the inscription according to I.179.1ab of the dialogue-hymn of Agastya and Lopāmudrā:

Old age impairs the beauty of the bodies,
therefore the bull-like men should go to their wives.

The first sign, that can be explained as a phallus hanging down, renders old age. The second sign can be read as śri, beauty, if it is interpreted as a veil or curtain. The cup-sign with a stroke represents the womb awaiting fecundation. The bull-like men are rendered by the field-sign and the hand-sign, whose basic reading is upholder of the law. Agastya is called a tamed bull in I.179.4. The sign of the water-carrier refers to Lopāmudrā.

It is not clear from the hymn, when the dialogue took place. If the woman on the tablet carries twigs on her head as is suggested by Franke-Vogt, it happened, when Lopāmudrā was going to prepare the Soma juice, whose twigs she brought on her head. This can also be deduced from I.179.4, because her desire coming *from here and there* is a reference to the pressing boards (cf. the reading of seal 1586 in chapter IV). The Soma is addressed directly in I.179.5:

To this Soma that I have drunk
with my innermost heart I say:
May he forgive the sin we have begot,
for the mortal has many desires.

It is surprising that Agastya thinks that he has begot a sin in having sexual intercourse with his wife Lopāmudrā. According to Vedic tradition, nobody commits a sin by having sexual intercourse with his wife. Agastya, however, may have looked upon her as his daughter, because he has created her. He purifies himself from the sin of incest by the notion that it was love that compelled him to do this. Through this love the vaginal fluid is turned into Soma. This is depicted in the motif of the reverse by a Soma-plant or Soma-leaf growing from the womb of the woman. In this way, divine and mortal love are reconciled. The relation of Agastya and Lopāmudrā is similar to that of Prajāpati and Uṣas, the goddess of Dawn, who is both, a virgin and a prostitute. Nobody who lives on the sexual plane alone will be able to understand this dichotomy. However, everybody has the potential to go beyond the bonds of nature and dance like the two tigers on the tablet.

It is impossible to explain every facet of the tablets with compound motifs and the symbolism of their signs in this chapter. It is hoped, however, that it has become clear by now that the Veda generally gives a true description of the motifs and the signs of the Indus seals whose meaning is focused on the cosmic man in his androgyn form.[19]

[19] The cosmic man is the precondition for the shamanic voyages to heaven and the underworld, too, but the shaman belongs to a tribal religion. This must be objected against E.C.L. During Casper's statement that the bow-man, the man in yoga posture and the deity in the tree are shamans (op. cit. passim).

IV. SEALS AND TABLETS WITH COMPOSITE ANIMALS

There are three main classes of composite animals on the Indus seals and tablets: A tiger with the horns of a bull or zebu and sometimes with bovine legs, a three-headed bovine animal and a fabulous animal consisting of seven parts, namely those of a tiger, a bull, a goat and an elephant that can also be regarded as a centaur, with which we have dealt in the preceding chapter.[1] According to the Indian concordance the motif of the horned tiger occurs five times on the whole, twice on seals from Mohenjo Daro (1357, 2360), once on a seal from Banawali (8521) and twice on copper tablets (1594 and 1599). On the seals, the animal has the long horns of the zebu, on the copper tablets the short horns and the hind legs of a bull. On the two copper tablets 1608 and 2810 the hind-part of a rhino is combined with the fore-part of a dog, on the copper tablet 1598 a bull and a markhor are forged together in the same way. The most interesting motif is found on seal 1357. Here a horned tiger stands in front of a horned deity with a tail, to be recognized as female by its bosom. Standing under a kino tree, the deity either tries to chase the tiger away or to catch it. There are other seals with a similar motif, but this seal is unique, because the tiger has horns and the deity is certainly female.

If we take the religious function of the seals for granted, the composite animals must be aspects of the godhead called Puruṣa in the Veda. This agrees with the fact that the animals consist either of two, three or seven parts. The two parts of the horned tiger have opposite connotations, for the tiger is the enemy of the bull, the bull is its food. The same opposition applies to the Puruṣa and the food in ṚV X.90.2:

The Puruṣa is all this
and what was and what will be;
he is the lord (of the draught) of immortality,
when he grows beyond (food) through food.

[1] For the seven parts of the animal cf. Finnish Concordance 1, p. xxxi.

This dichotomy is solved here through the agency of the draught of immortality, the amṛta or Soma.

The Puruṣa-hymn contains a certain amount of abstract thought, but this does not prove its relative young age, because there is a concrete meaning behind the abstractions. Abstract thought in a rudimentary form pertains to human existence from the very beginning, as it is illustrated by the geometrical signs of the cave-paintings. We find similar signs in the Indus script, and without doubt there is a concrete meaning behind them, too.

In ṚV X.90.5 the relation of the male and the female principle is stated as:

From the Puruṣa the Virāj (fem.) came forth,
and then from the Virāj the Puruṣa;
being born he expanded beyond
the earth behind and in front.

This is again a rather abstract description of the two principles that are found in concrete form on the Indus seals. In X.90.2 the Puruṣa is said to grow through food beyond food. To do this, he must split himself into two parts and then reunite. This is described in Bṛhad Āraṇyaka Upaniṣad I.2.4,5 in the following way:

The Puruṣa desired: May I have a second being. Death, who is hunger, united in mind with Vāc, the goddess of language. From the seed was born the year. Before that the year was not there. He nourished it for the appropriate time. After the appropriate time he produced it. When it was born he opened his mouth (to swallow it). It said 'bhan'. From this Vāc originated. (4)

He thought: When I eat it, little food is left behind. So he created through Vāc and that being [the year] all that is: The hymns of the Ṛg-Veda, the Yajur-Veda and the Sāma-Veda, the sacrifices, the (human) beings and the cattle. Whatever he created he retained to eat it. As he eats everything, he is the aditihood. He becomes the eater of everything, for him everything becomes food, who thus realizes the aditihood of Aditi. (5)

The aditihood of Aditi is the abstract equivalence of Aditi. As a philosophic treatise the Upaniṣad is still more abstract than the Vedic hymn. Here, the Puruṣa creates the world by the help of the goddess of language, Vāc. Vāc is another name of Aditi or Virāj. With the help of the female principle the Puruṣa divides himself at first into the eater and the food and through the union with it he transcends creation. Food is not only the object. Every food retained, can become a subject that needs others as food for its maintenance. In this way, the wheel of life and death goes on. But in the midst of his enjoying and being enjoyed, the Puruṣa can realize his eternal being, in the Veda through the draught of immortality, in the Upaniṣads through meditation.

In the frame of the first book of the Pañcatantra,[2] the horned tiger is split up into its two halves, the bull and the tiger, whereby the tiger becomes a lion.[3] The bull is a zebu. Its name is Saṃjīvaka, that of the lion Piṅgalaka. The names recall the two nāḍīs said to move along the spinal cord in the Haṭha Yoga treatises (cf. chapter VIII). Saṃjīvaka means 'animating'. That is another name for Iḍā, the animating beverage and the left nāḍī. The right nāḍī is called Piṅgalā in the Yoga treatises. Lion and bull become intimate friends through the mediation of a jackal, called Damanaka, the subdued, but then he brings about the dissension of the two by reciprocal slander, because he wants to become the chief minister. Eventually, the lion kills the bull. After having committed this sinful deed, he feels remorse. In this situation the jackal consoles him with these words:[4]

A kingdom cannot be ruled after the manner of human beings,
since the faults of human beings are virtues for a king.
The policy (nīti) of a king be manifold like the behaviour of a prostitute,
truthful and untruthful, speaking rough and polite,
cruel and compassionate, intent on money and generous,
always spending money and looking for revenue of all kinds.

After these words the first book closes with the remark: Having heard this Piṅgalaka regained his nature (prakṛtim āpannaḥ). In quite a similar way Arjuna turns to his nature (prakṛtiṃ gataḥ) in Bhagavadgītā 11.51 after having listened to the teaching of Lord Kṛṣṇa. Arjuna is a king like Piṅgalaka and he is sad for having to kill his friends and relatives in a war, but certainly the author of the Pañcatantra and the author of the Gītā have quite different aims in mind, when they speak of prakṛti. The

---

[2] For a critical edition see J. Hertel, Tantrākhyāyika, Die älteste Fassung des Pañcatantra, Darmstadt [2]1970.

[3] The related story of Mahābhārata XII.112 retains the tiger. Cf. H. Falck, Quellen des Pañcatantra, Wiesbaden 1978.

[4] Cf. Pañcatantra I.184,185 (ed. J. Hertel).

prakr̥ti of Arjuna is divine, the prakr̥ti, Piṅgalaka regains with the help of the jackal, is demonical. The Gītā deals with these two natures in chapter 16. Whether divine or demonical, the primordial Prakr̥ti is inherent the Puruṣa before he splits up into subject and object in the course of creation (cf. chapter XI).

In the hymn to Vāc, R̥V X.125.6c, the goddess says of herself: *I create strife among men*. In the preceding verse she praises herself, however, because it is she who says what is pleasing to gods and men. Her ambivalent behaviour is similar to that of a prostitute. The same ambiguity is found with the goddess on seal 1357, but whether she caresses or drives the tiger away, she will always split up creation, or in psychological terms, she will split up the mind or heart into two halves. In this connection we read in Bhagavadgītā 6.5,6:

The Self can be the friend or foe of the self; for him who subdues the self by the Self, the Self is a friend; in the enmity of the non-self the Self, too, behaves like a foe.

The non-self is here the unsubdued self, the body on its natural level. The senses and the mind behave like a foe, when they are not subdued. Subsequently, the Self apparently behaves like a foe, too. Damanaka is, as his name implies, a subdued and learned being, but he runs after profit like the unwise (avipaścita) mentioned in Gītā 2.41. In the Pañcatantra, Damanaka gains the victory, though he behaves in opposition to the general moral standards, but this ambiguity pertains to the whole Indian tradition. Even Lord Kr̥ṣṇa is criticized by Arjuna in Gītā 3.2 for his double-bound words. Similarly, we cannot explain the behaviour of the characters of this seal in one way only. The only thing which is certain so far is, that they are prototypes of Puruṣa and Prakr̥ti.

This is also confirmed by the symbolic values of its inscription reading 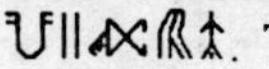. The first and the last sign are broken off or heavily damaged, but probably the first is a man with a stroke between the legs, the last the cup-sign. Interpreted logographically, the first sign can be read as Puruṣa, the second as a sitting ape representing the lower self, the third as the goddess of food, the two long strokes like the intersected circles they often follow as heaven and earth, the last as the Lord. This leads to the following paraphrase:

The Puruṣa, who having separated into a higher and a lower self by the goddess of food, is the Lord beyond heaven and earth.

This is contained in R̥V X.90.2 and X.90.5. If we look at the inscription from the standpoint of the Pañcatantra, we get:

The Puruṣa, who is divided into a bull and a tiger to obtain food, is the Lord of heaven and earth.

The phonetic reading does not correspond to one of the verses of R̥V X.90, however, but to a verse of the Vr̥śākapi-hymn X.86 dealing with the ape Vr̥śakapi and his relation to Indra's wife Indrāṇī. The Veda gives two renderings of the inscription in X.86.16,17:

na sa_īśe yasya rambate 'ntarā saktyā kapr̥t
sa_id īśe yasya romaśaṃ niṣeduṣo vijr̥mbati
viśvasmād indra uttaraḥ
na ya_īśe yasya romaśaṃ niṣeduṣo jr̥mbati
sa_id īśe yasya rambate 'ntarā saktyā kapr̥d
viśvasmād indra uttaraḥ
He is not the master, whose virile member hangs between his thighs,
he is the master, whom the hairy slot opens when he sits down on it,
Indra is higher than everything.
He is not the master, whom the hairy slot opens when he sits down on it,
he is the master, whose virile member hangs between his thighs,
Indra is higher than everything.

The first sign is equal to the first line of X.86.16,17. The sign of the sitting ape renders to sit. The third sign can be read as to touch the vulva. The refrain agrees with the last two signs: The cup-sign stands for Indra, the two long strokes are equal to higher than everything.

The meaning of these verses corresponds to the ambiguity of the motif. A man may be like a master or not, he may be potent or impotent, he will find a woman, who opens her womb for him, because women are like prostitutes. Indra's wife is another example for this behaviour that is likewise found in the goddess of the Dawn and of Language. The same is said by Urvaṣī in X.95.15 (cf. chapter VI).

It is significant that man and woman are only characterised by their sexual organ and therefore this is true only in relation to the sexual plane. It should also be noted that this truth is realized by the seer only. For the normal man his potency and the attractiveness of a woman are inseparably interwoven. This means, that he will never be able to ascertain, whether a woman wants to catch him or to drive him away. If the woman is stronger, the man is the sacrifice, if the man is stronger the woman will have to suffer. Urvaśī is right, when she says, that there is no friendship with women. She is right, however, only on the plane of sexuality.

A seer in the true sense of the word has gone beyond the pairs of opposite. The horns of the tiger are a symbol of its divinity as with the deities on seal 2420 and 2430. In the western world horns may be a symbol of virility as with the German warriors, but nowadays they have become a sign of stupidity, as in the metaphor of a man who was deceived by his wife. In this case the Puruṣa is not in the position of the master.

It is, of course, the idea of transcending the pairs of opposites that is referred to in the inscriptions going along with this motif. For the same reason the inscription of seal 8521 (B-17) from Banawali 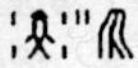 can be related to ṚV X.86.19a:

ayam emi vicākaśad vicinvan dāsam āryam

I travel and look around distinguishing between Dāsa and Āryan.

It is known that Indra travels around the world in disguise to find out which men are on the lower level, called the Dāsa here, and which are on the higher called the Āryan here. This is not a question of race, but of character. In the course of history the so-called barbarian have often shown to be the true noblemen. This holds good for the Vedic times, too.

The first sign stands for Indra here who goes over the earth, the Dāsa is written by the ape-sign, the Āryan by the fish-sign. The four strokes surrounding it can be explained as his radiance. He also wears a tiara. The two short strokes in the middle designate Indra's examining eyes.

There are only the two signs  on seal 2360 (M-1168). They can be read according to ṚV X.142.6 directed to Agni: *Your energies, your flame shall grow up.* The first sign is equal to the fire-wood or the growing flame, the universal energy abiding in all forms like the tiger in the bull, the cup-sign refers to Agni as the god.

The two separate signs  of the inscription 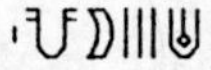 of the copper tablet 1594 direct us to ṚV IX.75.3:

Flashing up he roars into the vat,
clothed by the men in the golden veil;
the milker of the truth are calling him,
he is beaming on the threefold back of the Dawn.

The mortar-sign is equal to the vat, the three strokes to the men, the curve-sign renders the golden veil, the cup-sign and the single stroke that is omitted in the inscription of tablet 1601 is equal to the milkers of the truth, i.e. the gods. For the separate signs we get the threefold back of the Dawn. It is identical to the three layers of kuśa-grass used for the seats of the gods on the place of sacrifice. The opposition of eater and food is transcended by the draught of Soma called father of thought in IX.75.2.
In the same way the inscription 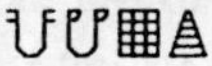 of the copper tablet 1598 can be related to the Soma-hymn IX.83.1:

Far extended is the sieve for you, father of the hymn!
From all sides you penetrate the limbs as the master;
The raw, whose body did not burn, does not obtain it,
only he who has burnt, the wandering (soul), achieves it.

The first sign is equal to the wandering soul and to be burnt, the second sign renders the sieve, master of the limbs is equal to the last two signs.
In X.28.4 the relation of food and eater is inverted by the speaker Indra:

Understand this well of me, my adorer:
The rivers push the water stream-up,
the antelope steals upon the lion from behind,
the jackal jumps out of the bush on the boar.

This agrees with the inscription of tablet 1599 (M-1518) 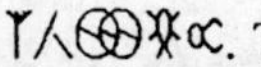. The crab-sign can be read as understand, the fish-sign as adorer. Since the intersected circles symbolize heaven and earth, the three additional strokes can indicate three heavens and earths. Normally, the relation between heaven and earth is that of eater and food, but it can be turned over, as it is done in the three similes of this verse. The following step-sign can be read as stream-up, steal upon and jump, the hand-sign as to push, from behind (from the tail) and as bush.

We can now take up the investigation of the animals with three heads, where as a rule a bull has two additional heads from a gazelle and a unicorn. The inscription on seal 7071 is arranged around the animal. It starts with the four signs  at the right border. The three short strokes in the middle can be read together with both lines, but are written here in front of the second: 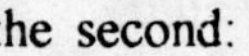. With regard to the three heads the motif can be explained as the bull Viśvarūpa that has three bellies, three udders and three faces according to ṚV III.56.3:

Three bellies has the bull Viśvarūpa
and three udders, he has manifold progeny;
having three faces he rules as the great (heaven and earth),
he is the seed-giving bull for all (the cows).

The two cup-signs are equal to the three bellies and the three udders. Manifold progeny is rendered by the two triangle-signs being a symbol for woman generally. The intersected circles stand for the three faces. To rule as the great is rendered by the last two signs.

The two lines 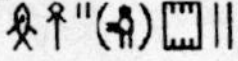 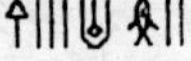 of the inscription of seal 2024 (M-1169) agree with the Soma-hymns ṚV IX.38.2,4:

The yellow (Soma) is urged to run
through the pressing stones by the women of Trita,
the sap to be drunken by Indra.
He alights on the places of Manu like a falcon (on the nest),
like a lover he goes to the woman.

The three-headed animal of the motif can be equated with Trita here. His women are the fingers that press and purify the Soma. The women are rendered by the dotted fish-sign, the two strokes represent the pressing stones or boards. The mortar-sign stands for the Soma, Trita himself corresponds to the three long strokes. The lance-sign renders to press and to urge. It can also represent Indra.

The first two signs of the second line are equal to the places of Manu, the first ancestor of the Āryans. To alight like a falcon (on the nest) is rendered by the bird-sign in brackets. For lover we get the dotted fish-sign, for women the penultimate sign that can be interpreted as a flower or bud. The two short strokes correspond to the two comparisons.

On seal 1382 (M-1170) from Mohenjo Daro we find the head of a gazelle twice along with the head of a bull. The seal has the sign for woman written over a tree-sign: . The sign can also be interpreted as a pillar or phallus. The compound can hence be a symbol of the androgyn cosmic being, the Puruṣa.

A three-headed bovine is found on tablet 8550* from Banawali exhibited at the 3rd World Congress of Archaeology held in Delhi 1994. The inscription, only partly readable , corresponds to ṚV III.56.8ab:

> *trir uttamā dūṇaśā rocanāni*
> *trayo rājanti asurasya vīrāḥ*
> *Threefold are the highest heavens that are difficult to reach,*
> *three heroes of the Asura are the rulers.*

For the three strokes and the cross-sign we get the three heavens difficult to reach. The fish-sign with an additional stroke at the bottom and the three strokes at the end correspond to the three heroes. The cup-sign represents the Asura.

We can now go on to the investigation of the composite animal with seven parts that we have already found on tablet 2734 and interpreted as an image of Lopāmudrā. Lopāmudrā is the substitute of the goddess of wisdom also called Kuṇḍalinī whose imaginative path along the spinal column consists of seven steps. The main part of the animal is a goat or bull as in the case of the unicorn. Hence we can call this animal a composite bull or goat. The Indian concordance has registered 20 seals and tablets with this motif, three more are contained in the Finnish. Five tablets have the same inscription. Of the rest, fifteen have been found in Mohenjo Daro, two in Harappa, one in Lothal. A rough design of this motif, exceptionally with a standard, is found on seal 8630 (Allahdino-8). On tablet 1586 we find the composite animal together with a bull.

Most of the inscriptions, that go together with this motif, are extremely short, five times they consist only of two signs, two inscriptions have six signs, two seven, the longest has nine signs. But possibly the broken inscription of seal 1191 (M-1173) had more than this. A composite animal with human face together with a leaf-sign is found on seal 7133 (K-35). It can be explained as the cosmic tree.

The inscriptions of two signs can be related to the bull Viśvarūpa, the all-formed. On this assumption, the first sign of the inscription of seal 2258 (M-301) can be interpreted as the dew-lap of a zebu or as the long neck hairs of the markhor. Viśvarūpa is a name of the Soma in ṚV VI.41.3. He is also known as an enemy of Indra like Vṛtra who can also be identified with this sign. Similarly, the two signs of seal 1252 (M-324), repeated on the reverse together with a unicorn, can be correlated to this mythical being. The first sign can then be interpreted as the three bellies or the three udders of the cosmic bull Viśvarūpa known from ṚV III.56.3.

In the last pada of this verse Viśvarūpa is called the seed-giving bull of all (the universe). This agrees with the inscription of seal 2493 (M-1176). The first sign can be read as all or the universe, the second as seed-giver and carrier of the two worlds. The two worlds are equal to the six worlds carried by the one according to ṚV III.56.2.

The two repeated signs of tablet 1563 (M-1399) occur also in the inscription of tablet 3309, which we discussed in chapter I.7. The second sign can be read as rodasī, the two halves of the world, the mortar-sign as to sacrifice, both is contained in the Soma-hymn ṚV IX.74.2cd:

> *seme mahī rodasī yakṣad avṛtā*
> *samīcīne dādhāra samiṣaḥ kaviḥ*
> ***Who sacrifices to the great world-halves turned to him,***
> ***he holds together the conjoined (halves) and all draughts, the seer.***

The inscription of the zebu-seal 2723 (M-1397) corresponds to the same verse. The first sign can be read as to hold together the two worlds, the second as to turn to.

On tablet 2754 (M-477) a woman-sign is added to the two signs of tablet 1563 to emphasize the female character of the world-halves. The two signs of tablet 2718 (M-436) can be read as apūrṇo aṃśuḥ, the full stalk of Soma mentioned in the first half of this verse.

There are two seals with three signs, 1380 (M-301) and 1381 (M-299). By the first sign of the inscription of seal 1381 we are directed to ṚV X.136.1ab:

> ***keśaya 'gni keśī viṣaṃ   keśī bibharti rodasī***

The long-haired is the fire, the long-haired is the poison,
the long-haired carries the two halves of the world.

The long-haired are the Vedic yogis. They are closely related to Rudra, the Vedic Śiva. The composite animal is especially suitable as their emblem, because the elephant is a symbol of austerity for the gnostic man up to the time of Christ.[5] Rudra or the long-haired is written by the guardian-sign. The second sign renders the two world-halves. The third sign, that is partly broken off, can be explained as a roost or, more likely, as the hand-sign. In both cases the meaning is to carry.

The inscription of seal 1380 can be affiliated to ṚV X.136.2ab:

munayo vātaraśanāḥ piśaṅgā vasate malā
The (long-haired) sages girded with the wind
are clad in red-yellow rags.

The first fish-sign renders the muni or sage, the dotted fish-sign is equal to girded with the wind (i.e. naked). The nakedness is hinted at by the dot that can be regarded as the navel. The lance-sign stands for piśaṅga mala, reddish rag. Since the root of mala, mla, means to get weak, the two words can be taken as a description of the phallus, which corresponds with the pictogram.

Several other inscriptions with this motif are also related to this hymn. The inscription on seal 1191 (M-1173) 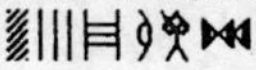 agrees with X.136.3:

unmaditā mauneyena vātān ā tasthimā vayam
śarīred asmakaṃ yūyaṃ martāso abhi paśyatha
Intoxicated through ecstasy we have mounted the winds,
only our bodies you mortals see.

Unmadita, intoxicated, is written by a sign that can be read as an enchanting ornament. Ecstasy, mauneya, is equal to the moon-sign. We, the munis, are written by the guardian-sign representing Rudra. To mount is equal to the following sign that can be regarded as a ladder. The winds are equal to the three strokes. The second half of the verse must have been contained in the lost part of the inscription, of which only one sign that can be read as a navel or naked body has survived.

---

[5] U. Ranke-Heinemann, Eunuchen für das Himmelreich, München 1990, p. 18.

The inscription of seal 8630  corresponds to ṚV X.136.4:

antarikṣeṇa atati viśvā rūpā_avacākaśat
munir devasya devasya saukṛtyāya sakhā hitaḥ
He flies through the air, looking down on all forms.
The muni intend on doing the good work, is the friend of all gods.

From the man-sign with an additional triangle we get the wandering (flying) muni, the rhombus-sign is equal to the air or the intermediate space. All forms (of the creatures) is rendered by the triangle-sign and the two strokes. To look down is written by a shadoof with a hook. The shadoof is personified in this way. The cup-sign renders friend of all gods here.

The inscription of the tablet 6044 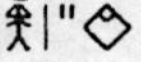 corresponds to X.136.5d:

ubhau samudrāvā kṣoti yaśca pūrva uta_aparaḥ
He lives at the two oceans, the eastern and the western.

The first two signs stand for the two oceans, the eastern and the western, the long stroke renders to live. The last sign symbolizes the long-haired.

The inscription of the tablet 2816 (M-571)  agrees with X.136.6:

apsarasāṃ gandharvāṇāṃ mṛgāṇāṃ caraṇe caran
keśī ketasya vidvānt sakhī svādur madintamaḥ
Following the track of the Apsaras,
the Gandharvas and the wild animals,
the longhaired, who knows the mind,
is (their) sweet, most enchanting friend.

The long strokes can be read as following the track, the muni is equal to the fish-sign, the Apasaras and Gandharvas correspond to the following compound being partly female and partly male. The cup-sign can be read as the sweet friend being equal to the Soma.

The inscription of seal 3249 (H-96) 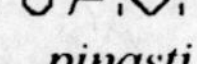 agrees with X.136.7ab:

vāyur asmā upāmanthat pinaṣṭi smā kunaṃnamā
The air has churned (the draught) for him,
Kunaṃnamā has quenched it for him.

The first sign can be read as Vāyu, the god of the air, the additional strokes and the circle render to churn the draught, the cup-sign represents the Soma and the nose-sign stands for Kunaṃnamā, a name of an Apsaras characterized by her long nose giving her the appearance of a witch.

The inscription 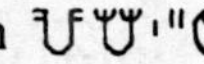 of seal 2450 (M-1177) corresponds to ṚV X.136.7cd:

keśī viṣasya pātreṇa yad rudreṇa apibat saha
The long-haired drinks the poison from the cup,
when he is together with Rudra.

The first sign can be read as long-haired, because the long hairs are equal to the beams of the sun, the two short strokes render together with, the single stroke is equal to poison, the womb-sign can be read as the cup containing the poison. Rudra is equal to the cup-sign.
The inscription  of seal 2636 can be read in two ways. The first reading agrees with ṚV I.105.10, where Trita in the well describes the planets above him as five bulls. Such a constellation is regarded as the beginning of an age. In this case it could refer to the era of Aries starting about 1500 B.C. The planets would be equal to the five strokes and to the composite animal in the motif. The second reading would follow ṚV III.59.3: *Mitra is searched for by the five tribes.* The two short strokes may be explained in this connection as the eyes of the sun called Mitra, friend, symbolized by the first sign. The tree-sign would render the tribes.
In the inscriptions of seal 2411 (M-303) 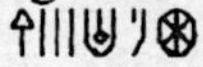 and 2521 (M-300) 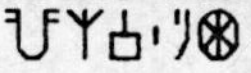 the king-sign , the mortar-sign and the tree-sign direct us to the Soma-hymn IX.89.2ab:

rājā sindhūnām avasiṣṭa vāsa
ṛtasya nāvam ārahad rajaṣṭhām
The king of the rivers has put on his cloth,
he has mounted the most direct ship of the ritual.

The first two signs of seal 2411 can be read as like a king. The cloth of the Soma is the mortar or the vat, into which the sap runs. Therefore it can be written as the mortar-sign. The same sign can also be rendered as ship of the ritual (of the Soma pressing). For the rivers we get the three long strokes, for to mount (the ship) the lance-sign. In case of seal 2521 the rivers have been omitted, the single drop is equal to the Soma here, the field-sign can be read as vāsa, cloth, because it is homophonous with vas, house, place to live. To put on is written by the hand-sign. The ship of the ritual corresponds to the cup-sign.

The rest of the inscription of the broken seal 2559 (M-1178)  renders R̥V III.56.7c: *Ratnaṃ bhikṣanta savitur savāya - they (heaven and earth) ask for Savitr̥'s jewel for its distribution.* The signs for ratna, jewel, and bhikṣanta, they ask, are obliterated, the two curves are equal to heaven and earth, for Savitr̥ we get the wheel-sign, savāya, for distribution, is equal to the two short strokes.

The broken seal 3250 with the inscription 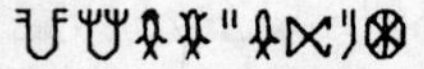 can be related to R̥V III.62.10, the famous Gāyatrī, the verse that is repeated every morning and evening by the brahmins until today:

tát savitúr váreṇyaṃ bhárgo devásya dhīmahi
dhiyo yó naḥ pracodáyāt
On the venerable effulgence of yonder sun,
of the god, let us meditate,
may he promote our understanding.

The first two signs are obliterated, of the third only the last stroke has been retained, but they can be restored through the Vedic verse. The first sign can be read as the sun. The second sign is equal to tat, that, yonder. The triangle-sign, that has a female connotation generally, stands for god as creator. For vareṇyam, venerable, we get the two short strokes. Bharga, effulgence, corresponds to the first fish-sign, dhīmahi, let us meditate, to the second and the third fish-sign. The womb-sign and the cup-sign agrees with promote our understanding.

Though the sun is male in the Veda, several signs in this inscriptions have a female connotation. This shows that the sun was conceived as androgyn by the seers. This is also underlined by the rhythm of the verse that I have indicated here exceptionally. The accent is only placed on short and mostly on odd syllables, in the case of pracodáyāt even between two long syllables. In this way, the rhythm that is female in its nature, serves to emphasize the female conception of the sun or its effulgence. There are other inscriptions that could be related to this verse, especially that of seal 3005, as I formerly did because of the three fish-signs, but the second half does not fit in with this affiliation.

The motif has a special relation to the Gāyatrī. On a painting made in Rajasthan in the 17th century a composite animal symbolizing the subtle cakras of the region of the head is identified with the Gāyatrī.[6]
The motif and the inscription of tablet 1586 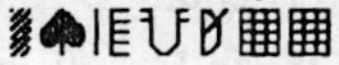 agrees with ṚV I.179.4:

> *After the tamed bull I am seized with desire,*
> *from here, from there, from everywhere it is born;*
> *Lopāmudrā squeezes out the bull-like man,*
> *the unwise sucks the panting wise man dry.*

The first line is contained in the motif of the bull representing Agastya followed by a composite animal, the symbol of Lopāmudrā. The two net-signs that are equal to the pressing boards (cf. I.28.2) render here and there. The bow-sign that can also be read as a womb is equal to everywhere, because it reminds Lopāmudrā all the time of cohabitation. The cup-sign renders it is born, the teeth-sign stands for Lopāmudrā, the stroke represents Agastya's manhood; he leaf-sign is equal to his name. The last line is obliterated.
Agastya carrying Lopāmudrā may be represented by the two gazelles standing over each other on the seal 2003 (M-233), that is partly broken off. The head and neck of the upper gazelle has been replaced by the leaf-sign, illustrating thus that it is composed of different parts.
There are two motifs with a different pattern. On the copper tablets 1608 and 2810 we find a composite animal of a rhino with the head and neck of a dog. On the copper tablet 1597 the composite animal is replaced by the sign . On seal 1383 (M-417) the heads of six bovines are arranged in a whirl.
The inscription of tablet 1597 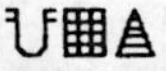 is almost identical to that on tablet 1598. It can likewise be related to ṚV IX.83.1. The singular sign can be read as the centaur or Gandharva mentioned as an image of the Soma in IX.83.4.
Tablet 1608 bears the inscription 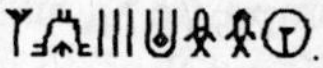. It can be read according to ṚV V.63.2ac:

[6] Cf. Ph. Rawson, Tantra, München 1974, fig. 56.

> *You are standing as rulers over this world, Mitra-Varuṇa,*
> *we ask for your rain as a gift of immortality.*

The first sign is equal to standing as rulers over this world, the two fish-signs represent Mitra-Varuṇa, the gift of immortality corresponds to the mortar-sign, the three strokes to rain, the head-sign to your and the hand-sign to we ask.

Tablet 2810 reads . It agrees with V.63.4:

> *Your magic power, Mitra-Varuṇa, is standing at the sky,*
> *as the sun, as light it appears, as a bright weapon;*
> *in the cloud, in the rain you hide the light at the sky,*
> *in drops of honey the rains falls down.*

Magic power is equal to the cup-sign, the sun at the sky is rendered by the fish-sign in brackets and by the rhombus-sign, the nose-sign can be read as bright weapon, the man-sign as to hide, the single stroke as drop of Soma, the two net-signs as rain and cloud. The motif of rhino and dog is explained in V.63.3 as *you are constantly watchful*.

The single stroke in the inscription of the two signs  of seal 1383 directs us to ṚV X.135.3, where a new car is mentioned manufactured by a boy. It has one shaft and no wheels, but can travel in all directions. One shaft means eka-īṣa. The guardian-sign can be read as īṣa, because it is homophonous with īśa, lord. The heads of the six bovines render all directions, the whirl, to which they are fastened, is equal to a car without wheels that is also a synonym of the whim (cf. chapter I. 7).

Thus we have got a lot of examples in this chapter to illustrate that the meaning of the signs in the Indus script depends on the symbolic value, and that, though different words may be written with the same sign and same words with different signs, the poet is able to make his idea understandable. We have even discovered a whole hymn in the inscriptions. This would have been impossible without the guidance of the motifs of the different composite animals. If the meaning of this symbol is discovered, it also confirms that the philosophy of the Indus civilization was indentical to Vedic thought. This means that a bilingual is not absolutely necessary.

V. THE BULL UPON THE WOMAN AND THE AŚVAMEDHA

The aśvamedha or horse-sacrifice is a Vedic ritual, but we know from the Rāmāyaṇa and the Mahābhārata that it was still executed in later times. According to the laws of Manu XI.75,83 it is one of the most effective means of expiation. In the Rāmāyaṇa it is applied to secure progeny for king Daśaratha and promotes the birth of Rāma and his brothers, who are all regarded as incarnations of god Viṣṇu. In the Mahābhārata it serves for the purification of the Pāṇḍavas after the great war against their cousins. When studying the central rite of this sacrifice, one feels abashed, however, to learn that the queen in order to "carry out the Dharma" has to spend a night in cohabitation with the immolated horse.[1] The aśvamedha is described in detail in the XIIIth book of the Śatapatha Brāhmaṇa. J. Eggeling, its translator, is not happy about this passage. Hence he leaves some sentences untranslated, and in regard to XIII.2.8.3 he remarks:[2]

This barbarous ceremony was evidently an old indigenous custom too firmly established in popular practice to be easily excluded from the sacrificial ritual. That it had nothing to do with Vedic religion and was distasteful to the author is evident from the brief way in which he refers to it, and from the far-fetched symbolic explanations attached to the formulas and discourses.

By expressing his disgust Eggeling protects the Vedic religion at the cost of an "indigenous custom", but what did he mean with that? Did he think of some pre-Āryan tribes? It is quite unlikely that some 'aborigines' were practising such a ritual, since they did not even use the horse for economic purposes. Or did he think of the Dasyus and Paṇis? The Veda does not say that they were possessors of horses, they are only combated by the Āryans in order to get their cattle. Though this might have included horses, it is quite certain that they did not celebrate a horse-sacrifice, as the Veda states that they had no sacrifices at all.

---

[1] Cf. Śrimad Vālmīki Rāmāyaṇa with Hindī translation ed. by C.D.P. Śarma, Allahabad 1958, Bālakāṇḍa XIV,32.

[2] Cf. Sacred Books of the East, Vol. XIII, Oxford 1882-1900, p. 322.

Hence only the Indus Valley civilization would remain. It was still unknown to Eggeling, but he may have had some anticipation of it. The inhabitants of the Indus towns were not barbarous, however, and according to the motifs of the seals they did not use the horse either. Instead we find the unicorn there in great number. On later Assyrian seals this animal is depicted as a deer or horse, sometimes with wings.[3] On the Indus seals it has similar features and its long neck is often decorated like that of a horse. And on the seals 2222 (M-1181) and 2430 (M-1186), which we have discussed in chapter III, we find a man with horns and the twig of a pipal tree on his head reminiscent of the horn of Ṛṣyaśṛṅga, the leading priest of Daśaratha's aśvamedha.

Vālmīki describes the rite in Bālakāṇḍa XIV,30-36 of the Rāmāyāṇa:

Three hundred animals were bound to the sacrificial posts
and likewise the highly estimated horse of king Daśaratha. (30)
After having venerated the horse from all sides queen Kausalyā
cut it in pieces with three swords[4] in greatest joy. (31)
With firmly established mind Kausalyā then spent one night
together with the horse desiring to fulfil the Dharma. (32)
Then the three priests[5] joined the favourite queen
as also the mahiṣā and the parivṛti[6] to the horse. (33)
Then the officiating priest[7] took with subdued mind
the omentum from the horse and burned it according to the laws. (34)
The king smelled the smoke of that fat, whereby his sins
were dispelled according to the time and to the rules. (35)
Then all the pieces of the horse were thrown into the fire
by the priests together with mantras of the sixteen priests.[8] (36)

---

[3] Cf. Frankfort XXXVa-k.

[4] The swords (kṛpāṇa) were used for making the marks on the horse. The actual cutting in pieces was done by 16 priests mentioned later. According to ŚB XIII.2.8.2 the horse was suffocated by the main priest before the queen was led to it. When she arrived at the horse she begged its pardon for the slaughtering.

[5] Hotṛ, Adhvaryu and Udgātṛ.

[6] These are the first and the third queen, the avoided queen (Sumitrā).

[7] The ṛtvij, here Ṛṣyaśṛṅga.

[8] The number of the priests agrees with the parts of the Puruṣa in Praśna Upaniṣad VI.2.

Usually the burnt offerings are served on pipal-leaves at the end of the sacrifice, in this case vetasa-leaves were used. The reason for this exception will be discussed later. After the meal the king gives the dakṣinā (cows, gold, women) to Ṛṣyaśṛṅga, the officiating priest, and accosts him with the following words:

You have fulfilled your duties well,
may you now act for the welfare of the family. (56)
Ṛṣyaśṛṅga replied: Be it so! You will have four sons,
by whom your family shall prosper. (57)

In the XVth chapter of the Bālakāṇḍa Vālmīki relates another ritual (iṣṭi) carried out under the leadership of Ṛṣyaśṛṅga. It is from the beginning of the Atharva-Veda, as he says. An iṣṭi is generally part of the animal sacrifices.[9] The verses recited in this ritual are normally taken from the Ṛg-Veda, not from the Atharva-Veda. The Atharva-Veda is regarded as later than the Ṛg-Veda, but the priest Atharvan, after whom it is named, belongs certainly to the eldest generation of the Āryans. In fact, the two Vedas were one in the beginning according to the Indian tradition.

In the fire of this iṣṭi a messenger of Viṣṇu or Viṣṇu himself appears holding a plate with gruel in his hand. He addresses the king with the following words (Bālakāṇḍa XVI.16-20):

I am Nara. I have come from Prajāpati, (the creator).
You shall see your desires fulfilled,
because you have sacrificed to the gods.
Take this divine gruel which gives wealth and health.
Offer it to your wives in due course,
then you will receive the sons for whom you have sacrificed.

The king did so. Thereafter his wives became pregnant, and from Kausalyā Rāma was born, from Sumitrā Lakṣmaṇa and from Kaikeyī Bharata and Śatrughna. All the sons are more or less incarnations of Viṣṇu. Nara is a name of Viṣṇu and of the cosmic man. Prajāpati is connected with the aśvamedha, because he is identified with the horse. The appearance of the god Nara or Viṣṇu in the fire can be compared to the epiphany of the deity in the tree on several Indus seals, notably on seal 2430. In the Ṛg-Veda idolatry was not practised. This form of

---

[9] Cf. Frits Staal, Rules without Meaning, New York 1989. p. 81.

worship is known only from later Hinduism, nevertheless the Veda is full of symbolic expressions that are similar to image-worship. It does not make much difference, whether the image is in the heart or outside. Where the image in the fire is seen by Daśaratha, inwardly or outwardly? If it is possible that the motif of this seal and of other seals reappears in the Rāmāyaṇa, it can also be found in the Ṛg-Veda, for in the epic there is no image-worship either.[10]

There is no horse on seal 2430, instead we find a markhor. The antelope, however, is an attribute of Brahmā-Prajāpati in later times, especially in his connection with his daughter Uṣas, as is told in the Maitrāyaṇī Saṃhitā and other texts. Uṣas is often compared to a cow or to cows and the male gods to bulls in the Veda. From all these reasons it is not unlikely that we find parallels in the Veda for the motif of seal 5013 from Chanhu Daro that depicts a bull standing over a prostrated woman:

Though the woman lies under a bull and not together with a horse, it was already supposed by H. Mode that the motif refers to the aśvamedha.[11] The inscription of seal 5013 is 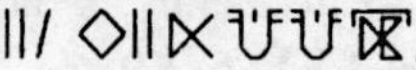. When read logographically the first sign can be interpreted as to be under a roof and represent Prajāpati coming together with his daughter Uṣas who could also be represented by the second sign. The third sign may stand for the fecundating god. The following triangle-sign can be interpreted as to create, as it is similar to a womb. The next two strokes can be explained as heaven and earth and the rhombus as the intermediate space. The last three strokes are found on many seals from Chanhu Daro and need not be part of a logographic rendering.

---

[10] In the Ṛg-Veda Agni is called iṣṭi, promoter, helper, the personification of the iṣṭi (fem.), the sacrifice. The word iṣṭa, explained by Grassmann as desire' only, means correctly 'desiring prayer' addressed to a beloved godhead, the iṣṭā devatā in later literature (cf. ṚV X.82.2 chapter I.5).

[11] Op. cit. p. 69. The impression of the seal has been taken from there, too.

When we form a sentence of these names and words, it would have the following shape:

Who is under a roof (married) with his daughter Uṣas, is the fecundating god who created heaven and earth and the intermediate space.

The act of creation is described with sexual metaphors in Ṛ̥V X.61.5-8:

After it had been stretched out and inserted
the manly one took the erected member back;
that what the irresistible one had put
into the virgin daughter he took back. (5)

In the midst of this act, when the father
had thrown his whole energy on his daughter,
it happened that the two lost some seed in separating,
which fell on the earth in the womb of the good deed. (6)

When the father united with his daughter
they spilt some seed on the earth;
with good thoughts the gods created a sacred verse (thereof),
the protector of the sacred law, Vāstoṣpati they formed. (7)

He vomited foam like a bull in fighting
and run hither and thither with confused mind;
like an exile he ran to the southern places -
my caresses could not hold him back. (8)

The phonetic reading of the inscription of seal 5013 goes parallel with verse 6 of this hymn.

The first sign is equal to the first two lines, the two lost some seed to the two cup-signs. The triangle-sign renders separating. The long strokes can be read as to fall. Earth and womb are equal to the rhombus-sign. The three last strokes can be read as the good deed here, because it is a symbol of the town Chanhu Daro, which means literally 'hill with a place of shelter' or 'hill with huts' (Hindi chāṃhā). It could have been the earliest inhabited place in the Indus Valley.

The two prototypes of creation are also referred to by the two signs  of the unicorn-seal 7103 (K-17), where the sign for separation is duplicated and combined with a long stroke indicating cohabitation. The cup-sign can be read as the father.

Separation and combination are also the main aspects of language. Hence the compound can also be interpreted as a twofold mouth. The Sanskrit root for to speak is brū. It is related to the root brah that is also found in the German word Sprache (language). The compound can be read as brahman, which means derived from brah, from speaking. Brahman in the sense of sacred verse is mentioned in X.61.7. The brahman is sacred as it is indicated by the cup-sign. Brahmaṇaspati, lord of the sacred verse, is another name for the father of the sky, called Prajāpati in the Brāhmaṇas.

Since Prajāpati is identified with the horse of the aśvamedha, the queen lying with it can be regarded as his daughter. We have then only to explain why on seal 5013 the woman lies under a bull and not under a horse. For this it is necessary to look into the history of religions. The marriage between a queen and a bull is also found in the Near East and in the Minoic civilization. The Indus civilization is the intermediary link between the bull-cum-queen and the horse-cum-queen relation, because the unicorn, the most frequent motif there, is a composite animal with traits of a bull and a horse, as we have seen already.

O'Flaherty, who explains the aśvamedha as a replacement of the Celtic ritual of the mare and the king, thinks it possible that the "invading Āryans" might have been influenced by the Indus Valley civilization or that they have taken "the raw material" for the aśvamedha from its mythology,[12] but she does not realize that the unicorn contains the elements of the bull and the horse. It is also quite unlikely that there have been "invading Āryans" in greater number before the decline of the Indus cities, and one should also take into account that the "raw materials" were already highly refined in the Indus Valley. At any rate, the aśvamedha cannot be called barbarous, as Eggeling did, since the Indus civilization had a high social standard. Hence there must be a deeper sense behind it.

---

[12] Cf. W.D. O'Flaherty, Women, Androgynes and Other Mythical Beasts, Chicago/London 1980, p. 209; for similar Greek rituals cf. J.J. Meyer, Trilogie altindischer Mächte und Feste der Vegetation, Zürich 1937, p. 248.

In ṚV X.61.6 the union of father sky and his daughter is called a *good deed*, but in I.71.5 Prajāpati is punished by an archer, who is a form of Rudra or Śiva:

After having created seed for the great father, the sky,
and having noticed his desire, he crept near (like a hunter);
boldly the bowman shot the arrow at him,
(since) the god had approached the own daughter impetuously.

This variant of the creation-story must be rather old, since it is referred to in the inscription of the copper-tablet 1606 (cf. chapter III,3).

According to *popular traditions*, reported by H. Mode,[13] the last kings of the Indus cities were killed by Śiva on behalf of their incestuous relations with the daughters of their sisters. In the Indus cities such relations might have been allowed, but only as long as they served for securing fertility for the country, as in the case of the Mesopotamian sacred marriage.

If this ritual was performed in the Indus Valley, it does not mean, that it was carried out in the same way as the aśvamedha of the Brāhmaṇa. The mind of the Indus priests was probably on a higher level than that of the Āryan priests in the time of the Brāhmaṇa. It should be noted in this connection that the fragment of a bull has been found in Mohenjo Daro (Aachen, fig.. 150) wearing the same trefoil garment as the so-called priest-king (Marshall pl. XCVIII). This makes it likely that the bull was joined to the queen symbolically, the real partner being the priest-king. In this way we arrive at the sacred marriage as it was celebrated in Mesopotamia. We shall hence study this rite a little more closely.

In the Mesopotamian sacred marriage the female partner is the Great Goddess called Inanna by the Sumerians and Ištar by the Akkadians. But her human substitute was a close relative of the king.[14] Thus we arrive at the same pattern we have come across in the popular traditions

---

[13] Op. cit. p. 14,15.

[14] Cf. E.D. van Buren, The Sacred Marriage in Early Times in Mesopotamia, Orientalia 13, 1944, p. 65: "Thus the 'high-priest'...was always a high-priestess and generally the sister or (eldest) daughter of the reigning king."

of the last Indus kings. However, Dumuzi, the prototype of the male partner of the goddess, is always called her "youthful lover". According to the myth of Inanna's Descent to the Netherworld Inanna sends him there, because he did not mourn for her, when she herself had gone to that place out of a whim and was killed by her sister. But Dumuzi's sister Geštinanna or Belili in the Akkadian version, with whom Dumuzi wanted to celebrate the sacred marriage in the absence of Inanna, weeps for him and tries to save him from this fate, that she regards as an injustice done by him to her. Like Uṣas or like Yamī in ṚV X.10 she is not against incest, but puts on her bridal attire for the occasion. At the end of the Akkadian version Ištar declares that Dumuzi shall come up again together with his ring and staff and the lamenting priests and priestesses at the New Year festival:

Belili had completed her (bridal) attire.
Her lap was full with eye-stones.
She heard her brother's lament. She struck the attire of her body,
the eye-stones filling the (sur)face of the wild cow.
My only brother, may you not do an injustice to me.
(Ištar:) At that day, when Dumuzi comes up,
when the lapislazuli-staff and the carnelian-ring come up,
when the lamenting priests and priestesses come up,
then the death shall come up, too, smelling the incense.[15]

Lapislazuli and carnelian are mentioned in the lists of gifts given to temples and in litanies as coming from Meluḫḫa, the Akkadian name of the Indus cities.[16] The Akkadian word for incense, qutrinu, has been derived from the Arabian peninsula Qatar, which was a staple-place of the Indus merchants.[17] The *eye-stones filling the (sur)face of the wild*

---

[15] Cf. Ištar's Descent into the Netherworld, l. 131-138, ed. by R. Borger, Babylonisch-Assyrische Lesestücke, Rome 1979 (transl. E. Richter-Ushanas).

[16] For the trade connections between Mesopotamia and Meluḫḫa cf. W. Heimpel, op. cit. (1987), p. 22.

[17] Cf. H.J. Nissen, Frühe Hochkulturen im Nahen und Mittleren Osten, in: Vergessene Städte am Indus, Aachen 1987, p. 48.

cow are difficult to explain.[18] Most likely they refer to the stars being stuck in the lap of the sky, as it were. Their form is similar to a vulva. The most prominent star is the Venus, the star of Ištar. The Akkadian word for face, pa-an, can also be read as the Sumerian word for the me, the divine powers. Because of their forming a vulva the eye-stones are filled with this power and are a symbol of fertility. At the end of the Sumerian version of the myth Ereškigal, the goddess of Death, grants Geštinanna to stay alternatively with Dumuzi six months of the year in the Netherworld.[19]

The two halves of the year are similar to the two ways after death, the way to the sun and the way to the moon, in Bṛhad Āraṇyaka Upaniṣad 6.2-15, Chandogya Upaniṣad 5.10.3-6 and Bhagavadgītā 8.23. They are first mentioned in ṚV X.88.15,16. In the Upaniṣads sun and moon are brought in relation to the final human resurrection. The souls that go to the sun are liberated, those that go to the moon will be born again. This evaluation exceeds a vegetation rite, as the sacred marriage is called by T. Jacobsen.[20]

The aim of the aśvamedha was to secure progeny. This agrees with the way to the moon. But this was not the only aim. Aśvamedha and sacred marriage had also to do with human resurrection. This is their deeper meaning. The idea of resurrection is not reserved to Christianity as interpretations like that of Jacobsen suggest.

The Vedic society in later time had no sacred kingdom as we find it in the Near East. Priesthood and kingdom were separate institutions. It was regarded as an awful sin for the king to think even of having sexual relations with his daughter. According to IX.4,49 of the Law of Manu the daughter has to be given in marriage at the appropriate time, i.e. after her first menses in the age of 12, sometimes already earlier, whereas men are enjoined to marry between the age of 24 to 30.

---

[18] For a discussion of the end of the Akkadian version cf. A. Falkenstein, Der Sumerische und Akkadische Mythos von Inannas Gang zur Unterwelt, Festschrift W. Caskel, Leiden 1968, p. 96.

[19] Cf. W.R. Sladek, Inanna's Descent to the Netherworld, Ann Arbor 1974.

[20] Cf. The Treasures of Darkness, New Haven 1976.

This is degrading for women from the modern point of view, but it is a custom that was followed in the whole archaic world, including Rome and Greece. Nor was it unusual or forbidden, that the man was much older than 30, though cohabitation with an unripe maiden is regarded as equal to incest (Law of Manu XI.171).

Apart from the fear of incestuous relations, these marriage-rules may have been caused by the general fear of the power of virginity and of the possibility that a maiden becomes a prostitute. In the Indian epics, however, we have another date for marriage at least for women of the noble class, the blossom of her youth, vayas (cf. the stories of Rāma's marriage in the Rāmāyāṇa and that of Nala and Damayantī and of Sāvitrī in the Mahābhārata). According to the context this must have been the age of 16 to 18. These stories are full of romanticism, but the normal marriage had nothing to do with love in ancient times.

Incest was regarded as one of the greatest crimes by Manu and other law-givers. Equally bad were relations of a woman with a man of low caste and abortion.[21] On the other hand, raping a maiden was recorded among the forms of marriage, to sell her, however, was regarded as very mean. Though from the modern point of view such rules may discredit the whole codex of Manu and though somebody who is interested in spiritual aims may find many things there, which seem dry to him or may even hurt his feeling for righteousness, there cannot be any doubt that at the time, when it was composed, most probably around 300 ante our era, it excelled all other works in this field,[22] because of the philosophical and ethic concepts expounded in its first and last chapter, where Manu refers to the Puruṣa, too.

Besides, modern laws often agree with the laws of Manu. It is possible that the human rights in democratic societies have evolved from the invulnerability granted by Manu to the brahmins and by their search for inner freedom that had become attainable for everybody in the time of

---

[21] Cf. J.J. Meyer, Sexual Life in Ancient India, New Delhi 1989, p. 372.

[22] Cf. R. Lingat, The classical law of India, Berkeley 1973, p. 86.

Hellenism notably through the Gnostic movement with its strong roots in Indian philosophy.

Probably for the reason of avoiding an incestuous relation Śāntā, the daughter of Daśaratha, is given in adoption to king Romapada at an early age, some time before she becomes the wife of Ṛṣyaśṛṅga, but after she had been brought to Romapada's place a great drought occurred, which could only be removed by bringing the chaste boy Ṛṣyaśṛṅga to the town.[23] The giving away of a maiden is also part of the aśvamedha sacrifice according to Śatapatha Brāhmaṇa XIII.5.4.27:

When the closing offering is completed, they give four women with a maiden as the fifth and 400 female attendants according to agreement as a sacrificial gift.

The maiden in Daśaratha's aśvamedha was Śāntā. She was given to Ṛṣyaśṛṅga already before the sacrifice together with the attending women on the occasion of his seduction in the forest, as the Rāmāyaṇa and other texts report. As we know from the role the Dasyus and the Paṇis play in the Ṛg-Veda and the Rakṣasas in the Rāmāyaṇa, the later Āryans were opposed to a free behaviour of women. In the Rāmāyaṇa this is evident from the episode of the Rakṣasa-princess Śūrpanakhā. On the other hand, they were aware of the higher standard of living in the communities of the Dasyus, who may have been in connection with the Indus civilization before the arrival of the later Āryans (cf. chapter I.1 and VI). In the process of acculturation the later Āryans adopted many features from the Dasyus, especially the caste system, which the Dasyus probably inherited from the Indus civilization, but the later Āryans rejected what they deemed to be morally bad.

The aśvamedha as described by the Brāhmaṇa can be explained as a result of this process. On the one hand it was an improvement in the eyes of the later Āryans, that the king was no longer allowed to have intimate relations with his niece or daughter. On the other hand - and this was not a deterioration in their eyes, as it is in ours -, the queen had to lie with the corpse of the horse and to regard it as Prajāpati. That this

---

[23] The texts do not declare Śāntā the reason for the drought, but an offence of Romapada to his leading priest. It can be inferred from the status the virgin had in ancient India, however.

was not felt as discriminating by the queen herself may be due to the fact, that she was made to lie beside the dead horse only after she had done the slaughtering, at least in a symbolic way. This might have given her the impression that she was free of any compulsion like the priestesses of the Near East and in the Indus society.

In order that the aśvamedha ritual could be carried out effectively, Daśaratha secured a priest with a horn on his head similar to that of the priests and deities on the Indus seals, who often wear the twig of a pipal tree in addition. We find a similar twig on the head of the prostrated woman on seal 5013. The pipal or aśvattha is the tree, where the horse (aśva) stands (sthā), which can be referred to the unicorn and the standard in front of it. On seal 2430 and other tablets a deity with horns stands under an arch of a pipal. Nevertheless the offerings in Daśaratha's aśvamedha are served on vetasa-leaves. The vetasa is a reed. ṚV IV.58.5 speaks of a golden vetasa that stands "in the midst of the streams of melted butter (ghṛta)". From this verse its male symbolism is clear. By serving the offerings on these leaves the guests partake of the king's potency and restore it, vice versa.

When we have in mind that the bull-sacrifice as carried out in the Indus society was regarded as immoral by the later Āryans, but still too powerful to be totally abolished, as Eggeling supposes, then the only way to make it acceptable to them was to replace the bull by a horse and to make the queen lie with it. But in this way the sacrifice was brought from the symbolic sphere down to that of barbarous idolatry.

This is how the process of acculturation often works, when the giving society is on a higher standard of organisation than the taking society. This process may be one of the reasons for the "dark spots" in the Indian tradition, Dvivedi mentions.[24] They cannot be removed simply by meditating on the parts of the immolated horse, as the Bṛhad Āraṇyaka Upaniṣad enjoins. Nor can we blame the giving society for the deficiencies of the taking, as Eggeling did.

---

[24] Cf. H.P. Dvivedi, Jīvema śarada śatam - May we live hundred years, in: Hindi Gadya Padya Samgraha, Calcutta 1960, p. 102. On the other hand, there are dark spots in every tradition sometimes without anybody being aware of it.

It is also no way out of the situation, if we keep silent about it or try to play the whole rite down as the author of the aśvamedha-chapter of the Mahābhārata did by telling the story of the weasel. This tiny animal comes to the big sacrifice simply to remark that it is a trifle compared to the hospitality of a poor man, who gave his life to feed his guest. Similarly Manu declares in IV.53 that a man living without meat gets the same reward as somebody offering the aśvamedha for a hundred years. In both texts, the degradation of women implied in this sacrifice is not mentioned with a single word. But the setting up of an ideal how lofty it is cannot make up for the deficiencies of the actual situation. Eventually, there is no other way out of it, but to know how it came into being. This would also mean to understand the incest rite of the sacred marriage in a symbolic way and not as a sinful act that gives other nations the right to suppress the nations practising it, as M. Buber declares in respect to the Canaanitans.[25]

A bowman shots the father according to R̥V I.71.5. In later mythology he is identified with Rudra who is declared to be the son born from the seed that has fallen on the earth on the place, where the cohabitation of the father of the sky and his daughter took place. It is said that he kills his father by beheading, which is an euphemism for castration. In R̥V X.61.7 the son is called Vāstoṣpati, father of the house, and vratapā, protector of the law. According to X.61.2 he is adored on an altar made of rubbish.[26] Śiva is known for standing outside society, but that he punishes or kills his father is not mentioned at all. It would be against the nature of this god.

The father himself seems to be aware of his transgression, though it may have been inevitable at the beginning of creation, for in R̥V X.61.8 he is said to *run hither and thither with confused mind*. A feeling of remorse seems to speak from the eyes of the bull on seal 5013 in a mixture of shame and surprise. Shame may have been felt by the father of the sky

---

[25] Cf. Die Sprache der Botschaft, München 1964, p. 1099.

[26] Sūda, what has been crushed. This may also include sherds. In this sense it is homophonous with arma (cf. chapter I.1). This explains that many seals have been found at rubbish heaps (cf. chapter I.1).

over his own deed, surprise that the woman made things so easy for him. According to ṚV X.61.8 she tries to console him with her caresses. Instead of accepting this he runs away to the *southern places*, the realm of death. This seems to be the older variant of his beheading.

Geldner thinks that the daughter runs away after she tried in vain to prevent the father from forsaking her.[27] J. Deppert identifies the Dawn with the star Rohiṇī in the constellation of Taurus.[28] Rohiṇī, the Aldebaran of the Arabian astrologers, is indeed the main star of this constellation, but as the daughter of the sun who is married by the Aśvins she can also be identified with the Venus star.

Rohiṇī is a fix star. Like the woman lying prostrated under the bull on the Indus seal she does not move. The moon, who is her husband in later mythology, moves from one constellation to the other. In the Upaniṣads Prajāpati is also called the year and the Dawn as the planet Venus is identified with the first day of the year. As both are transitory, they are both liable *to run away*. When this is done by Prajāpati, the transitoriness of the whole creation is referred to.

All commentaries agree in the point that it was the daughter who seduced the father and that she tries to console him, because she feels guilty. The woman on the seal, however, looks as if she is violated. It seems likely hence that there was a basic incompatibility between the sexuality of the father and the daughter and not mutual love. The father's violence is hinted at by his vomiting foam in X.61.8. Perhaps, the daughter wanted to attract him, but in view of his violent response she is overwhelmed by frigidity.

Neither of the two seems to have any feeling of responsibility in respect to the world they are going to create. This feeling comes in only in later mythology through their son, Rudra, but at the cost of another act of violence. Violence seems to be inseparably interwoven with creation. In the creation myth of the churning of the milk-ocean, however, Śiva, Rudra's place-holder, swallows in an act of utmost benevolence the poison coming up from the churned ocean.

---

[27] Note to X.61.8.

[28] Cf. Rudras Geburt, Wiesbaden 1977, p. 194.

In the aśvamedha it is the horse, which has to bear the responsibility, as it is the substitute of Prajāpati according to the Brāhmaṇa. In the eyes of the feministic ideology this would not be sufficient, of course. Like the poet of R̥V I.71 its followers think that Prajāpati has to be punished, since a father who makes love with his daughter is immoral, in any case. It does not matter at all, whether he was seduced by the daughter or not. She is exempt from any responsibility like Urvaśī in R̥V X.95 who does not even show motherly affection for her child, when she is going to leave her lover Purūravas for ever. Her callousness would make violence against her understandable or excusable at least, but Purūravas can threaten with violence only against himself. Urvaśī is out of his reach. The only excuse for her behaviour is to blame the faithlessness of women in general (cf. chapter VI). We have to admit, however, that the inconsistency which we find between male and female sexuality in the cosmogonic myths exists only from the modern point of view. In the frame of the archaic world Prajāpati and Uṣas and Purūravas and Urvaśī are simply executing their part in the cosmic play of the sacrifice of the Puruṣa.

Under these presuppositions it would not be surprising, if the woman under the bull on seal 5013 would have opened her womb deliberately to its seed. This assumption is confirmed by a similar scenery on tablet 1574 (M-489), where a woman exposes her back to a man with hoofs. Probably, the cosmic male is hiding behind him as Prajāpati hides himself in a deer in later mythology. The animal with three heads at the right of this side of the tablet would exactly fit in the frame of a fertility rite as it was carried out at the New Year festival in Akkad, the additional heads could be substitutes of the two years.[29] The motif is repeated in the two goats eating from a kino tree on the left side, a motif that is also found on Akkadian seals (cf. chapter VII.1). Two goats or gazelles stand also beside a kino tree on tablet 2719. The Agastya-myth that is illustrated here is but another version of the myth of Prajāpati (cf. chapter I.4).

Besides, the two gazelles and the two heads of the composite animal can be explained as the channels of Iḍā and Piṅgalā and the tree or the

---

[29] The relation of the Purūravas-Urvaśī-story with the New Year has been hinted at by G. Dumézil, op. cit. p. 140.

animal in between as the Kuṇḍalinī (cf. chapter VIII). The bird in the middle of the erotic scenery of tablet 1574 could hence be a representative of the phoenix that is a symbol of human resurrection. It is reached when the Kuṇḍalinī has arrived at the highest plane.

From the same reason it is not to be wondered at that the goddess of Dawn is praised in many Vedic hymns for her purity without admonishing her role as a seductrice. Like the Dawn the Apsaras, her companions, live near the waters, as their name implies. Purūravas recovers Urvaśī in a bathing tank according to Śatapatha Brāhmaṇa XI.5.4 and his son is born "in the waters" according to ṚV X.95.10. The same is said of the sage Vasiṣṭha in ṚV VII.33.1, if we read puṣkara, lotus-flower, as its synonym lotus-pond.

Like the bathing of the Dawn and of the Apsaras the aśvamedha is carried out as an act of purification, as stated in Rāmāyaṇa I.14.35. In the Indus cities it was the Great Bath in the midst of the citadel that served for this purpose, but the bath was likewise a place of seduction and enjoyment, as we can infer from the Veda. This is also true for the Mesopotamian sacred marriage.[30] In ṚV V.80.6ab we read:

> *Like a beautiful woman the daughter of the sky*
> *turns against the men and uncovers her breast.*

Apsas, breast, is explained by Grassmann in his dictionary as: "(Es) scheint den Busen oder vielmehr den Teil des Gewandes zu bezeichnen, der den Busen verhüllt." (It seems to be the bosom or rather the part of the garment veiling the bosom). It is highly improbable, however, that the goddess of Dawn wore an upper garment. Neither the female figurines found in the Indus Valley nor the women in later Indian art wear an upper garment or if they do, it does not veil the bosom.[31] Apsas should be translated therefore as 'spending wetness' like the related word apsā. This is also in accordance with ni-ri, to uncover, meaning literally to run or trickle down, which can be referred to the milk of the

---

[30] The parallels of the Mesopotamian sacred marriage with the Indus Valley have already been hinted at by D.D. Kosambi, Myth and Reality, Bombay ³1992, p. 42.

[31] Cf. Vergessene Städte am Indus, fig. C 108-120.

swelling bosom of the Dawn. The meaning is that the Dawn with her dew refreshes the worshipper like Soma.

The dreadful aspects of the Dawn are also present for the poets, when they describe her as shortening their life-time, whenever she appears anew. In R̥V I.124.4cd she is even compared to a fly:

> *Like an onrushing ship (nodhas) she exposes her treasures,*
> *like a fly she awakes the sleeping.*

The fly lives on cadavers and rubbish and transfers illnesses like the mosquito, her relative. The reading of nodhas as ship follows from the cup-sign on the related rhino-seal 1347 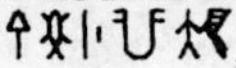. Nodhas is the name of a merchant and seer, who must have been the owner of beautiful see-going ships. The compound in the beginning can be read as to expose the limbs to everybody, the short stroke as she, the long stroke as a corpse or to sleep, the bee-sign as a fly, the lance-sign as to awake.

Whether pleasant or unpleasant, whether she comes or goes away, the Dawn fulfils the law and still she behaves as an independent woman as it is to be expected from the women of the Indus society.[32] Perhaps it is because of this behaviour, that Indra smashes her cart (R̥V IV.30.8-11). After this 'punishment' she runs away to distant places like the father of the sky in X.61.8 to the southern. But her behaviour in relation to the Vedic seers and to Purūravas is the same.

A woman who has the right to attract a man, must be prepared to be rejected, as it happened to Śūrpanakhā. It is not easy to put up with rejection. Śūrpanakhā slandered Rāma and his wife in an act of revenge that led to Sītā's rape by Ravaṇa and to the great war between him and Rāma. This sort of slander occurs even in modern societies, though today it should not be necessary any more on account of the better social position women have. Nevertheless a young woman might feel compelled to take to this means in the fear of being blamed by society, when she admits that she has sexual desires of her own. It seems, that in the Indus civilization female sexuality was accepted. This may be the reason why we find no signs of violence in this society.

---

[32] The goddess of luck, Śrī, is praised for her 'not going away' (R̥V V.87.2,15), but everybody knows that nothing is as transitory as luck.

If all men are declared as violent and all women as victims, as by the feministic movement, violence increases even. The blaming of the other sex is no way out of it. The war between the sexes can end only by the realization of androgyny. This would mean that man and woman try to help each other, not only in regard to this world, but still more in order to reach the world beyond. Regardless the environment in which they lived, regardless the riches they could accumulate, a lot of men in India and elsewhere have always felt society a burden and a bondage and searched for inner freedom. A woman can help a man to achieve this aim, if she wants to, sometimes even at the cost of giving up the aim of her own social and inner liberation, for when a man has won inner freedom the woman too will be free, out- and inwardly. A woman should have the right, however, to strife for this aim independently and to forsake a man, if he is an obstacle in the way of her inner liberation. That she can do it for profane aims is no longer discussed in the West. The aim of inner freedom has not yet come in view to most of the modern women. It is much harder to be won than outward liberty, and certainly it cannot be reached as long as the world is considered as the only reality.

The world is a simile, it is real because something beyond or behind it is real, like the image in a mirror is real only because somebody looking into it is more real than the reflection. When taken as real, the world gives rise to endless strife, but when taken as unreal, not even as a simile, it will give neither experience nor knowledge like a dry fruit. This knowledge can be won from the Indus seals, but it should not remain merely theoretical. One should try to realize it by daily exercise. This is called ūrdhvaretas in the later Indian tradition, drawing the seed upwards (cf. chapter VIII). Through this exercise the splitting of the object seen and the seer is minimized. Then the arrow reaches the aim in one's own hand, as is said in ṚV X.61.3 in similar words as in Zen texts. Then it will become unnecessary to direct it so somebody else in order to punish him as Rudra did according to later mythology. From this point of view life and death, separation and union are a play.

Rituals serve for remembrance. They are made unnecessary by meditation. This is the teaching of the Upaniṣads. It seems to me that it was taught already by the priests and seers of the Indus civilization.

VI. PURŪRAVAS AND URVAŚĪ

(ṚG-VEDA X.95)

The dialogue-hymn ṚV X.95 that we shall study in detail in this chapter has often been analysed and commented upon. In my opinion, the commentary of H.J. de Zwart, though the shortest, is the most helpful for the understanding of crucial points.[1] G. Dumézil has thrown much light on the mythological and ritual background of this hymn, although he only dwells on the parallels in the Indo-European world.[2] As far as I know, the only commentator who saw the relation of the Vedic hymn to the Mesopotamian religion, is D.D. Kosambi.[3] He also mentions the Indus Valley as a possible source of the "parallelism with Ištar-Inanna".[4] My earlier attempt to explain the dialogue on the ground of the logographic reading of several Indus seals with the motif of a dog or bird was published eight years ago.[5] It was the starting point for the investigation of this hymn in the first edition of this volume. The results achieved therein are now revised here in the light of the logophonetic method developed in the meantime.

The Śatapatha Brāhmaṇa says that the dialogue, of which it quotes verse 1,2,14,15 and 16, consists of 15 verses, but the Vedic hymn has 18. Geldner believes that 15 verses are part of the dialogue and that

---

[1] Cf. Ṛgveda X.95. Purūravas and Urvaśī, in: Orientalia Neerlandica, Leiden 1948, p. 363-371. Here a list of literature is given, too.

[2] Op. cit. p. 140.

[3] Op. cit. (1992). Kosambi's investigation has been discussed by me already in regard to the Vedic hymn in Die Dreigestalt des Seins und ihr androgyner Ursprung, Bremen 1983, and Die Sakrale Liebe im Alten und Neuen Testament, im Alten Orient und im Rig-Veda, Bremen 1987.

[4] Op. cit. p. 67,68.

[5] Cf. Der Fünfte Veda, p. 66. The dog under consideration belongs to a small species, for the mastiff as part of a composite animal on some copper plates related to Mitra and Varuṇa cf. chapter IV.

verses 4, 6 and 18 do not belong to it, because they are of narrative character,[6] but this does not mean that these verses are of later origin. Notably verse 4 contains an old trait of the story. There are no objections against verse 18 either, even if it was not spoken by Urvaśī. For this reason it may not have been counted by the author of the Brahmaṇa as part of the hymn. Verses 6 and 7 have probably been inserted in a later time, however, because verse 6 contains a rather rude insult of the water-women that could have had only a bad effect on Urvaśī and because the *annihilation of the Dasyus* in verse 7 cannot have been requested by an Apsaras. I could not find an Indus equivalence for these two verses either.

The names of the speakers have been added by me in brackets in the following translation, in which the results of the investigation of the Indus seals have been duly considered:

1 (P.) Alas, woman, have a heart, stay, cruel one!
Let us exchange words with each other!
If these things remain unsaid,
they will not cause us joy at any future day.

2 (U.) Why shall I exchange words with you?
I have gone like the first of the Dawns.
Purūravas, go back home!
I am as difficult to catch as the wind.

3 (P.) Like the lucky arrow, the missile from the quiver,
like a race-horse winning a hundred of cows;
after having made an unmanly design it flashed up somehow,
and the blowing ones let it roar as from a sheep.

4 (U.) She gave wealth and youth to the father-in-law;
whenever the lover wished she came from the inner house
to the house, where she found joy,
day and night pierced by the rod.

---

[6] Cf. R. Pischel/K.F. Geldner, Vedische Studien I, Stuttgart 1889, p. 293.

5 (U.) Thrice a day, indeed, you have pierced me with the rod,
even when I did not desire it, you filled me;
Purūravas, I surrendered to your will,
you, hero, were the king of my body.

[6 (P.) The glowing one, she with the line of beauty, the graceful,
she with eyes like a lotus-pond, she who goes with a hair-knot,
they melted away like rosy paint,
like cows full with milk they mooed for satisfaction.]

[7 (U.) The heavenly women will sit near his side, when he is born,
the rivers that purify themselves will let him grow;
likewise the gods have given strength to you, Purūravas,
for the great struggle, the annihilation of the Dasyus.]

8 (P.:) As I, the mortal, mixed with the immortals,
when they had stripped off their [feather]dress,
they ran trembling away from me like [gazelles] bowing down,
like young mares fearing to be yoked to the car.

9 (U.) When a [worthy] mortal feels desire for the immortals
and mixes with the onrushing according to their desires,
then they polish themselves like ducks,
like young mares the play and bite.

10 (P.) She who flashed up [and disappeared] like lightning,
the water-woman, who brought me her lovely things,
may bring forth from the waters a manly, well-born (son),
Urvaśī may have a long life!

11 (U.) You have been born to rule, really,
but you gave me your virile strength;
I, the knowing one, advised you this day,
but you did not listen - why do you speak now for in vain?

12 (P.) Won't the new-born son when seeking the father
shed tears like a cakra[vāka-bird] hearing this?
Who can separate husband and wife who are of one mind,
as long as the fire burns with the parents-in-law?

13 (U.) I will tell him, that he sheds tears
like a cakra[vāka-bird] crying for loving care;
I shall send you what is with us belonging to you,
go back home, you won't get me, you fool!

14 (P.) And when your lover runs away now
to the farthest distance, never to come back,
when he falls in the womb of the goddess of Death,
when the wild wolves eat him up?

15 (U.) Purūravas, you won't run away, you won't die,
the cruel wolves won't eat you up!
Really, there is no friendship with women,
they have the hearts of bristly wolves.

16 (U.) When in another appearance I stayed
four years among the mortals,
I ate a drop of melted butter once a day,
and I am still satiated with that.

17 (P.) She, who flies in the air, she, who goes at the sky,
Urvaśī I adore, the best [of her lovers];
so that the reward of the good deed may reach you,
return! My heart is burning up!

18 (U.) Thus the gods speak to you, son of Iḷā:
Since you are a companion of death,
your offspring shall offer Soma to the gods
and you shall enjoy heaven.

In order to understand the hymn it is necessary to study Śatapatha Brāhmaṇa XI.5.1-17, where the background of the dialogue is given. Here we learn that Urvaśī married Purūravas on three conditions: Three times a day he shall beat or pierce her with a rod; he shall not come to her without her consent; he shall not appear naked before her. Moreover, she asks him to protect the two rams she has brought with her, probably from the meadow, where she was tending them. After Urvaśī has become pregnant by Purūravas, the Gandharvas, her heavenly companions, want her back. They agree upon a ruse (the unmanly design of verse 3), rob one of the two lambs that are fastened to Urvaśī's bed and imitate their bleating. Urvaśī reacts thereupon in the following way according to the Brahmaṇa:

As if I had no man, no hero, they rob my son. She said the same after the Gandharvas had robbed the second lamb. Now Purūravas jumped up from the bed, naked as he was, to bring the lambs back. In this moment the Gandharvas sent a lightning, Urvaśī saw him naked and disappeared on the spot. After a long search he met her and four of her companions when they were bathing in a lotus-lake. They decided to appear before him in their human form. Then he accosted Urvaśī with the verses of the Vedic hymn.

1-2: Manasā tiṣṭha ghore - [if you] have a heart, stay, cruel one, recalls *manasā hi dhīraḥ - wise in mind* of R̥V X.82.1, said there of the all-maker Viśvakarman. But here manas means heart. Urvaśī has no heart for Purūravas' problems, she is *cruel*, because of the dark aspect of her nature, because the mind of women in general is unsteady (cañcala). Urvaśī confirms this involuntarily, when she compares herself with the wind. In this regard, Arjuna says in Bhagavadgītā 6.34:

For unsteady is the mind, Kr̥ṣṇa, and very easily set in motion:
its restraint methinks is as difficult as of the wind.

But for Urvaśī the wind is of divine nature like the goddess of Dawn. *First of the Dawns* may refer to the festival of the New Year as celebrated in Akkad.

3: This is the most difficult verse of the hymn. I take 'na' in the first half of the verse as a particle of comparison. Purūravas uses this particle in the same way as Urvaśī did in the last line of the previous verse. She leaves Purūravas like a lucky arrow that comes to a hunter only once in his life, or like a race-horse that has once won a hundred of cows, but which then for unknown reasons does not win any more and has become entirely useless for the owner. The *blowing ones* are the Gandharvas who go with the wind like the munis as described in R̥V X.136. On account of their super-human nature Purūravas is not able to catch them after they have robbed the rams and imitated their bleating. Instead of the rams of the Brāhmaṇa we find urā, sheep, in the Veda. The sheep or markhor is similar to the unicorn.

In tales all over the world this fabulous animal is mentioned together with a virgin who is a form of the goddess like the Apsaras. Urvaśī's name can be explained as mistress (vaśī) of the sheep or unicorn (ura). Purūravas is a prototype of this animal. His name means 'crying often, crying loud'. That Purūravas went away naked and that the Gandharvas sent the lightning when he brings the sheep back is not stated in the Vedic hymn, but it is certainly an original trait of the story. It shows that there must have been a tradition separate from that of the hymn. The words Urvaśī said according to this tradition (I have no man) are transformed by Purūravas into *the unmanly design.* This is another arrow from his quiver. He hunts Urvaśī like a gazelle (cf. verse 8).
In regard to the nakedness Kosambi quotes ṚV VIII.33.19:[7]

Look downwards, not upwards,
hold your feet closely together!
let not your naked hinder part be seen,
for you, o brahmin, have become a woman.

The nakedness of a man is obviously a matter of ridicule here. Manu treats nakedness as something immoral. In IV.53,75 he prescribes that a man should not see his wife naked nor that he should sleep naked, but in the Veda the nakedness of the Dawn is referred to in various hymns. According to X.95.8 it is reserved to the goddess and her companions. Urvaśī is like a daughter to Purūravas. To see him naked would remind her of an incestuous relation. This was a problem only from the Brāhmaṇa-time onwards, not for the Indus civilization. Perhaps this is the reason, why it is not mentioned in the Vedic hymn.
4: This verse retains the ancient trait of the relation of Urvaśī to her father-in-law, i.e. to Budha, the planet Mercury according to the Harivaṃśa. She treats him almost like a lover and that is why he regains his youth and potency. In behaving like this she obeys the social rules of that time. Likewise it is said of the Dawn that she follows the Law. According to the later versions of the story Urvaśī lived with Purūravas alone in the woods, not together with his family.

---

[7] Op. cit. (1992), p. 29.

Inner house, antigṛha, demonstrates that there were separate houses for women in the Vedic society as in later time. Certainly these were not simply cottages, as W. Rau maintains.[8]

5: The rod is the vetasa that is used according to ṚV IV.58.5 for churning butter . It is a drop of butter, on which Urvaśī lived according to verse 16. To be beaten or pierced by the vetasa is part of the ceremony of churning butter, hence she has not regarded it as an act of violence against her as long as Purūravas was the *king of her body*. Nevertheless he should not have beaten her or pierced her with the rod against her will. Even if the Gandharvas had not brought her back by a ruse, Purūravas has no right to expect her to live together with him any longer, because he did not obey this condition.

6: The names of the Apsaras who may be identical to the companions of Urvaśī mentioned in the Brāhmaṇa are fanciful The *line of beauty*, śreṇī, could refer to the three lines around the navel regarded as a sign of beauty in later literature.[9] The number five of the companions corresponds to the five subtle cakras on the spinal cord passed by the Kuṇḍalinī on her way to the seventh cakra at the skull. This last cakra and the first would then be represented by Urvaśī herself. Purūravas wants to say here that these ladies were not prude at all, but behaved like 'painted women', i.e. like prostitutes. They even obtruded themselves upon him like a cow that wants to be milked. This is a conventional description of the Apsaras in classical time, when they are regarded as 'common property'. Purūravas is boasting with his love adventures to make Urvaśī jealous, which is, of course, a useless means to get her back.

7: This verse seems to have been inserted for two reasons: One is the announcement that Urvaśī is pregnant, the other is the annihilation of the Dasyus that should be a more worthwhile aim in the life of Purūravas than the pursuit of a woman. But this does not sound a good argument for a woman whose moral standards are certainly different from that of the later Āryan society. The author of this verse tries to

---

[8] Cf. Zur vedischen Altertumskunde, Mainz 1983, p. 34.

[9] Cf. Bhartṛhari, Poems, ed. B. S. Miller, London 1967, no. 78.

direct Purūravas' wrath for Urvaśī against the innocent Dasyus. But if Purūravas would be able to do such a cruel deed as to annihilate them, he could not be Urvaśī's best lover (verse 17), nor would the Gandharvas, to whom Urvaśī belonged, request such atrocities.
The rivers mentioned here may be caused by the name of the Apsaras that can be explained as 'flowing like water'.
8: The Apsaras are furnished with opposite qualities. On the one hand, they behave like 'painted women' or prostitutes, on the other, like innocent virgins. Like gazelles they incite the hearts of a man, but they are also dangerous for him. The cruel aspect of their nature is described by Urvaśī in verse 15.
Bowing down (bhujyu) is the position of eating and also of awaiting sexual approach. The gazelle-like woman has carnal desires, though Urvaśī declares that she lived on *a drop of butter* only (cf. v. 16). The Apsaras behaved to Purūravas like *young mares fearing to be yoked to the car*,[10] though they are divine women. The word 'gazelle' is not used by Purūravas, perhaps because it is synonymous with prostitute. He prefers the word horse instead.
9: Urvaśī confirms the description of Purūravas in a way, but she adds that the mortal man who deserves these women has to surrender to their will, when they 'rush on him' like waves (kṣoṇi) of polished ducks. Generally, the swan, not the duck, is the bird of the Apsaras who are called swan-maiden hence, but the duck is also found on the related Indus-seal. What Urvaśī says here, is not contrary to what she has said in verse 5, according to which Purūravas was the *king of her body*, as if she was a mortal, for even if the Apsaras accept the sovereignty of a man, they do this on their own free will. Purūravas did not realize this, because he had lost his mind through Urvaśī's beauty. The horse is used by Urvaśī for comparison, too, but she turns Purūravas' words into another direction. The word caress (ratha) that can also mean car,

[10] Rathaspṛś may also mean 'eager for caress' according to J. Hertel, Rathaspṛś oder rathaspṛh, Indogermanische Forschungen XXI, p. 143. But this assumption is not corroborated by the related Indus seal.

is omitted by her. For her, the horse is a simile of freedom. She thinks of the wild horse, not of the domesticated horse of the later Āryans that was yoked to a car.

10: The *lightning* has been mentioned in verse 3 already. Purūravas supposes that Urvaśī is pregnant, because he deems this a powerful argument to bring her back. The *waters* recall the Great Bath of Mohenjo Daro. It was probably here, where Purūravas meets Urvaśī again. His son is going to be born there in the same way as Vasiṣṭha in ṚV VII.33.11, who is said to be born in a puṣkara, a lotus-lake.

11: What Urvaśī has communicated to Purūravas *this day* (when they met for the first time, probably at the New Year's day) was - apart from her conditions - to retain his male energy, when uniting with her. This is called ūrdhvaretas in later Indian tradition, drawing the seed up, i.e. retain it. But Purūravas being *the king of her body* did not listen to her, that means, ūrdhvaretas did not work, because he could not restrain himself.

12: For cakra, wheel, meaning cakravāka here cf. de Zwart. Her explanation is supported by an Indus seal, as we shall see later on. The cakravāka cries like a wheel, cakra, for his beloved. Like a wheel will run the tears of the child after it is born. A rather artful simile, through which Urvaśī as the goddess of speech shall be convinced at last that she has not the right to leave Purūravas. Padas 12cd refer to the ancient custom of kindling a new fire only after the decease of a householder. As long as the fire burns he is alive.

13: In the Viṣṇu Purāṇa Śiva's Vedic name Rudra is derived from the root rud, to weep, because Rudra wept, when he was born without any one to take care of him. Urvaśī refers to this story, when she ironically speaks of *loving care* for the weeping son, for this means also 'care of Śiva'. Purūravas is a fool, because he does not realize that sexual love is transitory. A child cannot be used for repairing broken love, still less, if the woman is a goddess who can easily cut off the bonds to a mortal.

14: If this is the nature of love, Purūravas does not want to live any longer. But the goddess of Death is merely the other aspect of the Dawn, who shortens the days of the seers whenever she appears (cf. ṚV I.124.10).

15: Urvaśī compares women to sālā-vṛka, sālā-wolves, an epithet found only twice in the Ṛg-Veda. According to Monier-Williams it is identical to śālā and means house, but 'house-wolf' does not make any sense here. A better explanation is obtained from Greek 'hyena', which is the equivalence given in Grassmann's dictionary. Hyena, the female form of hys (Latin sus), means sow, and refers to the bristly neck-hairs of this animal. Consequently, it is used here and in later Indian literature as a simile for the obstinate character of certain women otherwise called prostitutes in later time. In the Greek word the initial sa has become ha. In the Śatapatha Brāhmaṇa we find the related word śalalī, quill of the porcupine.[11] In Bhāgavata Purāṇa IX.14.37,38 Urvaśī says in regard to the sālāvṛkīs:

(These) women have no compassion, they are cruel and obstinate
and have no respect for a friend; for a little offence they kill
the husband or the brother who entrusted faith into them.
Having false confidence in unknown persons
they abandon their friends; they are prostitutes (puṃścala),
ever looking for another man, because they cannot live on their own means.

What Urvaśī says is in agreement with the words of the goddess of Language, Vāc, in ṚV X.125.5ab,6cd, whose representative she is:

I myself am she, who says, what is
agreeable to gods and to men;
I create quarrel among men,
I penetrate heaven and earth.

The goddess behaves like a prostitute, when she entices gods and men with flattering words and incites quarrel among them on the other hand. The Dawn, too, is compared to a *brotherless woman* in ṚV I.124.7, i.e. to someone behaving like a prostitute, because she appears to every men alike.
16: Butter stands for immortality in the Veda like the Soma, it is hence a fit nourishment for an immortal woman, though it does not sound probable that Urvaśī lived from one drop of melted butter alone. By this exaggeration she wants to make clear that she is really fed up with the world, in such a way that even sacrificial food does not attract her any more.

---

[11] Cf. A. Keith/A. Macdonell, op. cit., p. 365.

17: Purūravas recognizes Urvaśī now in her higher nature as an Apsaras, who are known as being able to fly (cf. X.136.4,6). Still he does not want to let her go. As ultimate means he takes resort to her divine nature, adoring her as a divine image, as his iṣṭā devatā. He wants her to come to the fire of his burning heart and to stay there and receive the oblations from the sacrifice as the results of their *good deed*. The same words are used in relation to the union of Prajāpati and his daughter (cf. chapter V). But even if Purūravas' seed is equal to a drop of butter, Urvaśī has enough of it. That does not mean that she breaks the laws of nature, on the contrary, it is the law of her nature, that gives her the right to behave in this way.
18: Purūravas would not suffer from the pain of separation, if he had practised ūrdhvaretas (cf. v. 11). But he preferred to remain a mortal, a companion of Death. Now what can a man do, when ūrdhvaretas did not work? He is advised to offer Soma in the fire in order to reach heaven after death. The triple fire and the Soma belong to the Indus civilization. It is significant that Purūravas is called after his mother here. His father is of no importance. This means that he lived in a matrilineal society.
According to the Brāhmaṇa Urvaśī invites Purūravas to come again after a year and spend one more night with her. After that the Gandharvas give him a fire-vessel, sthāli, literally a stand that can be identified with the standard in front of the unicorn. But Purūravas forgets it in the forest, and is then taught the use of fire-sticks. After he has made a triple fire with them, he ascends to the world of the Gandharvas and is united with Urvaśī again. But fire-sticks are nothing new. They are used already in tribal societies.
Let us study now the Indus seals that I have found in relation to this dialogue. Most of them are from Mohenjo Daro, two are from Harappa, one is from Lothal, but this seems to be a remake only.
1251 (unicorn) 

haye jāye manasā tiṣṭha ghore (1a)
Alas, woman, have a heart, stay, cruel one!

The fish-sign with an additional stroke that can be explained as a mouth renders the vocative haye, alas. To lament much is the explanation of the name of Purūravas. As a pictogram of the womb the mortar-sign can stand for jāyā, woman. For the three strokes we get manasā, because the mind is wavering like the wind represented by the lines. The lance-sign renders tiṣṭha, stay, the teeth-sign ghore, cruel.

2190 (unicorn) 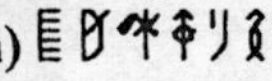

na nau mantrā anuditāsa ete
mayas karau paratare canāhan (1cd)
If these things remain unsaid,
they will not cause us joy at any future day.

From the first two signs we get na nau, like a ship, from the arrow in the target mantra, literally word, because the words of Purūravas are like arrows. The fourth sign that can be explained as a flagstaff renders joy, since it can have been used at the procession of the New Year that is related to Urvaśī. The bow-sign, which can also be read as a womb (cf. ṚV VI.75.3) can be read as to cause, since the womb is the cause of everything. The last sign corresponds to at any future day. Time is an attribute of the Dawn.

2482 (ivory rod) 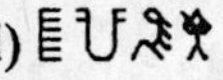

durāpanā vāta iva aham asmi (2d)
I am as difficult to catch as the wind.

The first sign renders durāpanā, literally protecting the door. The second sign which can be explained as a snake has been replaced by the wind in the hymn. From the two last signs we get aham asmi, I am, denoting Urvaśī as a goddess and a woman.

4144 (unicorn) 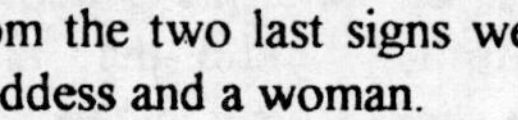 6094 (unicorn) 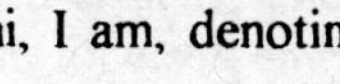

iṣur na śriya iṣudher asānā
goṣāḥ śatasā na raṃhiḥ
avīre kratau vi davidyutan na
urā na māyum citayanta dhunayaḥ (3)
Like the lucky arrow, the missile from the quiver,
like a race-horse winning a hundred of cows;
after having made an unmanly design it flashed up somehow,
and the blowing ones let it roar as from a sheep.

To a certain degree the two inscriptions explain each other mutually. Iṣur na śriya iṣudher asānā - like the lucky arrow, the weapon from the quiver, is written by the compound sign in the beginning of the main line of seal 4144 and by the third sign on seal 6094. It has been explained in chapter III.3 as to seize the womb of a flower-bud. Here the flower-bud is Urvaśī whose womb is compared to a quiver. The arrow is equal to the pistil, the crab-sign can be read as to seize. The horse-sign renders raṃhiḥ, the race-horse that wins a hundred of cows. The two strokes refer to the two comparisons. The long stroke is equal to flash up, the bee-sign on seal 4144 and the mortar-sign on seal 6094 have a female character and can hence be read as unmanly. The following field-sign on seal 4144 renders design. On seal 6094 we find a simple field-sign in place of it. The cup-sign at the end of seal 4144 refers to the Gandharvas called the blowing ones in verse 3, because they are companions of the wind. A similar sign must be supplemented on seal 6094. The sheep is a variant of the unicorn.

The separate signs on seal 4144 render the name of king Purūravas. On seal 6094 we find the rhombus-sign instead.

2518 (tiger) 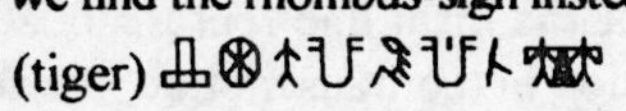

> *sā vasu dadhati śvaśurāya vaya*
> *uṣo yadi vaṣṭy antigṛhāt (4ab)*
> *She gave wealth and youth to the father-in-law;*
> *whenever the lover wished, (she came) from the inner house.*

The compound in the beginning can be read as to (let) bring goods or wealth, the stroke-sign is equal to the personal pronoun, the cup-sign with a stroke renders vayas, youth, the attribute of Urvaśī. Father-in-law is written by the snake-sign that is a synonym for forefather. It also contains the word for thread (German Schnur). He wishes is equal to the second cup-sign and the man-sign, the king-sign written separately over the tiger is equal to uṣo, lover, here the king, whose image is the tiger. For *inner house* we get the brickwork under the head of the tiger. Its two elements can also be read as the fire-sticks, because they are the inner house of Urvaśī.

3229 (elephant) 

triḥ sma mā 'hnaḥ śnathayo vaitasena (5a)

Thrice a day, indeed, you have pierced me with the rod.

From the first sign we get thrice, the short strokes render day (and night) here. The personal pronoun mā, me, is equal to the banner-sign, the fish-sign stands for you, Purūravas, here. From the arrow-sign we get śnatayo, beat or pierce. The male organ is piercing the vulva like an arrow. The penultimate sign can be read as veta, rod, reed, here, because the reed is similar to a snake. The water-carrier renders sena, servant, it refers to Purūravas here like the elephant of the motif. Purūravas is the king, but in relation to Urvaśī he is the servant.

1099 (unicorn) 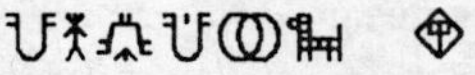

apa sma mat tarasantī na bhujyus

tā atrasan rathaspṛśo na_aśvāḥ (8cd)

They ran trembling away from me like [gazelles] bowing down,

like young mares fearing to be yoked to the car.

The hammer inside the rhombus that can be read as a house (math) is a simile of Purūravas. The first sign of the main line represents a trembling gazelle, though it appears as a dog in the transcription, the second sign renders bhujyu, being bent. The gazelles are bent like heaven and earth, otherwise written by this sign whose parts are united as in cohabitation. The cup-sign with a stroke is equal to the female personal pronoun they here. The following sign can be read as Vasiṣṭha, the best one. It is a name of Purūravas in verse 17. The horned man-sign is equal to ratha-spṛśo, to touch the car, because it can be read as car-driver, again referring to Purūravas. The young mares are equal to the cup-sign, because they are the divine water-women.

1093 (unicorn) 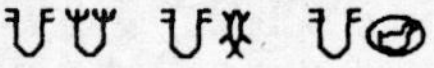

tā ātayo na tanvaḥ śuṃbhata svā (9a)

They polish themselves like ducks.

The three lines can be read as: The goddesses are rendered by the fish-sign and they polish themselves like ducks. The first sign is equivalent to the ducks of the Vedic verse, the fish-sign renders to polish, the womb-sign is equal to themselves.

0126 (unicorn) 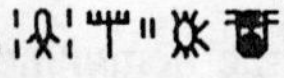 1017 (unicorn) 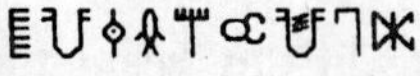

vidyun na yā patantī davidyod
bharantī me apyā kāmyāni
janiṣṭo apo naryaḥ sujātaḥ
pra_urvaśī tirata dīrgham āyuḥ (10cd)
She who flashed up like lightning,
the water-woman, who brought me her lovely things,
may bring forth from the waters a manly, well-born (son),
Urvaśī may have a long life!

For this verse we get again two Indus seals. Seal 0126 renders he whole verse, seal 1017 the last half. The compound in the beginning of seal 0126 is equal to Urvaśī (the banner-sign) brought me (the king-sign) her lovely things (the cup-sign). The second sign can be read as flashed up, the two short strokes as eyes, the single banner-sign as lightning. The last sign, the fish surrounded by (water-)drops, renders the son born from the waters.

The last two signs of seal 1017 are missing, but they can be restored by the cup-sign and the woman-sign. From the first sign we get janiṣṭa, equal to jani, woman, and sthā, stand. The second sign can be read as a shadoof, used for fetching water that is symbolized by the strokes in the following cup-sign to be read as a womb. Narya sujāta, well-born son, is equal to the crab-sign that can be read as a bull. From the banner-sign we get lightning again, from the fish-sign flash up. The pointed stroke corresponds to dīrgha, long, the restored cup-sign to āyu, life, the restored woman-sign to the personal pronoun she.

1237 (unicorn) 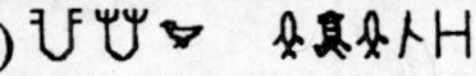

prati bravāṇi vartayate aśru
cakran na krandad ādhye śivāyai (13ab)
I will tell him, that he sheds tears
like a cakra[vāka-bird] crying for loving care.

From the second sign we get I, from the first prati bravāṇi, to answer him. The pictogram can be explained as a mouth. The first fish-sign agrees with varta as vrata means vow, religious observance. Yate, homophonous with yati, leader (of a horse), magician, corresponds to the horse-sign The second fish-sign is equal to aśru, tear, being homophonous with śru, hear, study. The bird in the beginning of the second line can be a cakravāka, at any rate it is not a wheel. From the womb-sign we get krandad, cry, being natural for women. The cup-sign is equal to ādhye śivāyai, for loving care, denoting Śiva.

2527 (tiger)  2313 (bull) 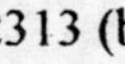 0102 (unicorn) 

na vai straiṇāni sakhyāni santi (15c)

Really, there is no friendship with women.

There are three seals that can be affiliated to this verse. This means that this sentence was already very famous in ancient times. In all these inscriptions the dog-sign occurs. It always corresponds to sakhi, friend, which is an attribute of this animal till modern times. A Meluḫḫa-dog occurs in Akkadian lists of merchandise. The drawn pictogram looks like a terrier, but the original resembles a gazelle. Contrarily to its being a friend of man, the dog has also been known since ancient times for its shamelessness. This is the reason why a Greek school of philosophy was called the cynics after the Greek name for dog.

On seal 2527 the thigh-sign agrees with straiṇāni, belonging to women, strī. From the dog-sign we get sakhyāni, friends, and from the teeth-sign na santi, not being, as a female quality. On seal 2313 the thigh-sign is replaced by a step-sign, the teeth-sign by the navel-sign that have the same meanings. On seal 0102 straiṇāni agrees with the first sign, which can be interpreted as a woman with ornaments. Na vai is equal to the two strokes of the second sign, santi, being, corresponds with the cup-sign.

2305 (unicorn) 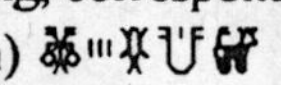 2219 (unicorn) 

sālāvṛkāṇāṃ hṛdayāny etā (15d)

They have the hearts of bristly wolves.

For line 15d I have found two seals. Again we meet the dog-sign, but here it stands for hyena, because this animal has bristly neck-hairs like a terrier. On both seals, the accented cup-sign stands for vṛka. The word can be derived from vṛ, enclose. On the ground of the pictograms, a sālāvṛkā is a woman who attracts a man by her bristly hairs and then sucks the marrow out of his bones like a hyena, when he yields to her. The bee-sign on seal 2305 and the first wheel-sign on seal 2219 can be interpreted as kānam, one-eyed, or cana, lovely. From the water-carrier on seal 2305 we get hr̥dayāni, literally go (away) with a heart, which is a description of the prostitutes constantly stealing away the hearts of men. The heart is equal to the cup-sign on the top, the three strokes represent the seed here, because this it is what these women really take. On seal 2219 the two wheel-signs can be read as the bosom, that is helpful in stealing the hearts of men. The bird in brackets that can be interpreted as the egg-shells is another simile of these women, who appear as helpless young birds, but draw men into an abyss represented by the cup-sign here.

2069 (unicorn) 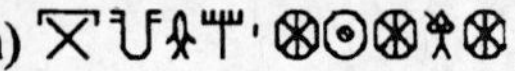

antarikṣaprām rajaso vimānīm
upa śikṣāmy urvaśī vasiṣṭhaḥ (17ab)
She, who flies in the air, she, who goes at the sky,
Urvaśī I adore, the best [of her lovers].

On this seal the king-sign that can also mean queen, occurs thrice. In the first and the third position it refers to Urvaśī as flying in the air and going at the sky, in the fifth position it is equal to Purūravas. The guardian-sign depicting Rudra or the long-haired is omitted in the Vedic verse. We have quoted R̥V X.136.4, where the long-haired is said to fly in the air. The bosom-sign refers to Urvaśī again. The single stroke can be read as the personal pronoun I. The sequence of the next two signs is already known to us as rendering Urvaśī. From the cup-sign and the cross-sign with bar we get Vasiṣṭha, best of lovers.

2228 (blank) 

prajā te devān hāviṣā yajāti
svarga u tvam api mādayāse (18cd)
Your offspring shall offer Soma to the gods
and you shall enjoy heaven.

Seal 2228 has three lines, which have to be read from the bottom to the top as usual. The lowest line consists of one sign only, that is broken off, however. It can be read as a bee or as a rhombus-sign with additional strokes. In both cases it renders prajā, offspring. The bee is a symbol of fertility as well as the rhombus with strokes or hairs representing the vulva. The bowman in the second line stands for te, your, referring to Purūravas. Haviṣā yajāti, offer with Soma, is equal to the two strokes and the field-sign, the place of sacrifice or the pressing board. The hand-sign represents the gods as the supporters. From the field-sign and the bird-sign of the uppermost line we get svarga, bird, whose literal meaning is to go to heaven (by sacrificing). The two short strokes are equal to tvam, you, the bee-sign that is a variant of the fish-sign, renders mādayāse, you enjoy (the honey, madhu) referring to Purūravas again. We see again from these examples that the same sign can be interpreted in several ways, but the readings are consistent because of the Vedic context.

The Bhāgavata Purāṇa states at the end of the Purūravas-episode that Purūravas lived *in the beginning of the Tretā-Yuga*, and that before this time the Veda and the syllable OM (ॐ) and all languages had been one like the sacrificial fire, that was made thrice by Purūravas. We do not know when the Tretā-Yuga began, but it is possible to associate it with the end of the Indus civilization, since the story of Purūravas could well have taken place in the ancient cities furnished with baths and hierodules.

The same applies to the story behind the rape of Tārā - the wife of the divine priest Br̥haspati - by Soma reported in R̥V X.109 in a very cryptic form[12] and narrated in the Bhāgavata Purāṇa in the previous chapter. Through the raped Tārā, who is another representative of Language (Vāc), Budha or Mercury was born. Through Iḷā, the daughter and wife of Manu, the ancestor of the Āryans, Budha became father of Purūravas. Manu's father was Vivasvat, the sun. Manu and Purūravas were the first in this genealogy who had a human body and lived on earth, their forefathers are personified planets abiding in heaven. Purūravas is the grandson of Manu and the half-brother of his children simultaneously.

The extraterrestrial beginning of the solar and the lunar race does not explain how human civilization started on earth and how it rose to the higher level of urban communities like those of the Indus cities. We can only assume that it occurred through intercourse between immortals

---

[12] A. Parpola (1994, p. 262) identifies Tārā with Rohiṇī (Aldebaran) and explains the story with the replacement of the sun-calendar through the moon-calendar, the sun being represented by Br̥haspati. He is not able, however, to state a reason for this replacement.

and mortals like it happened between Urvaśī and Purūravas. But how the gods and goddesses appeared on earth, is said nowhere. The only connection between the divine worlds and the earth is sacrifice and the ground of sacrifice is poetical imagination and yoga.

The next steps of the cultural evolution are quite easy to be explained as a process of acculturation of tribal and urban communities. In this cultural evolution the Atharva-Veda split from the Ṛg-Veda, thereafter the Sāma-Veda and the Yajur-Veda,[13] followed by a diversity of languages. The gods had only one language, in the big cities of the Indus Valley many nationalities with different languages were grouped together. The language employed in the sacrifices must have been as near as possible to the language of the gods, that was Sanskrit, but it also incorporated Dravidian traits. The inscriptions of the seals were written in the same vernacular, since they had a religious function. The priests could be Āryans or Dravidians, too. Even in later time, a lot of non-Āryan names are found among the Vedic poets and others might have adopted an Āryan name though they were non-Āryan by birth. It is most likely also that non-Āryan women married Āryan men, who took them for immortal, since they came from a higher social order. Purūravas and Urvaśī may be prototypes of such a 'mixed' relation.

In the Veda the Dāsa-king Vṛtra is described as a lecherous man, who keeps the women imprisoned (cf. ṚV I.32.11). This sort of slander is a stereotype and is in praxis even now, as is seen in today's psychological war between religions and sects. However, Urvaśī is free to forsake a man, in the same way as the Mesopotamian goddess was capable of doing it. The Purūravas-Urvaśī-legend can be regarded as a 'civilized' way of dealing with the problem of separation.

Already during the era of the Brāhmaṇas Urvaśī's behaviour had become intolerable. Consequently, she had to come back to Purūravas after a year and to spend one more night with him. Even then, she failed to gain back her freedom, because Purūravas ascended to the world of

---

[13] The Yajur-Veda, as it is known today, has quite a modern form. Its verses are not identical to the ancient yajus or sacrificial mantras that are contained in the Indus seals.

the Gandharvas, where she might again be under his control. This implies that love becomes a sort of bondage and is no longer a way to freedom as it was in the Indus civilization. It is surprising that in later time in India, where liberation or mokṣa was looked upon as the highest achievement in life, women were not allowed to strive for and achieve it independently of a man. The devaluation of women went along with the upgrading of homosexual relationships. The reason for this is that homosexuality can better be associated with an ascetic life than heterosexuality. We find the same phenomenon in the Catholic church. In the course of this development heterosexual and romantic love are denunciated as immoral or foolish, except if they lead to marriage. If one gets married, however, one is an object of ridicule by one's fellowmen. If one is unable to forget a woman, one is still more a fool, as Purūravas is already called by Urvaśī. After all, this is nothing but the play of Nature, by which she wants to perpetuate herself. Only in a few cases she reveals her higher nature leading to the knowledge of the self behind the screen.

This knowledge is also manifested in the whim for generating fire and pressing Soma that was invented by the Gandharvas (cf. chapter I.7) and given to Purūravas according to the Brāhmaṇa, but was forgotten by him, as the whole Indus society was forgotten by the later Āryans, in spite of the teaching of reincarnation that should be a means against this sort of oblivion. The name of the Gandharvas meaning cohabitator (from the root gadh, cf. German Gatte) is a reminiscence of their invention, because cohabitation works after the same principle as the whim (cf. note 83 in chapter I.7). This principle and its application for transcending the dual world through ūrdhvaretas is the deeper meaning behind this ancient love-story. We shall come across this principle in the next chapter again.

VII. GILGAMEŠ AND ANCIENT INDIA

1. The jewel-tree and the ale-wife Siduri

(Epic of Gilgameš, tablet IX and X)

We know from the age of the ramparts of Uruk built during the lifetime of Gilgameš and referred to in the first tablet of the Gilgameš epic that Gilgameš lived some time between 2750 and 2600 ante our era, but the first testimonies of the epic are from the end of the 3rd millennium.[1] This means that it is contemporary with the mature Harappa civilisation. It is possible hence that the epic was influenced or inspired by the poets of the Indus Valley. This assumption gets further supply from the name of Gilgameš that is explained like the Greek word Cyclops as 'he, who looks around'.[2] The single eye that is attributed to the Cyclops in Greek mythology recalls the third eye of Śiva and the yogi. To look around means here to look in both directions, outside and inside.

Moreover, in Mesopotamia several seals with religious motifs were found that also appear on Indus seals: The hero between two lions or bulls (Frankfort XIm), a tree flanked by two goats (Frankfort IIIa, IVj),[3] a file of bulls or goats with a plant between each of them (Frankfort Vb,f) and a horned elephant (Frankfort VIc). There is a unicorn with the body of a deer, too (Frankfort IVk,m). Frankfort dates these seals in the Uruk- or Jemdet-Nasr-period which he states to have been earlier than 3000 ante, but with regard to the Indus seals it was probably 250 years later.[4] Like the script the Indus glyptic can have been influenced by the Sumerian, but since the religious motifs are the most frequent, if not the only type, it is likely that they have developed independently.

---

[1] Cf. Schott/Von Soden, Das Gilgamesch-Epos, Stuttgart 1980, p. 4.

[2] Cf. K. Oberhuber, Der Kyklop Polyphem in altorientalischer Sicht, in: Antiquitates Indogermanicae, Innsbruck 1974, p. 153.

[3] This motif is also found on a seal from Susa. Cf. E. Paroda, Alt-Iran, Baden-Baden 1962, p. 26. It is dated in the same time as the Uruk seal.

[4] Cf. H.G. Gundel, Der alte Vordere Orient, in: Studienbuch Geschichte, Stuttgart 1974, p. 14.

We have studied the figure of Enkidu in regard to its parallels with the Indian tradition in the 2nd chapter. Now we shall investigate the figure of Gilgameš in relation to other persons and motifs of the epic under the same aspect. At first we shall deal with the jewel-tree and the ale-wife Siduri.

Gilgameš is deeply hurt by the death of his friend Enkidu. The whole 8th tablet is filled with his lamentations. Eventually, he runs into the steppe, that is to the place where Enkidu spent his youth. The steppe is also known as the place of death. Gilgameš, however, does not want to commit suicide there, he wants to overcome death, he wants to know what is behind or beyond it.[5] Therefore he looks for the way to his ancestor Utnapištim, who survived the Great Flood with his wife in an ark and was brought by the gods to the "mouth of the streams" afterwards. The way to this place is not only unknown to him, but also dangerous. Gilgameš meets lions in the night, prays to the gods for help and drives them away with his sword and his axe (IX.i.9-18). The detailed description of his search is lost, but after some time he arrives at a huge mountain, whose peak touches the sky, the Mašu. Because of its height it could be compared to the Himalayas, but from the following lines we learn that the Mašu is a mythical mountain like the Indian Meru, to which it also seems to be related etymologically. Every morning the sun rises from behind the Mašu and disappears behind it every evening. This is illustrated on several Akkadian seals (Boehmer XXXIV,392-415).

On seal 409 the sun-god, to be recognized by the rays emanating from his shoulders, puts his right foot on the slopes of the mountain. Two minor gods open the door of heaven supervised by a third. The sun-god holds a key in his hand that looks like the Indus sign for woman,[6] a club

---

[5] A similar desire is uttered by the boy Naciketas to the god of Death, as told in the beginning of the Kaṭha Upaniṣad. It is supposed that the story is based on ṚV X.135.

[6] Cf. F.M. Feldhaus, Die Technik der Antike und des Mittelalters, Hildesheim 1971, p. 87. He thinks that the key serves for opening the door of heaven According to D. Edzard this instrument is a saw (cf. Mesopotamien, in: H.W. Haussig, Wörterbuch für Mythologie I, Stuttgart 1965, S. 126), but Feldhaus` explanation seems more convincing.

which may serve for dispelling the darkness stands outside the door-wings. Two 'standards' are placed at both sides of the god. They consist of the signs for god and the sun in respect to its rising and setting. In IX.ii.6-9 of the epic we learn that the door of the mountain is guarded by scorpion-men. Their effulgence is so great that human beings cannot bear it. To look at them means to die. Gilgameš, however, who is a god by two thirds of his being (IX.ii.15) has only to cover his face for some time. Then he is addressed by a scorpion-man with the following words (IX.ii.18-21):[7]

[Why did you go] this long way? [Why have you] come to me?
[Beyond many] hills that are difficult to cross?
[The reason thereof] I want to know.

Gilgameš replies that he is looking for the way to Utnapištim. The scorpion-man tells him, that he must pass underneath the mountain Mašu to come to his place and that no human being has gone there so far. He adds that the way extends from the emerging to the setting sun (IX.ii.12,13). Hence the Mašu must follow the direction from east to west. This agrees again with the Himalaya. According to this description the sun goes back the way in the night, it made in day-time. This is possible, no matter whether the earth is believed to be a disk or a globe. The way is 12 double hours long. One double hour is the twelfth part of the day or the night at the time of the equinoxes. It seems that Gilgameš arrives at this favourable time and that this is the reason, why the scorpion-man does not block his way. Gilgameš takes the direction to the east, for it is getting brighter more and more in the course of his wandering. The 12 double hours that he passes underneath the Mašu are dream-time. When he wakes up, he is in another world. There he sees a tree described in tablet IX.iv.47-51:

He goes [to the place] of the tree, to see [it].
Carneol it has as its fruit,
a grape hangs down from it.
Lapislazuli it has as foliage,
the fruits it bears are to behold with joy.

---

[7] Translated from R.C. Thompson, The Epic of Gilgamesh, Oxford 1930.

In all sentences only one tree is mentioned, not many, nor a garden of trees.[8] The fruits were explained by Oppenheim as the apples of the Hesperides, and he concluded that Gilgameš found a means of reaching immortality in the tree.[9] If Oppenheim was right in this point, and I think that he is, Utnapištim must be in a close connection with this tree, too. Gilgameš does not meet Utnapištim there, however, but the ale-wife Siduri. Though we are in a dream-world, she is more real than the hierodule, who brought Enkidu into the city of Uruk, for she has a name, the name of a goddess even, to be recognized by the determinative in front of it. Speiser thinks of a Hurritic word for "young women", who is a "form of Ištar".[10] In Sanskrit, there are the words siddha and sindhura in this connection. A siddha is a human being with extraordinary powers, mostly gained by yoga exercises. Sindhura with the female form sindhurī means elephant. We find this animal as door-keeper at the doors of Indian temples. The name Siduri could be explained with the help of the Vedic etymology as woman (strī) at the door (dūr). In X.i.15,16 we read that she closed her door, when she saw Gilgameš, and that he tries to make her open it with the same words Ištar used at the door of the Netherworld: "I smash the door, I break the bar."[11]

The second name of the ale-wife, Šabita, has also Indian connotations. It recalls the Indian tribe Śabara that is mentioned by Hiltebeitel.[12] Moreover, it is contained in the name of the wishing-cow Śabardugh. The Indus country is also referred to by the names of the jewels, carnelian and lapislazuli, which are both imports from Meluḫḫa.[13] Mohenjo

[8] Cf. A.L. Oppenheim, Mesopotamian Mythology II, Orientalia 4,1948, p. 47. It is impossible to read "gods" here, as Thompson notes. 'Issi' cannot be a plural, but only genitive singular.

[9] Op. cit. p. 48

[10] Cf. The Epic of Gilgamesh, ANET, Princeton 1955.

[11] Cf. Ištar's Descent to the Netherworld, obv. line 17.

[12] Cf. Rāma and Gilgameš, The Sacrifice of the Water-Buffalo and the Bull of Heaven, History of Religions 19,1980, p. 206.

[13] Cf. H. Heimpel, op. cit. (1987), p. 51.

Daro is known for its tree-worship. Hence there are several reasons to locate the dreamland of Gilgameš at the Indus. This would be in correspondence with the "lowlands at the border of the sea", as the place of Siduri is called in X.i.1 of the epic. If we translate this passage as "who dwells in the depths of the sea", as Thompson suggests,[14] we are in agreement with R̥V X.125.7, where the goddess of language (Vāc) describes her residence as: *My womb is in the water, within the ocean.* This may also refer to an over-flooded town. Like Indian village-goddesses Siduri has connections with a pot (X.i.3). And the "veils" Siduri wears (X.i.4) are very likely identical to an Indian sari. After opening her door reluctantly, Siduri addresses Gilgameš with the famous words of X.iii.1-14:

Gilgameš, where are you going?
That life you are looking for you will not find.
When the gods created man,
they have allotted death to him,
life they took in their own hand.
Your belly be full, Gilgameš!
Be happy at day and night,
celebrate a banquet every day,
dance and play at day and night!
Your clothes shall be clean, your head washed,
in flowing water you shall bathe;
look at the little one at your hand,
your wife be happy on your lap!
That is the lot of man.

With similar words Yama, the god of Death, tries in the Kaṭha Upaniṣad to lure the boy Naciketas away from his search after what is beyond death. Like Naciketas Gilgameš insists on his desire (X.ii.16-19):

Ale-wife, what is the way to Utnapištim?
What is its sign? Tell it to me, tell it to me!
If it is useful, I will cross the ocean,
if it is not, I will run through the steppe.

The two ways Gilgameš is thinking of are identical to those, between which Alexander could choose on his way back from India.

---

[14] Cf. Epic of Gilgameš, p. 84.

The relation between the jewel tree and India will become still more obvious, when we study the tree-seal 1387. The leaves indicate that it is a pipal tree, though the two fruits hanging down from the middle twig look a bit too big to represent the berries that grow on this tree. The circle in the middle of the tree could be part of the standard and the berries of the fig tree might have been used for making the sweet Soma juice (cf. chapter I.7). An equivalence of the Soma in Mesopotamia and Greece is wine, hence 'grape of wine' in line 49 would correspond to the berries of the fig tree. Grape of wine means geštin in Akkadian. This word is contained in the first part of the name of the goddess Geštin-anna, the sister of Dumuzi. Her exact function is unknown, but when the last letter of the first half of her name is regarded as omitted as it often happens with the last letter of a syllable in Sumerian, we would get Geštin-nanna. Nanna is the name of the moon-god. Gešti(n)-nanna could be explained then as the goddess of wine and of the moon. The moon is identified with the Soma in the Veda.

The 'lamellas' or incisions under the circle in the middle of the tree on the Indus seal have also an equivalence in the description of the jewel tree. In line 48 we read: *Carneol it bears as its fruit.* Carneol was made into pearls of oblong form in the Indus cities and exported to Mesopotamia.[15] By its reddish colour it can be regarded as a symbol of blood and of the pith of the tree. It was obtained by incising the bark of certain acacia trees that yielded perhaps the bitter ingredients of the Soma. In line 51 the foliage of the tree is compared to lapislazuli. This stone was used in Mesopotamia as a face brick for the temples. In Bhagavadgītā 15.1 the leaves of the eternal aśvattha or pipal tree are regarded as the hymns of the Veda. Hence the foliage is sacred in both traditions. The aśvattha tree can also be explained as the archetype of all plants. Consequently, it can be a composite plant as the unicorn is a composite animal. Therefore, its fruits can be from other trees than the leaves.

That the standard in front of the unicorn symbolizes a tree is confirmed by several seals, where it is replaced by it. It can also be a whim, as on the sherd from Mehi, where a bull is tied to it (cf. chapter I.7). The whim may

---

[15] For a picture of the pearls cf. Vergessene Städte am Indus, fig. 26-28.

also be identified with the car of the sun-daughter. It is drawn by two oxen along the ecliptic, when she travels to the house of her bridegrooms, the Aśvins, as is reported in the marriage-hymn ṚV X.85. The inscription of seal 1387 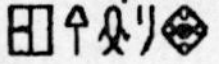 can be affiliated to X.85.13, X.125.3 and X.135.1 (cf. chapter I.7). If the motif is explained as the cosmic tree, the two unicorn-heads correspond to heaven and earth that look back to their origin in the stem. The motif can then be correlated to the Viśvakarman-hymn X.81, where the cosmic tree appears in verse 4. In X.81.2, the fundament and the pillar of the world are mentioned that agree with the last two signs. The first sign can be read as the sun at the sky, the seer of the world or king of the universe, the second sign is related to the number-sign for one. It can be rendered as first or former. The fish-sign is a symbol of the seer, as usual. With regard to X.81.1-2 we can translate the inscription as:

The sun-like one, who has sacrificed these worlds
(after hiding) the former ones, the seer,
he is the pillar and the fundament.

With regard to the Akkadian mythology the first sign of the inscription can be explained as the sun coming out of the mountain. The second sign could be explained as sparks or to appear. The fish-sign that is written at the root of the tree would correspond to Utnapištim in the epic of Gilgameš. The last sign is used instead of a plate or trough in front of a bull on seal 2279 depicting a bull-sacrifice. This can be explained with the fact that food is the fundament of life for the bull. The inscription 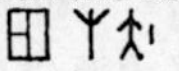 can also be read according to ṚV X.81.2: The All-maker (the One, the cosmic man) is the pillar and the fundament. He is the sacrifice.

Gilgameš does not meet Utnapištim under the jewel tree, but the ale-wife Siduri, as we know already. Likewise Indra meets the goddess Umā in his search after the eternal Brahman in the Kena Upaniṣad. A goddess could also have been depicted in the upper register of the cylinder seal 9006 from Ur as giving birth to a tree. Because of her long legs drawn back behind her head she can be compared to the Vedic goddess of creation Uttānapad: she, who draws her legs apart (for giving birth). In her hand she holds a stick with which she beats a zebu standing in the middle of the lower register in front of a date tree. A trough or bundle of grass is placed under its head.

The date tree in front of the animal can be compared to the jewel tree and the bundle of grass under its head to a sparkling jewel. The bull is followed by a scorpion which the goddess treads upon with the toes of her right foot. Two snakes on either side of the scorpion complete the scenery. The scorpion is known as an attribute of the goddess Ištar in Akkadian mythology. On several Akkadian seals it is found under the bed of the sacred marriage (Boehmer 690,691; Frankfort XVI). It could stand for the dark aspect of the goddess or for death, which is closely related to marriage. On the other hand, the goddess is in opposition to death, which is expressed on the seal by her treading the scorpion under her foot. The two aspects of the goddess are repeated in the zodiac, where Taurus and Scorpio are opposite signs. According to verse 13cd of the marriage-hymn R̥V X.85 the bulls are killed under the constellation of the (M)aghās equal to Scorpio, whereas under the constellation of the two Arjunīs, equal to Taurus, the bride is led to the house of the bridegroom.[16] That the bull is going to be sacrificed is indicated by the stick in the hand of the goddess and by the scorpion behind it.

A scorpion is also found on the round seals 9011 and 9015 from Ur. On the signless seal 9011 it has an egg behind its tail, on seal 9015 the egg is part of the inscription reading 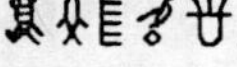. It can be translated according to R̥V X.85.34:

> *Scratching it is, biting it is,*
> *it has barbs, like poison it is uneatable;*
> *only the brahmin who knows the wedding hymn,*
> *deserves to receive the bridal shirt.*

Scratching and biting is not the bridal shirt, but the virgin, in particular if she is unwilling to marry. The brahmin 'purifies' it, as is said in the next verse. This he does by deflorating her with his supernatural power, as we learn from the inscription. After defloration she will become peaceful.

For the first sign, that can be interpreted as a thorny flower or as the paw of a cat, we get tr̥ṣṭam, scratching. Kaṭukam, biting, is rendered by a bird defending his egg like a girl her virginity. Having barbs is equal to

[16] For a discussion of this verse cf. chapter III.4.

the woman-sign itself. The fish-sign stands for the brahmin, the horse-sign renders his supernatural power.

If the scenery of seal 9006 depicts the sacred marriage, there is no objection of identifying the bull and the goddess with one of their prototypes like Gilgameš and Siduri or Purūravas and Urvaśī. At the same time, the seal is another proof of the close connections of the Akkadian and the Old Vedic mythology. This makes it likely that, if not Gilgameš himself, at least the author of the Gilgameš epic was in India, and that he adorned the figure of Gilgameš with the ideas and images he found there. We shall come across more similarities, when studying the further story of Gilgameš' search after Utnapištim and the narration of the Great Flood contained in the following tablets of the epic.

2. The ship and the Great Flood

(Epic of Gilgameš tablet X and XI)

As she is unable to prevent Gilgameš from his search for Utnapištim, not even by the description of how far his place is and of the dangers of the 'ocean of death', the ale-wife Siduri says all of a sudden:

Gilgameš, there is Uršanabi, Utnapištim's skipper,
to him belong the šu.ud.tak (those of stone).
He has gone to the forest to catch an urnu..

Gilgameš' former question, whether he shall take the sea- or the land-route, is thus answered by Siduri in the first alternative, and this is quite in agreement with the fact that Utnapištim lives at the "mouth of the streams", as we learn afterwards. In Old Babylonian tablets the name of the skipper is written 'šuršunabu'. This is explained by Thompson as 'servant of Ea', but it could also be interpreted as a derivation of Sanskrit vr̥ṣanābhi, 'having strong axes', which is said of the storms in the R̥g-Veda. It is quite suitable for a skipper, who must be acquainted with the storms. The word can also be translated as 'being from a high family'. This would be equally suitable for the skipper of Utnapištim.

Uršanabi is not only in possession of a ship, but also of the šu.ud.tak, which in Akkadian are written as 'šût abni', those of stone. Von Soden explains them as "gewaltige Ruderstangen" (huge poles).[17] It is not very likely, however, that poles are made of stone. A better explanation is obtained from the Akkadian dictionary published by the same author.[18] Abnum is explained there not simply as stone, but also as precious stone and stone for amulets. This means that it could be steatite, the material, of which most of the Indus seals are made, or even ivory. We have mentioned already that an ivory standard has been found recently in Harappa (cf. chapter I.7). 'Those of stones' could hence be identical to this 'cult-object' in front of the unicorn. This supposition is supported by a cylinder seal from Failaka, on whose preserved half the prow of a boat is to be recognized furnished with a moon-standard and a plant, that could be the plant of life. Two men have just left the ship. They could be Uršanabi and Gilgameš.[19] Moreover, the motif is bordered by a row of circles similar to the upper part of the moon-standard on the Failaka seals. H. Frankfort believes, that Gilgameš is depicted on plate XIm sitting together with Utnapištim and the plant of immortality on the ship pooled by Uršanabi.[20]
In the Veda stones (adri) are used for pressing the Soma. The mortar and the whim are constructed after the same principle (cf. chapter I.7). On some seals the 'vessel' has simply the form of a drill-hole that can be compared to the ring the goddess Ištar holds in her hand together with a rope. Frankfort explains them as measuring instruments,[21] but they could also be identified with a whim.

---

[17] Op. cit., note on X.ii.29.

[18] Cf. W. von Soden, Akkadisches Handwörterbuch, Wiesbaden 1965.

[19] For an illustration of the seal cf. P. Kjærum, op. cit. fig. 404.

[20]. That the situation is not identical to that described in the epic is explained by him with reference to medieval iconography, where "painters would thus bring persons together ... in order to make their representation intelligible" (op. cit. p. 67). This explanation holds good also for the crow sitting on the stern of the boat.

[21] Ibid. p. 179.

Ring-stones of different size, whose function is unknown, have been found in Harappa and Mohenjo Daro, eighteen of them in one room there.[22] It is known, that the Hindu temple developed from the Vedic altar. Therefore it has an imaginative central post built of ring-stones placed one above the other. They had no technical function, but served only as the mythical door to the sun for the figure of a golden man lying buried under the foot of this pillar.[23] If the ring-stones from Mohenjo Daro would all have been used for this purpose the temple would have reached a height of nine meter, since one stone has the average height of 50 cm. This would be quite a normal height for such a building, but walls of this size have not been found in the Indus cities. Hence it is more probable that these ring-stones were used as the lower part of a whim.[24]

The Vedic altar called vedi, mould, in Sanskrit has the form of a hyperboloid.[25] We find the similar form  on seal 5076 from Chanhu Daro (C-23). The only difference are the convex horizontal lines, but this agrees with Āpastamba Śrauta 2.3.1, according to which the Adhvaryu priest lifts up the two 'shoulder'-points in the east and the two 'thigh'-

[22] Cf. Vergessene Städte am Indus, fig. C 97.

[23] Cf. St. Kramrisch, Indische Kunst, Köln 1965, p. 15.

[24] There is the possibility, too, that they were used as coins which has already been discussed by J. Marshall (op. cit. p. 61). Stone money of similar size is still in use on the Pacific island Uap. A small coin, the obolos, had to be given to the ferryman Charon by the dead according to Greek mythology, to bring them over the stream of Hades (cf. R. Ranke-Graves, op. cit. p. 105). These oboloi were not perforated, but made from a pointed rod that was used for roasting meat originally. It is similar to the Indus sign  that may have been used as number-sign, too. The male symbolism of the rod is equally obvious as the female of the stone-rings. In China such 'tool' money was still used in the time of 1000 to 200 ante (cf. T. Kroha, Lexikon der Numismatik, Gütersloh 1977). The whim has a similar function as the Greek coins in the Vedic hymn X.135, as it opens the way to heaven. The stone money from Uap may have served for the same purpose originally.

[25] Cf. A. Hillebrandt, Das Altindische Neu- und Vollmondsopfer, Jena 1879, p. 191.

points in the west of the vedi.[26] As the upper and lower sides are called the shoulders and the thighs, their central points correspond to the third eye and the womb. In the central point under the shoulder-line a post could be erected that may have been fastened with the help of a ring-stone. The vedi is compared to a woman in RV X.114.3. The inscription of seal 5076  can be related to ṚV X.86.3. The sign for vedi can be identified with Indra's wife. The Vedic verse reads:

> *kim ayaṃ tvāṃ vṛṣākapiś cakāra harito mṛgaḥ*
> *yasme irasyasi īd u nv aryo vā puṣṭimad vasu*
> *What has done this Vṛṣākapi to you,*
> *the yellowish animal (of the forest),*
> *that you are angry with him,*
> *or what (has he done) to the blooming property of the lord?*[27]

As usual, the reading starts from the bottom. The man with two bows is a symbol of Indra, the following sign that can be explained as a mouth renders to speak. The two strokes are equal to the particle vā, or, referring to the two alternatives. The third sign of this line depicts a sitting ape (cf. chapter III,2). The first damaged sign of the third line stands for harito, yellowish. This can also be said of the gazelle depicted in the motif. The ape represents a male hierodule, the gazelle a female. Both animals belong to the forest. This is indicated by a tree here. The three following strokes indicate plurality. The big eye is a symbol of anger, the bowman stands for lord in general or for Indra again. The last sign can be interpreted as a blooming flower, to which the property is compared here. This refers to the *painted things* Indrāṇī (X.86.5) has made for her husband, i.e. pots painted with flowers.

---

[26] In the commentary to Śatapatha Brāhmaṇa I.2.5.18 cited by Hillebrandt on p. 190 this is explained as: "The shoulder-points of the vedi should be in touch with the Āhavanīya-fire (the fire in the east of the vedi)." Hillebrandt concedes not to understand these instructions, but the Indus seal makes it evident that shoulder and thigh are the respective lines here.

[27] My translation follows grammatically P. Thieme, Der Fremdling im Ṛgveda, Leipzig 1938, p. 13.

We know from the Gilgameš epic that the cabin of the ship of Ut-napištim was built like a ziggurat. Likewise there was a cabin in the middle of the Indus ships. The imaginative pillar is here sometimes visible as the mast. A car without wheels that can be explained as a whim, is brought by a boy on a mythical ship according to R̥V X.135.4.[28] In R̥V I.140.12 Agni is asked:

> *Give us for our car and for our house, Agni,*
> *a ship with its own oars and feet*
> *that carries our men and our generous lords*
> *and all human beings across and gives shelter to them.*

A ship for a car and a house must have been a house-boat like that on the Indus tablet 2828 (M-1429). It is used in a similar form on the Indus till today. *Carry across* may be interpreted in regard to the eternal world as in R̥V X.135, but in respect to the Indus ships it could mean to cross the Indian ocean and the Persian gulf on the way to Akkad. The Sumero-Akkadian word for the Indus ship was magilum. Ma_2 means ship in Sumerian, gilu means joy, perhaps because these ships were a cause of joy to the citizens of Akkad. Gilu may also be a variant of gala, great, for according to a fragment of the Sumerian Gilgameš-story these ships had to be towed into the harbour on account of their size.[29] Some of them might have been moved by a whim as the ship constructed by a boy in R̥V X.135.4. Uršanabi's mythical ship might have been equipped with the same contrivance. Instead of oxen it could have been driven by a mythical animal, the urnu, which may be the Akkadian version of the unicorn.

V. Soden translates this word as varan here (a species of a lizard), but in X.iii.38,39 as fetters. This is an unnecessary deviation from the rule of retaining the same or a similar word for the original. The urnu is said to live in the wood. This would be appropriate for a deer. The word could also be related to Sanskrit ura, sheep, a substitute of the unicorn (cf. chapter VI). On an Akkadian seal (Frankfort XIj) we find two lions

---

[28] For a Roman ship driven by a whim cf. F.M. Feldhaus, op.cit. p. 225.

[29] Cf. W. Heimpel, Tierbilder in der sumerischen Literatur, Rom 1968, p. 46. The towing of a ship is illustrated on a seal from Fara (Frankfort XIm).

harnessed to a plough like bulls. A composite animal is also found on the sun-boat (Frankfort XIXe,f).[30]
Uršanabi would not have had any difficulty to discover this urnu, if he had not been disturbed by Gilgameš, who arrives exactly in the moment when he is in search of the animal. Gilgameš enters the ship, goes to the stone objects and crushes them to pieces with his sword in a rush of anger. No reason is stated for his behaviour, but it seems that he has an aversion against unknown objects that might have a religious function. Surely, tolerance was not practised at that time outside India. After having destroyed the stony ones, Gilgameš runs into the wood crying for Uršanabi. When Uršanabi hears him, he comes at once, but he cannot save the stone objects. Nevertheless he friendly asks Gilgameš after his name and where-abouts. Such a behaviour recalls that of an Indian sage, who remains peaceful, even if he is insulted or his property is attacked.
Out of compassion for Gilgameš he is ready then to bring him across the water to Utnapištim, but since the stone objects are missing, it is impossible to cross the Sea of Death. Instead of them, Gilgameš has to procure poles, 120 in number (cf. Gilg. epic X.ii.4). In order to cross the Sea of Death, he is enjoined to use each of the poles only once.[31]
With the poles Gilgameš crosses the sea safely. When he comes near to Utnapištim's place at the mouth of the sea, Utnapištim sees the boat from afar and is surprised that he cannot recognize the stone objects. From this he infers that a foreigner has come without having the right to see him (X.iv.15-17). But after Gilgameš has gone ashore, Utnapištim too feels compassion for him and listens to his life-story. Then he gives him some advice in respect to the life of a king and to a human being in general. Eventually, Gilgameš asks him to tell him the story of the Great Flood, and Utnapištim narrates it in the following passage (XI.14-31):

---

[30] Cf. H. Frankfort's explanations of this animal, op. cit. p. 68,69.

[31] In Greek mythology an alive person wanting to cross the river of Hades had to show a golden bough to Charon. Cf. H. Jens, Mythologisches Lexikon, München 1958, p. 25. Frankfort takes recourse to this myth (op. cit. p. 136).

It was decided in the heart of the great gods to produce a flood.
Their father Anu made this decision
together with Enlil, the hero, their counsellor,
with Ninurta, their secretary, and Ennugi, their irrigator.
Ninšiku-Ea was also among them.
He imparted their words to a reed-house:
Reed-house, reed-house! Wall, wall!
Reed-house, listen! Wall, understand!
Man of Šurippak, son of Ubar-Tutu,
tear down this house, build a ship!
Renounce wealth, seek life!
Hate property, keep the soul alive!
Take the seed of all living beings aboard the ship!
The ship that you shall build,
its dimension shall be measured out,
it shall be equal in width and in length,
furnish it with a (cubical) roof like the Abzu.

Like the Paṇis in the Veda the Mesopotamians are described as being attached to wealth and property and this is said to be the reason for the flood. The ship or better the cabin of the ship that Utnapištim is asked to build shall have cubic form like the cabin of the Indus house-boats. It would be against technical knowledge to believe the trunk of the ship could have been cubical. The biblical ark had a cabin, too, but here it was rectangular. The cubical form of the Akkadian ship has mythical reasons. It agrees with the fundament of the ziggurat built above the fresh water-ocean called Abzu. The ship is hence a swimming temple.

The similarity of the Akkadian ark and the Indus ships is not confined to the cabin. In XI.146-153 the epic mentions three birds, which Utnapištim lets free in search of land, a dove, a swallow and a crow. This is also told in the biblical story, only the birds are a crow and two doves. We find three birds on the Indus ship-tablet 2828, two sit beside the cabin, one sits on the beach in front of the prow of the ship, its head pointing in the direction of the ship, as if it is on the verge to enter it. The birds are difficult to identify, but it is quite likely that they are fowls as they are still found on ships of this type. In the biblical and the Akkadian flood-story the birds are used for finding land. The birds on tablet 2828 are too plump to fulfil this purpose. No birds are mentioned in the Indian flood-stories. Instead a fish draws the ship of Manu, the Indian hero of the flood, through the waters and at last to a peak of the Himalayas. Before the flood the fish came in his young tiny form to Manu and said to him according to Śatapatha Brāhmaṇa I.8.1:

Foster me! Then I will save you from a great flood, in which all these beings will be drowned. Manu asked: Why should I foster you? The fish answered: As long as we are small, there are many dangers for us: fish swallows fish. Foster me at first in a jar. When I have become too big for it, dig a trench and foster me there, when I have become too big for it too, bring me to the ocean. Then I am rescued.

That the big animals swallow the tiny is illustrated on the second side of tablet 2828 by the gharial with a fish in its jaw. The Śatapatha Brāhmaṇa contains the first Indian version of the Great Flood, but an inundation is mentioned already in ṚV I.32.8:

Like a cut off reed Vṛtra lay there,
rising to his heart the waters flowed over him;
now Vṛtra lies at the feet of those waters
he has enclosed with his power formerly.

The translation of line b follows the padapātha, the word-reading of the Veda. If the waters are compared to women, as in verse 11 of the hymn, it is quite possible that they rise to the heart of the demon identifiable with his virile member. In this way the women become his masters. ṚV I.32 is addressed to Indra, the king of the gods. It describes his fight and victory over Vṛtra, the king of the demons. Like the Akkadian god Anu, Vṛtra is the lord of the waters, Indra like Marduk becomes their lord only afterwards.

According to the Gilgameš epic the god of wisdom, Ea, rescues Utnapištim and his wife. In the later Indian versions the saviour god is Viṣṇu. The fish is regarded as his first incarnation. The growing of the fish can be compared to the swelling of the waters of the flood. The destructive principle is also life-giving. In the Gilgameš epic this double principle is personified in the goddess Ištar, it is also contained in the crocodile and the fish of the Indus tablet.

For the survival of humanity a god, Ea or Viṣṇu, teaches a man to build a ship. Since the best and biggest ships of that time came from the river Indus, we can expect that the motif of a ship plays a prominent role on the Indus seals, but only two seals with the image of a bigger ship have come to light so far. Two others depict smaller boats, of which one looks like a galley. The other is a sailing-boat roughly drawn on a sherd. A reason for this scarcity could be that no profane motifs were pictured on the seals. This explains also, that there are no cars.

There are several verses in the Veda, in which the ship is mentioned as a means for rescue and welfare. Its negative aspect is not referred to, as the Vedic poets apparently had unlimited confidence in technical inventions. This confidence is still found in modern India. We have already mentioned that the motif of the crocodile eating a fish on tablet 2828 is occurring in the plot of the Indian flood-story. Therefore its contents could be contained in the inscription 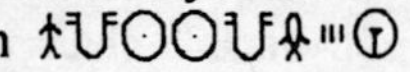 of this tablet. Indeed we find the fish as the third sign and the pot as the fourth and the last but one. The first sign, a hand in a circle, can then be interpreted as the hand of Manu, and the three short strokes as the teeth of the fish or its ability to speak. The first half of the inscription can then be translated logographically as: By the hands of Manu the speaking fish was put in a pot.

Now we come across the two wheel-signs that may be interpreted as a car. The car is connected with the root vah, to draw. Vahana means ship and vessel. Augha, as the flood is called in the Brāhmaṇa, is derived from the same root. It is related to the German word Auge (eye). Hence we can translate the second half of the inscription as: The pot is the vehicle in the flood for the man (Manu). If the two halves are combined we get:

The speaking fish placed by Manu in a pot became the vehicle for drawing him through the flood.

It is also possible to give a rendering of this inscription in relation to the Gilgameš epic: The first sign can be interpreted as carrying something, the three short strokes of the second sign as the seed, the fish as a prototype for being, the two cup-signs as a ship. This would be another instance for the compatibility of the cup-sign with the Sumerian ship-sign. The two circles can be interpreted in the same way as in the Indian version. This is equal to:

Who carried the seed of all beings on the ship, he was rescued by this ship.

This can be related without problem to Utnapištim, who is told by Ea in Gilgameš epic XI.27 to carry the seed of all living beings on the ship. Seeds may have been in the vessels of the Akkadian sun-boat, too.[32]

There is also a climatic reason for the origin of the flood-story in India. Only in the Indus Valley occur such ample rains as they are mentioned in the beginning of the story of the Great Flood in the Akkadian and the biblical story. On the other hand, they are not mentioned in the Brāhmaṇa, probably because they are self-evident in the Indus Valley. It is stated by S.R. Rao that there was a great flood about 1900 ante.[33] The Akkadian story refers to a flood that took place much earlier than this, no doubt, but this is merely a fabulous time. After the recoil of the flood the gods make Utnapištim settle at the "mouth of the streams". By his settlement at this place Utnapištim becomes similar to an Indian seer. His name has become true: He has found (uta) [eternal] life (napištim).

It is not to be expected that a Vedic reading of the inscription of tablet 2828 refers to a flood, since the waters are mentioned in the Veda only as beneficial for the Āryans. An indicator for a Vedic reading are the two wheel-signs and the number-sign for three. Both direct us to the Ṛbhu-hymn IV.33. In verse 8 of this hymn we read:

ratham ye cakruḥ suvṛtaṃ nareṣṭhāṃ
ye dhenuṃ viśvajuvaṃ viśvarūpām
ta ā takṣantv_ṛbhavo rayiṃ naḥ
svavasaḥ svapasaḥ suhastāḥ
The Ṛbhus constructed the smooth-running car, fit for men,
they created the all-invigorating cow Viśvarūpā,
the Ṛbhus shall render us riche,
who are always helpful and have skilful hands for to work.

---

[32] Frankfort infers this from the plough on the boat. Cf. op. cit. p. 108.

[33] Cf. Dawn and Devolution, p. 326. G.F. Dales, the excavator of the tablet, dates it to about 1900. Cf. New Inscriptions from Mohenjodaro, Kramer Anniversary Volume, Neukirchen-Vlyn 1976, p. 111

The hand-sign in a circle can be read as R̥bhu, because it can be divided in a hand and a circle. The hand is equal to the root grah, so seize, the circle to bhu, become, with its derivation bhū, the earth. The three strokes must be read together with this sign. The fish-sign stands for smooth-running, the cup-sign renders fit for men. The two wheel-signs represent the car. The second cup-sign can be read as the cow Viśvarūpā and as riches. The man-sign and the cup-sign are equal to the second half of the verse.

The motif of the crocodile with a fish in its mouth on the third side can be explained in relation to this hymn as a symbol of initiation (cf. chapter XI). The R̥bhus were initiated in the house of Agohya according to R̥V IV.33.6. The name whose literal meaning is not to be hidden is explained as an epithet of the sun, but it could also be related to the Dawn, the mother of the sun, whose 'cruel' aspect is represented by the crocodile. By their deeds the R̥bhus overcome the cruel aspect of the Dawn and the law that the big eat the small to a certain extent. Therefore they are regarded as benefactors of humanity.

Birds are not mentioned in the hymn, but the R̥bhus are described as cultivators of the land who made blooming fields out of deserts in IV.33.7. Through this verse the cross-lines on the reverse of the boat-seal 2014 (M-1349) can be explained as the fields the R̥bhus have cultivated.

That the car they constructed was a ship is confirmed by the two signs 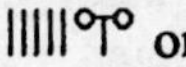 on the sherd 2714. The most appropriate verse relating to them is found in R̥V II.40.3d: *The car (of Soma and Pūṣan) has five reins*. Pūṣan's car is compared with golden ships in R̥V VI.58.3. Since Pūṣan is a name of the sun, the five strokes can be referred to it. According to the commentator Sāyaṇa the number five stands for the seasons. They depend on the apparent movement of the sun around the earth. Like Pūṣan's car the car of the Aśvins went over the sea (cf. chapter III.7).

The rescuing aspect of the ship-motif is also valid for the two signs of seal 3223 (H-99) 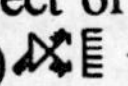 that can be read as R̥V X.101.2b: *Build a ship with oars that takes us across!* The woman-sign stands for taking across here, the triangle-sign with additional strokes renders a ship with oars, the extension at the back of the sign, that can be read as a hand, stands for to build.

The small museum of Mohenjo Daro possesses another seal with a house-boat made of reed apparently, which has not been published so far in any manual, but I happened to see a picture of it in a television spot about Mohenjo Daro.[34] To record it I give it the number 2829*. It has an inscription of five signs . Obviously, none of the signs can be read as ship, but the first two signs have certainly to do with woman, the ship is compared with in many traditions. Since the first sign can be read as a mouth or as the female organ, the Vedic equivalence can be found in X.125, the hymn to the goddess of language, Vāc. In X.125.7bc she says:

mama yonir apsu antaḥ samudre
tato vi tiṣṭhe bhuvanā anu viśve
My womb is in the water, inside the ocean,
from there I spread over all the worlds.

For mama, my, we get the woman-sign, the womb is equal to the rhombus-sign. In the water inside the ocean is rendered by the circle-sign with additional strokes. All the worlds are equal to the simple cup-sign with three additional strokes. The two long strokes render vi tiṣṭhe, I spread, whose root is sthā, to stand.

That there is an erotic aspect in the ship on the account of its female qualities is not surprising. It is rather unexpected, however, to find it in the biblical story of the Great Flood. In the introductory chapter the sons of the god El (beni elohim) are said to have married the beautiful daughters of men. It is not said there, from where the sons of El came, but we can infer that they came by ship from the same region, where the greatest floods take place, the Indus Valley.

This sort of marriage is against the will of the god El, and he knows no other means against it, but to send a huge flood. Hereafter it is no longer possible for the daughters of Israel to indulge in such connections, obviously similar to the sacred prostitution. In the flood story of the Gilgameš epic the erotic aspect is referred to by the reed-house that is also a place for the sacred marriage. The relation of Gilgameš with Siduri can also be classified under this headline.

---

[34] Cf. R. Schirra, Im Tal des Indus, Baden-Baden 1994.

At the end of the epic Gilgameš returns with Uršanabi in his ship to his city Uruk. On the way a snake takes away the plant of life called šammu, the Akkadian equivalent of the Soma, he has brought up from a deep well on Utnapištim's advice. The well is a synonym for the mortar, in which the Soma is pressed. Both can be rendered by the sign . To have found this plant was the greatest achievement of his voyage to his ancestor. But the friendship with Uršanabi who stays with him in Uruk makes up for the loss of the plant. In this friendship Akkadian power and Indus Valley spirituality meet. To bring about it was perhaps the main aim of this great piece of literature.

3. Gilgameš and Ištar

(Epic of Gilgameš tablet VI)

The investigation of relations between the epic of Gilgameš and the records of the Indus seals and tablets cannot be closed without dealing with the abusing speech of Gilgameš against the goddess Ištar in the first half of the sixth tablet. After Gilgameš and Enkidu have killed the ogre Ḫuwawa in the forest, Gilgameš washes himself, puts on new clothes and sits down on the throne with the tiara on his head. Now Ištar invites him to celebrate the sacred marriage with her (VI.i.7-9):

Come, Gilgameš, be my lover!
Give me, give me all you have!
You shall be my husband and I your wife.

But Gilgameš does not response to her desire, because he fears to be treated with the same bad behaviour she has shown to her former lovers. He may be intoxicated with his victory, too, or he may feel despise for a woman who expresses her desire for him in such plain words, as the goddess does. The main reason of his refusal is, however, that he has looked behind the mirror, as it were. He does not believe that to love the goddess (or her priestess, of course) will yield any happiness to him. The illusionary character of worldly happiness is an Indian teaching from times immemorial. On the other hand, the abuse of a god is a general topic in Mesopotamian literature, that even found its way into the Old Testament in the book of Job.

Whereas the sovereignty of the Jewish creator-god is re-established at the end of the dialogue with Job like that of Marduk at the end of the New Year ceremony, in the abuse of the goddess Ištar matriarchy as a whole is challenged and eventually abolished.

A suitable form for the abuse of the gods is the ironic dissimulation that can easily be derived from the symbolic way of archaic expression. For establishing a link between the speech of Gilgameš and an Indus inscription it would be sufficient, if some signs are ironically misused. Thus the circle on the leg of the man-sign of the inscription 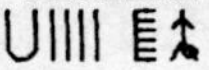 of tablet 4120 may be read as a snare, in which the man is bound by a woman represented by the second sign. But the woman may also save him from a snare by preparing Soma for him, as is indicated by the next two signs. The woman that catches a man in a snare is called a witch in ṚV X.85.28 that can be correlated to this inscription.

The ambiguity of the signs may be the reason, why the introductory verses and the similes of line 24-41 of the epic are all found in the sealing 7064 (K-89). Several signs are difficult to read here, however. I have reconstructed them with the help of the related Vedic verse that shall be discussed later on. The Vedic reading of the four inscriptions starts at the left and goes on boustrophedonly, the Akkadian has no certain rule:

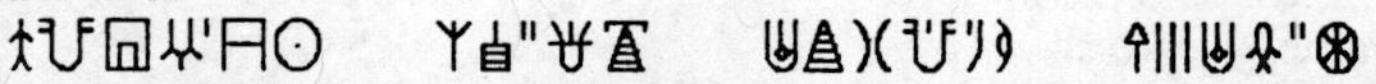

Gilgameš starts his speech with a short description of the sacred prostitution. Then follow nine ironic similes:

What am I to give you, when I take you in marriage?
Shall I give you oil for your body and garments?
Shall I give you bread and a soup for your hunger?
[I have got] food fit for divinity,
[I have got things] worthy of a king.

This agrees roughly with the logographic reading of the first line of the Kalibangan sealing. The first two signs can be read as worthy of a king, the fish-sign as food, the pot-sign as the oil made in it, the long strokes as garments, the lance-sign as fit for divinity.

The epic goes on (line 30-41):

[...] Sit down in a corner!
[...] Clad yourself in a cloak!
[...] Let take you!
[You are] the winter-ice, [that makes one slip],.
a back door, that does not keep out the wind and bad smells,
a palace that crushes the heroes to pieces,
a pit made invisible by a covering [of grass],
pitch that makes its bearer [dirty],
a waterskin that makes its bearer [wet],
limestone by which the walls [are destroyed],
a jasper seal betraying [its bearer] in a foreign country,
a shoe that [pinches the foot] of its owner.

The first three lines refer to the Akkadian custom of defloration, for which the young women of the upper classes sat down at the street leading to the temple clad only in a cloak to wait for some foreigner to „let take her". The story of Judah and Thamar in the Old Testament is based on this custom.[35]

The following lines correspond to line 3 and 4 of the sealing from Kalibangan. The first sign of line 4 can be read as winter-ice on account of the homophone surinû, emblem of the sun, for the second sign we get back-door, for the third sign bad, for the fourth smell, if it is interpreted as a nose, for the fifth sign we get palace, the last two signs can be read as divine men, heroes. From line 3 we get the pit covered with grass, limestone that crushes the walls to dust, the jasper seal and its bearer. It must be pointed out that these interpretations have merely the purpose to explain similes used in the Gilgameš epic with the help of Indus signs. These investigations have a purpose only, if they lead to a Vedic hymn that deals with the sacred marriage in a critical view. The Veda has no critical outlook at all, but the marriage-hymn contains several verses that can be called misogyn. One of them, X.85.34, we have come across in the foregoing paragraph. The longest description of a dangerous woman is contained in the verses 28-30, of which we just quoted verse 28. The first half of X.85.44 goes in the same direction. It is contained in the fourth line of this sealing. The two padas of the verse read:

---

[35] Cf. E. Richter-Ushanas, Die sakrale Liebe, Bremen 1987, p. 34

Be without evil eye, do not kill the husband!

The first sign of 7064,4 is equal to eye, the second one can be read as evil. For the Vedic seer evil was something that was blocking his way, a closed entrance for instance, and this is illustrated by the sign. It is a variant of the second sign of tablet 3304 (cf. chapter III, 7). In relation to the eye it represents stiffness. The evil eye is equal to the obstinate look of the woman. The single stroke renders without here. For to kill we get a womb-sign with additional strokes at the bottom. They refer to the dangerous fluids of the virgin referred to in ṚV X.85.30. The last three signs are equal to divine owner of the house. The husband had to be treated like a god by the wife.

The other lines of the sealing can be affiliated to verse 37, 39 and 40 of the marriage-hymn that have beneficial character. X.85.37 reads:

Bring her hither, Pūṣan, the most beautiful,
into whom we men sow the seed,
who opens us her thighs with love,
into whom we insert our members with love.

Obviously, the verse refers to a polygynic society, where one woman has several husbands. This verse agrees with 7064,1. The first sign, whose meaning is king or queen in general, can be read as the most beautiful, the woman is like a queen in a matriarchic society. The two strokes refer to men and women, both represented by the mortar-sign that is a simile of cohabitation. The fish-sign renders the god Pūṣan. The three strokes and the lance-sign correspond to the last line of the verse. X.85.39 and 40 have been interchanged in the Veda. This means that verse 40 corresponds to 7064,2. The Vedic verse reads:

Soma got her as the first,
the Gandharva got her as the next,
the third husband was Agni,
the fourth one is the human.

The first sign renders Soma, the second means first, it is omitted in the concordances. The third refers to the woman. The following sign is hardly readable. With regard to the Vedic verse I have restored it as two curves that represent the rainbow being also called Gandharva in the Veda (cf. X.123). The triangle-sign stands for Agni. The last sign that is also hardly readable, may be a mortar-sign again. It renders the human husband here. X.85.39 reads:

Agni gave the woman back
with long life and with beauty;
a long life may also obtained by the husband,
hundred autumns he may live!

The triangle-sign under a bar refers to the domestic Agni. The second sign that we read in 9015 as thorny flower is here the beautiful flower or a beautiful vessel. The two strokes refer to husband and wife here. The field-sign that can be read as an inscribed amulet, is equal to immortality. Obviously, the writers of the seal attributed immortality to the script, which has proved to be true in the course of the millennia. The tree-sign refers to the husband. Like a tree he shall live hundred years.

For the stories of Dumuzi and Išullânu told by Gilgameš in 1.42-57 of this tablet we find parallels on several other Indus seals:

Which lover did you love for ever?
Where is the bird having mounted up to you?
Well, I will name your lovers.
Dumuzi, your youthful lover,
him you have ordained wailing every year.
When you loved the dappled shepherd-bird,
you broke his wings.
Now he sits in the forest crying 'kappi' (my wing).
You loved a lion, perfect in strength,
and dug out seven and seven pits for him.
You loved a horse, famous in battle,
and ordained the spur, the belt and the whip for him.
You decreed for him to run seven double hours
and to drink muddy water,
and for his mother Silili you ordained to weep.

Dumuzi is the central male figure of the Sumero-Akkadian rite of the sacred marriage. His special feature is his youth. In the Veda the sun-god is the son and also the lover of the Dawn. His youth is often mentioned in his form of Agni, the sacrificial fire, but the tertium comparationis is always his strength, even when he is called many-coloured, citra-bhānu. The prototype of a wailing lover in the Veda is Purūravas, with whom we have dealt in the previous chapter. Purūravas inaugurates the Soma sacrifice for the Āryans, but in pursuing Urvaśī he does not set an example that is followed by other kings as Dumuzi does, with whom the Mesopotamian kings identify themselves in the sacred marriage. It seems, that the Sumerian and Akkadian kings wanted to appear unmanly and weak, because they believed this to be a feature of a lover of the goddess Ištar.

It is likely that the sacred marriage and myths connected with it like Ištar's Descent to the Netherworld were also depicted on Akkadian cylinder seals, though it is still difficult to explain their motifs, the more so as the inscriptions, when read phonetically, contain little more than the names of the scribes or owners of the seals. Sometimes the mythological meaning of a motif can be ascertained, however, when the signs are read as logograms.

For example, there seems to be a close connection between line 46-52 and seal 377, which according to Boehmer belongs to the group 'martial Ištar'.[36] In the centre of the seal the sun-god emerges from the mount Mašu with his key and his club. At his right side the god Ea ascends the mythical mount surrounded by six fishes emanating from his shoulders that can be explained as the planets. At his left the goddess Ištar stands near a tree followed by a man with bow and arrow and a lion. The man could be Gilgameš. In his hand the god Ea bears the bird Imdugud that is on the verge to attack a bull lying prostrated under the foot of the god.[37] At the right end of the seal a god with two faces is standing who is an attendant of Ea.[38] The four signs of the seal have been translated as ad-da, dub-sar: Adda, writer.[39] The readings are based on the pictograms liṅga or father for ad, arm for da, tablet for

---

[36] Op. cit. plate XXXII. For a better photograph cf. H. Frankfort, pl. XIXa.

[37] This part of the motif recalls a similar scene on seal 9910*.

[38] For the interpretation of the seal cf. H. Frankfort, op. cit. p. 105.

[39] Cf. D.O. Edzard, op. cit.

dub and watered tree-garden for sar.[40] This is logographically equal to: The arm of the father waters the garden of the earth.
With regard to the sacred marriage the father can be said to be identical to the male partner of the ceremony, the priest or the king. As we know from the myth of Gilgameš, Enkidu and the Netherworld, the bird Imdugud dwells on a tree in the garden of Inanna. When she wants to make a chair and a bed of its timber, the bird prevents her from hewing the tree down. Gilgameš comes to her help and drives the bird away. As a reward Ištar gives him a drum and a drum-stick made of the wood of the tree, as the epic describes in the 12th tablet. But he loses them to the Netherworld like the plant of life. Thereupon Enkidu descends into it to bring them back.
The descent of the king to the Netherworld was part of the Akkadian New Year festival and Dumuzi is sent down to it by Inanna, because he did not mourn for her whilst she was staying at this place. In the Sumerian version Dumuzi has to stay there only half the year in turn with his sister Geštinanna who is ready to relieve his lot.[41] Probably Dumuzi can be identified with the calf in the centre of the seal under the feet of Ea, because one of his names is amar.utu, calf of the sun.[42]
Though the Akkadian kings executed this ceremony in the conscience that sovereignty has to be based on sacrifice for its justification, Gilgameš lays the responsibility for Dumuzi's death on Ištar, as it is untimely in his eyes and hence not justified. He should have noticed, however, that the goddess descends into the Netherworld in order to fight with her sister Ereškigal, the goddess of Death, even if she does this only out of a whim. Gilgameš' behaviour is similar to that of Purūravas against Urvaśī. Both deny to recognize that the goddess has two aspects, the birth-giving and the death-giving, the lovely and the 'cruel', the sacrificing. The bird Imdugud has demoniac features in the Akkadian mythology. These traits do not occur on the Indus bird-seals, except perhaps on seal 9910* found in the Near East.

---

[40] Cf. A. Deimel, op. cit.

[41] Cf. W.R. Sladek, op. cit.

[42] For a somewhat different explanation cf. H. Frankfort, op. cit. p. 107.

The motif of the bird is equally rare in the Indus Valley as the motif of the ship. There have been found only three bird-seals so far. Their numbers are 0007 (M-451), 2780 (M-1390) and 3255 (H-166). In addition, there are birds on the boat-tablet 2828 (M-1148), on tablet 1574 (M-489) together with the motif of the sacred marriage, on tablet 2742 (M-1395) opposite a fish at the head of a crocodile, on tablet 2752/2753 (M-1428) over a crocodile. Here we shall only discuss seal 3255 and the tablets 2780 and 0007, as we have dealt already with the other seals and tablets in the previous chapters.

The bird on the signless seal 3255 that is similar to the bird on the Akkadian seal 377 and on the cylinder seal 9910* is probably an eagle. We have already found out in chapter III.2 that it is a symbol of the Gandharva or of the sun. The cross on the reverse of the seal can be interpreted as the car of the sun and as the dimensions the sun is crossing. The two snake-like lines on both sides of the head of the bird could be hills, but in the context of the Veda they can be explained as heaven and earth.

The bird on the round tablet 2780 and the oblong tablet 0007 is probably an eagle, too (Franke-Vogt, p. 73). The eagle is a symbol of strength and of oppression, in ṚV I.32.14 it is used as an image of fear, however. It could also be a mountain-cock that is known for its dancing and crying during the pairing-time. 'Kappi' in line 50 of the epic may refer to this behaviour of the bird. On the reverse of tablet 2780 we find the three signs 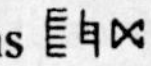 on the top of an elephant that was stamped on the tablet later. The first sign can be interpreted as grasping or stretching out. The central sign can be read as a hide. The last sign signifies the goddess in general and the earth in particular, whose attribute is the elephant, as said in ṚV V.87.3 in regard to the goddess Śrī. The bird would be equal to the sun. The inscription can be read according to ṚV V.85.1: *Varuṇa stretched out the earth like a hide under the sun.* The first sign would represent Varuṇa.

The goddess of earth is only passive in this hymn, but in X.125, where she is called Vāc, speech, it is she who creates heaven and earth. In this hymn, the two aspects of the goddess, the positive and the negative, that are also found with the Dawn, are mentioned, too.

Dumuzi stands between the friendly and the cruel aspect of the goddess Ištar. On the one hand, he enjoys his life, on the other he is sacrificed. As long as he sees the friendly aspect of the goddess, he plays on his flute and dances like a mountain-cock, but when he becomes aware of her devouring aspect, he does not want to submit to the role of being sacrificed and runs weepingly away. In his behaviour he can be compared to Purūravas, who is said to be "a companion of death" in R̥V X.95.18, but who eventually is not sent into the Netherworld like Dumuzi, but ascends to heaven.

Birds are mentioned in R̥V I.124.12 as flying up from their nest in the morning like the lords (nara) who distribute the food. According to the Akkadian mythology the sun distributes the food to the dead. In the Veda the sun assigns the work to all beings (cf. I.124.1). This implies the distribution of the food, as it is done in R̥V III.59.9 by the sun-god Mitra. In R̥V I.124.12 all gods in the form of birds are assigned this work.

It is true, that there is nothing demoniac in the birds of the Veda as is the case with the Akkadian Imdugud, but the Dawn does not only destroy the night, by her coming again every morning she reduces the life-span of the seer like that of an ordinary man (cf. I.124.2b). In the goddess Ištar the dark traits are more prominent, since she is a sovereign deity and not mainly a natural phenomenon like Uṣas. As a queen she can act according to her whims, as she even does in her descent to the Netherworld. Accordingly, Gilgameš says in verse 58 to 63:

You loved the keeper of the herd,
who ever has heaped up ash-cakes for you,
who daily has slaughtered goats for you.
You have beaten him and turned him into a wolf,
his own herd-boys drive him off now
and the dogs bite him in his thighs.

Line 63 is an exact rendering of the three signs of the tiger-seal 2527 (cf. the chapter VI), if we take the first sign as the pictogram of a thigh and the last as a row of teeth. In R̥V X.95 it is Urvaśī, who behaves according to her whims, as Purūravas accuses her to do. She does not turn him into a wolf, however, but uses a relative of this animal as a simile for the character of women in general. When Ištar turns her lover into a wolf, she might have done it, because he had behaved to her as a false lover in her opinion. In her eyes not women, but men are false. Perhaps she wanted to expose him to ridicule. Gilgameš knows of another case, where the goddess betrayed her lover (I.64-79):

You loved Išullânu, the gardener of your father,
who ever brought you baskets full of dates,
and daily wiped your table bright.
You raised your eyes at him, went [naked] to him:
My Išullânu, [you said], let us enjoy your vigour!
Stretch out your hand and touch my 'modesty'.
Išullânu said to her: What do you want from me?
Did my mother not bake, did I not eat,
that I should take my food in stench and foulness.
that halfa-grass should be my mattress in the winter?
After having heard what he said,
you beat him, you made him a poor one,
made him live amidst his work.
Neither come the liquids up nor go the jars down.
And if you would love me, you would treat me like them.

When we only take the main words, it seems as if they agree with the signs of tablet 0007, whose inscription is identical to that of tablet 2771 (M-1427). The bird on the reverse of tablet 0007 is similar to that on tablet 2780. The signs of tablet 0007 are: . With regard to the epic they can be read logographically as tree or gardener (1), akin of heaven (2), baskets, fields (3,4), date-twig (5), fish/to beam (6), eyes (7), man with staff, guardian (8); follow the line: touch the modesty (9/10). This could be translated with regard to the epic as:

The gardener, the kinsman of heaven, whose baskets are full of date(-twig)s, whose fields are bright, is the guardian raising his eyes, stretching out his hand/his organ to the modesty (of the goddess).

Here it is the gardener who desires the goddess as in the Sumerian version of Išullânu. The guardian-sign includes violence even. But we could also translate:

Who rises her eyes to the gardener, the kinsman of heaven with baskets full of dates and bright fields, who shows him her modesty, (is the goddess).

The second verb in line 67 is probably an irregular durative form of alaku, to go, with basic meaning. According to line 68/69 Ištar appears here as the unveiling goddess, as she is known from the Mesopotamian cylinder seals.[43]
The incest-problem is discussed in ṚV X.10, a dialogue-hymn between Yama and his sister Yamī. Yamī tries to make Yama her husband in order to secure the maintenance of the human race. Since Yama and Yamī are the first human beings according to later Indian mythology, she must have been successful, but in the Veda Yama refuses her desire vehemently. Yama is also the first mortal and hence the king of the dead. According to ṚV X.17.2 Yama and Yamī are the children of the sun-god Vivasvat. Like Išullânu Yama is a relative of the gods. The king of the dead can also be regarded as a gardener, for according to ṚV X.135.1 he sits *at the tree with beautiful leaves*. The *bright fields* of the epic are similar to the meadows of bright worlds in ṚV IX.113.9.
The words Yama says in X.10.12 are worthy of the god of Death, who is also the guardian of the Law. Išullânu's answer to Ištar is similar to Yama's. In his way he declares that a relation with the goddess would be incestuous for him. But Ištar cannot bear up with his words sounding as an insult in her ears. Whereas Yama is a eunuch by his own choice, Išullânu is made one by force. The poor one, dalalum, recalls the poor in the spirit of the Gospel of Matthew, though, of course, their austerity is a spiritual one. This interpretation is also confirmed by line 78, where two similes for impotence or castration are given. In later mythology Yama is cursed, too, in ṚV X.10.13 Yamī only joins him together with an entirely helpless woman who often becomes the 'fate' of an ascetic:

> *Woe, a coward is Yama, this is sure now,*
> *and never I could win his heart or his mind;*
> *certainly another woman will embrace you*
> *like the belt embracing a horse or a creeper a tree.*

These words are contained in the inscription  of the unicorn-seal 3037 (H-461). The first sign renders the embracing belt, the second

[43] Cf. the motif on a painted urn of cemetery H of Harappa. Here the goddess stands between two goats holding them by a rope. The Śatapatha Brāhmaṇa mentions the two lambs standing near the bed of Urvaśī.

the creeper, the horse is found in the motif, the two strokes indicate the two possibilities, the leaf-sign stands for the tree, for Yama we obtain the man-sign and for woman the cup-sign.

A tree-sign is also found at the beginning of the inscription of tablet 0007. But the second sign, though it has some similarities with the second sign of seal 3037, does not mean creeper, but rainbow, called Vena (lovely or beloved) and Gandharva in the Veda. This directs us to ṚV IX.12.7, where the Soma is called lord of the trees, Vanaspati. A sign for lord  is written twice on the back of tablet 2771. The inscription can hence be read according to IX.28.8:

To the beloved place of the sky,
the Soma rises up, urged to speed,
he, the poet in the stream of the enthusiastic.

The first sign stands for the Soma as lord of the tree, beloved is rendered by the two curves. The two field-signs representing the pressing boards are equal to the places of the sky here, the fish-sign refers to the Soma as poet. The oblique stroke-sign and the short strokes are equal to rise up. Urged to speed is rendered by the guardian-sign. The last two signs are equal to the stream of the enthusiastic.

Whereas Išullânu becomes a slave, the Soma and those who drink it rise up to the sky, to immortality and freedom. The eagle on the reverse of tablet 0007 can be interpreted as a symbol of this freedom. The Soma is brought to the children of Manu by this bird, as it is told in ṚV IV.26,27. The eagle is used as a symbol for freedom in many countries of the western world. In later India we find a haṃsa-goose instead. It is an attribute of the mother-goddess and her companions, the Apsaras.

Gilgameš is deluding himself in his belief to have a better fate by rejecting the goddess. Because of his rejection Išullânu is cursed. Gilgameš cannot escape her revenge. He is punished with the premature death of Enkidu. At first it makes him lose his mind, but then it leads him to the Indus. This is a place where the mind can meditate on the cosmic man, the Puruṣa, who is described in ṚV X.90 as time and space and beyond it. It is by his sacrifice that the laws of the world are inaugurated. Having reached there, Gilgameš is beyond suffering and joy and the curse of the goddess.

VIII. THE COSMIC MAN IN PATAÑJALI'S YOGA SŪTRAS

Like other ancient philosophical and religious systems the Yoga Sūtras are based on a mythical view of the world. It differs from the modern view mainly through the conception of the macroanthropos or cosmic man called Puruṣa in R̥V X.90. The microcosm or the human being is a reduced copy of the macroanthropos, the spinal cord corresponds to the axis mundi.[1] The explanation of the word puruṣa in Br̥had Āraṇyaka Upaniṣad IV.2.1 as "having burnt (uṣ) before (pūrva) creation all what is evil" is a good example for the ancient Indian etymology that does not only depend on the root, but on the sound of the word and the idea the philosopher wants to communicate.

According to R̥V X.90.2 the Puruṣa is "everything that is, was and will be, and he is the lord of (the draught of) immortality." This implies that the Puruṣa was before, pūrva, anything else. The explanation of uṣ as "having burnt what is evil" indicates that evil is something that is burnt up. The fire, in which this is done, is the primordial heat or tapas, as we know from R̥V X.190.1:

r̥taṃ ca satyaṃ cā bīddhāt tapaso 'dhyajāyat
tato rātry ajāyata tataḥ samudro arṇavaḥ
Law and Truth have been born from the enflamed heat,
from that was born the night, from that the ocean.

The word evil or something similar does neither occur in that hymn nor in R̥V X.90, however.[2]

There are other explanations possible. Thus Grassmann derives it from the root pur, to pervade (the body as the soul). In Bhagavadgītā 5.13 the Puruṣa is compared to the embodied one (dehī) living in the town

---

[1] Cf. M. Eliade, Yoga, Frankfurt 1985, p. 245.

[2] The purifying effect of the fire is also attested to by the Rāmāyāṇa (cf. Sītā's ordeal), the Mahābhārata and the Indian law books. Cf. J.J. Meyer, op. cit. p. 372, 527.

with nine gates, i.e. the body. That means that the Puruṣa is the entity that illumines the body and notably the mind. The Vedic man did not use clay images, but because of the conception of the Puruṣa all gods are images, especially the god of fire, Agni.

Like the human body, the body of the cosmic man is sustained by breathing. The cosmic breath is called prāṇa, vital energy. Inhaling and exhaling correspond to the cosmic periods of evolution and involution. According to modern science we are now in a period of exhaling, because the visible universe is expanding. At some unknown future the phase of absorption will follow it, though this is not accepted by most of the scientists so far. Like man the cosmic man can suspend his breathing, but in extension of human possibilities for an endless time. The suspension of the cosmic breath corresponds to the cosmic void. In spite of its vastness the universe is only one quarter of the Puruṣa according to ṚV X.90.3, three quarters are the immortality in heaven. Like heaven and the Netherworld the visible universe is divided into seven spheres corresponding to the seven orbits of the planets and the seven cakras of the subtle body. Like the planets revolving around an imaginative axis mundi the cakras are arranged along the spinal cord. Cakra means wheel and could be derived from the form of the planets, but in spite of the universal conception the ancients had of the essential identity of macrocosm and microcosm, the planets are not mentioned at all in Indian treatises dealing with the cakras.[3] On the other hand we find illustrations of the human body with the respective position of the planets in alchemistic books, but here the cakras are missing.[4] A reason for this mutual negligence could be that the Western mind is more outwardly drawn, the Indian mind more inwardly.

---

[3] The cakras are dealt with in detail only in Tantric treatises like the Śiva- and Gheraṇḍa Saṃhitā. Both have been published with an English translation by Ch. Vasu, Delhi 1979 and 1975 respectively.

[4] Cf. O.M. Hinze, Tantra Vidya, Freiburg 1983, p. 53. The illustration there has been taken from J.G. Gichtel, Theosophia Practica, Paris 1897.

According to the Tantric Saṃhitās the vital energy sleeps at the foot of the spinal cord in the form of a snake coiled up around a liṅga. This energy has many names, but mostly it is called Kuṇḍalinī.[5]

After the snake has been awakened through yoga or Tantric exercises she enters the liṅga from the top and climbs up the inner channel of the spinal cord called Suṣumnā.[6] As long as the mind is drawn to the outward world, the entrance of the Suṣumnā is closed. Then the vital energy passes through two other channels called Iḍā and Piṅgalā that accompany the Suṣumnā in a double helix of five turns. They correspond to the moon and the sun, signifying not the planets here, but the male and the female energy, though both channels are female in gender. From the modern point of view they can be compared to the two main fibres of the nervous system. The six junctions between these channels and the Suṣumnā are also called padma (lotus) or grantha (knots).

The Haṭha Yoga Pradīpikā says in III.2 that all cakras and granthas are pierced, when the Kuṇḍalinī climbs upwards. That means that there is no difference between the two words. In II.67 the same text speaks of three knots located in the area of the chest, the throat and the eyebrows. They are named after the gods Brahmā, Viṣṇu and Rudra and dealt with in detail in the fourth chapter. Here again the granthas are identical to the cakras of the same region. That means that grantha has no negative connotation, as it has in western psychological language.

When the Kuṇḍalinī has merged into the highest cakra called thousand-petalled all the vital energy is absorbed in the Suṣumnā. This is called pratiprasava (reabsorption) by Patañjali in sūtra IV.34, the last one of his treatise. Then only very little of this energy passes through the other two channels. The yogi has transcended the opposites. His ego is almost extinguished. The outward universe dissolves into the cosmic void called Nirvāṇa by the Buddhists and in Bhagavadgītā 2.72 and 5.24-26 and the whole (pūrṇa) in Bṛhad Āraṇyaka Upaniṣad V.1.1:

---

[5] Cf. Śiva Saṃhitā V.81. According to Indian etymology the name can be derived from kuṇḍa, water-pot. Hence it can be written by the cup-sign.

[6] Rawson, op. cit. p. 27. The image recalls the ithyphallic yogi on seal 2420.

This is the whole, that is the whole,
from the whole evolves the whole;
when the whole is taken from the whole,
as the whole the whole remains.

The void and the whole are not contradictions, but aspects of the same eternal substance regarded as abstract impersonal ideas. The Puruṣa can also be seen in personal form, as described in the 11th chapter of the Gītā. A similar vision is obtained by the yogi, when his Kuṇḍalinī pierces the highest cakra according to the Tantric Saṃhitās, but for the Yoga Sūtra this vision is of a lower degree, as we shall see later.

A yogi sitting between two snakes is depicted on tablet 2774 (M-453). The snakes can be identified with Iḍā and Piṅgalā, the yogi with the Kuṇḍalinī and the Suṣumnā. The inscription  can be read as the verse of the Upaniṣad: The first, the fourth and the last sign can be ideograms for pūrṇa, whole. The two long strokes of the fifth sign can represent the act of taking, the two short strokes of the second sign render this or that. The fish-sign can be read as evolve, since its root añj, to bend, describes the form and the movement of the fish.

The cosmic void is called the bottomless space in verse 7 of the Vedic hymn I.24 directed to Varuṇa. The first two padas of this verse and the first two of the following verse coincide with the inscription of the bull-seal 0002 (M-1424) 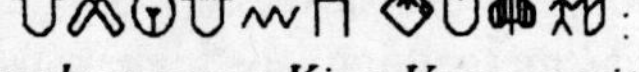:

In the bottomless space King Varuṇa with pure strength
holds the stem of the tree upside;
King Varuṇa has made the way broad for the sun,
so that she can walk on it.

The archer is an image of Varuṇa with pure strength. The stem and the tree are equal to the next two signs, the bottomless space is rendered by the variant of the rhombus-sign. For upside (on the top) we get the tower-sign, for the way the snake-like line, the cup-sign with three strokes stands for Varuṇa again, the hand in a circle is equal to the verb to make. For to go we get the step-sign, for the sun as an image of the Kuṇḍalinī the cup-sign at the end. The snake that is lying on the tower-sign is an image of the Kuṇḍalinī that has reached the top, the bull represents the cosmic energy.

The inverted cosmic tree is also symbolized in the first sign of the inscription of the unicorn-seal 2323 (M-151) 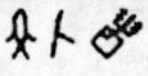. Here it is identified with the drawn up sexual energy of the seer.

The concrete image of the Puruṣa is older than the abstract ideas of the Upaniṣad. It took humanity some thousand years to elaborate abstract thinking. This is also illustrated by the development of writing from pictograms over ideograms and syllabic morphemes to letters. In the beginning of writing was the image, though it often has a geometric form. This form can be regarded as the seed of abstract thought.

The cosmic man is androgyn. Its female aspect, the mother-goddess, is referred to in ṚV X.72.4 as Uttānapad, she who spreads her legs apart (for giving birth). It is here, where we find a Vedic equivalence of the inscription of tablet 2774:

> *bhūr jajña uttānapado bhuvo āśā ajāyanta*
> *The earth was born by her who spreads apart her legs,*
> *from the earth the quarters of the sky were born.*

The earth, is equal to the first and the fifth sign. For Uttānapad, the mother-goddess, we get the bee-sign. The bee is known as an image of the goddess in the Veda and elsewhere. For āśā, the quarters of the sky, we get the intersected circles, the cup-sign renders the verbal forms. The short strokes indicate the twofold creation.

The androgyn nature of the Puruṣa is also pointed out in ṚV X.72.5 that corresponds to X.90.5, where Aditi, the female principle is born from Dakṣa, the male principle, and Dakṣa vice versa from Aditi. Patañjali, however, refers in sūtra II.23-25 only to the personal god in his male form (īśvara) as a means for attaining the highest stage of samādhi. The Kuṇḍalinī is not mentioned at all in the sūtras, perhaps because she is too mythical for a philosophic treatise. But moon and sun, that are equal to Iḍā and Piṅgalā in the Tantric Saṃhitās, and the pole-star, that is equal to the last stage of the Kuṇḍalinī, are referred to in the third chapter that deals with the acquisition of super-human powers. In sūtra III.26,27 Patañjali says, that by concentrating on the sun the yogi acquires knowledge of the universe, by concentrating on the moon knowledge of the arrangement of the stars, on the pole-star knowledge of their movements. The word for star is tārā here, which can also mean planet. Arrangement of the stars would then refer to the houses of the zodiac visited by the moon according to Indian astrology, surely not to the sun-systems and galaxies, as I.K. Taimni maintains,[7] since they have been discovered only in our era.

When speaking of the movement of the stars, Patañjali must have meant the planets, since the constellations or houses are formed by fixed stars. Sun, moon and the planets are mainly used as scientific entities by Patañjali and not as mythological symbols as in the Tantric Saṃhitās, but he also makes use of the astrological language. This is quite natural, as astronomy at that time was not yet separate from astrology.

The word cakra is used by Patañjali only once, but he refers to three more cakras by mentioning their respective place. The light of the head that appears according to the Tantric Saṃhitās, when the Kuṇḍalinī has merged into the highest cakra, is not identical to the highest samādhi for Patañjali, for by concentrating on this region only beings with extraordinary powers appear (III.32). In sūtra III.51 he warns against invitations of such higher beings, because they create pride and attachment. This refers especially to female beings. In the Śiva Saṃhitā, however, such acquaintances prove that the yogi has attained his aim, since these beings are aspects of the Kuṇḍalinī.

In sūtra III.29 Patañjali mentions the navel-cakra. By concentration thereon one acquires knowledge of the structure of the body. This is not meant in the sense of modern science, but in regard to the medical knowledge of that time as expounded in the Āyur-Veda.

In Gichtel's alchemist treatise just mentioned the planet Venus is affiliated to the third cakra. It occupies this place on account of the sequence of the planets starting with Saturn. Otherwise, Western astrology affiliates Venus to the fifth cakra and the moon to the third, but when regarded as the star of the mother-goddess, her affiliation to the third cakra is quite reasonable. As the moon is an aspect or symbol of the goddess, it can also be affiliated to the third cakra. In ṚV X.90.13 the moon is said to have been

---

[7] Cf. The Science of Yoga, Madras 1961. This is also clear from the commentaries. Cf. E.H. Woods, The Yoga-System of Patañjali, Delhi 1983.

born from the mind and the sun from the eyes of the cosmic man. The eyes and the mind belong to the region of the sixth cakra, the super-mind to the seventh. Here sun and moon are again personifications of the male and female energies. After all, Western astrology and Patañjali have the same fundament, the contradictions refer only to the details.

In the following two sūtras III.30-31 Patañjali mentions the pit of the throat together with the kūrma-nāḍī, the kūrma-channel. Kūrma means tortoise, which is identical to the form of the thyroid gland that is situated at the place of this cakra. Patañjali adds, that by concentrating on the pit of the throat hunger and thirst vanish and stability of the body is achieved. That these things are very important in meditation goes without saying. Especially the trembling of the body is an obstacle for concentration (cf. sūtra I.31). In Gītā 2.58 the tortoise is mentioned as a simile for the steadfast man. When the gods and the demons churn the milk-ocean the tortoise serves as supporter of the churning stick. Through this function it is connected with the first cakra. Another supporter, namely of the four quarters, is the elephant, which is associated with the fifth cakra in Tantric treatises.

According to the Purāṇas the seer Kaśyapa, whose name means tortoise, is the father of the gods, demons and men. The goddess of wisdom and language, Vāc, can be regarded as his consort. Language is formed at the fifth cakra. In Western astrology it is affiliated to the fifth cakra, too, but on account of Gichtel's sequence of the planets Mars occupies this place. Mars is an aspect of Indra. As the king of the gods Indra rides on an elephant. Hence his association with the fifth cakra is not unjustified.

In the Tantric Saṃhitās this cakra is called viśuddha, which means pure. It can be explained by its association with the element ether and by the mental purity achieved on this plane on account of the absence of hunger and thirst and the desire for procreation. In sūtra II.38 Patañjali declares that by sexual abstinence male energy (vīrya) is obtained. This is another word for steadfastness. The process that leads to sexual abstinence is called ūrdhvaretas or bindu siddhi in the Tantric Saṃhitas. The inverted tree of R̥V I.24.7 is an illustration of it. The realization of the cosmic man is based on continence. The Bengali saint Sri Ramakrishna says in this relation:[8]

---

[8] Cf. The Gospel of Sri Ramakrishna, Madras 1969, p. 362.

A man controlling the seminal fluid for twelve years develops a special power. He grows a new inner nerve called the nerve of memory. Through that nerve he remembers all, he understands all. Loss of semen impairs the strength. But it does not injure one, if one loses it in dream. That semen one gets from food. What remains after nocturnal discharge is enough. But one must not know a woman. The semen that remains after nocturnal discharge is very 'refined'.

He remembers all, he understands all agrees with Vyāsa's and Vācaspati-Miśra's commentaries on this sūtra.[9] The exemption of the nocturnal discharge refers to householders only, however. The monk should not even think or dream of a woman. For the householder, however, the 'refined' semen seems to be more valuable than not to think of a woman at all. At any rate, through Ramakrishna's teaching he is in a much better situation than the biblical Onan, who was killed by the god of the Jews, only because he had spoilt his seed on the earth instead of fecundating a woman. The retention of the semen through ūrdhvaretas and the 'refined' semen of nocturnal discharge are certainly not identical, though both are based on the idea that *loss of semen impairs the strength*. The Tantric practice of ūrdhvaretas can even be applied during cohabitation.

The Mahābhārata recommends the marriage-hymn to somebody who has lost his seed in sleep.[10] For the epic marriage was the solution of the problem. But Ramakrishna speaks of man, who is married already. In the Veda marriage is described in a cosmic sense, that means that it is identical with the sacred marriage known from Mesopoatamia. Its cosmic relation is indicated by the occurrence of satya and ṛta, truth and law, in the first verse of the marriage-hymn, ṚV X.85:

> *By the truth the earth is set up,*
> *by the sun the sky is set up,*
> *by the law the gods exist*
> *and the Soma is placed at the sky.*

The Yoga sūtras do not give any advice for achieving ūrdhvaretas. Even prāṇāyāma and āsanas are dealt with only casually. In the Tantric Saṃhitās they are all described in detail, together with the mudrās that

---

[9] Cf. J.H. Woods, op. cit., p. 187.

[10] Mahābhārata XII.34.26. Cf. J.J. Meyer, op.cit., p. 260.

may be even more helpful.[11] Abstinence is not only a question of philosophy for the authors of the Saṃhitās.

In Bṛhad Āraṇyaka Upaniṣad VI.4.3 the brahmin is told to look upon the lap of his wife as the sacrificial mound before intercourse. Its Sanskrit equivalence is adhopahāsa, literally 'smile downwards' (to the region below the navel). This is a much better word than 'to know a woman', that is used by Ramakrishna under Christian influence, since it is free from patriarchic connotations. To look on a woman in a symbolic way is also helpful for keeping continence, whereas it is evidently a cause of endless suffering to regard her as an obstacle to spiritual growth.

The Tantric exercises for retaining the semen are distasteful in the eyes of the educated Western man (and woman) and also physically impracticable. There is no doubt, however, that they are old. They might even have their roots in the Indus tradition. Like the aśvamedha ritual they can be related to the sacred marriage. D.D. Kosambi believes that the sacred marriage was carried out in the Great Bath of Mohenjo Daro by priestesses identical to the Vedic Apsaras.[12] Some of these rites reappear in the erotic sculptures on the walls of medieval Indian temples.

Though it is to be appreciated that sexual life is included in art and religion, there is no doubt that the retention of the seed under all circumstances is as difficult as the suppression of the movements of the mind, as is obvious from the stories of sages like Agastya, Viśvāmitra and Vibhaṇḍaka, Ṛṣyaśṛṅga's father. If it does not work, women cannot be held responsible for it, as Purūravas tried to do. If there is something like responsibility in love affairs, which Purūravas seems to believe, it should not be used as a means for suppressing or disciplining the other sex, but for a mutual agreement not to harm each other, especially after separation. Certainly, the fear of losing one's energy through the loss of the semen is one of the reasons for the idolization and on the other hand the degrading of the female sex.

---

[11] There are Chinese exercises for the same purpose. Cf. M. Chia, Taoist Secrets of Love, Cultivating Male Sex Energy, New York 1984 (with a similar book for women). It is reported that they guarantee a long life, when applied correctly.

[12] Op. cit. (1992), p. 71.

According to modern medicine the retention of the seed is poisonous for the body, but probably not more poisonous than the food taken regardless of its results by ordinary people. On the other hand, it could be a self-delusion to expect the realization of the truth from a sexual ritual. Certainly, the retention of the seed saves both sexes from many bad consequences, but for the realization of the truth love is at least of equal importance.

Like economics, religions promise more than they can keep. The Tantric ritual is no exception from this rule. Modern man is as easy or even easier to be cheated than the man of former ages, because he regards sensual pleasures as being much more satisfying than the realization of the truth. Especially a virgin seems to be irresistible, the more so, if she seduces an old man, as it is described in ṚV I.126. In the Yoga Saṃhitās the virgin is said to be the preferred form of the Kuṇḍalinī. If somebody would tell a man that he is going to be cheated he will not believe it. One may ask, why it is so difficult to achieve continence. According to the Indian tradition, Indra is afraid that the ascetic could become more powerful than he himself, and therefore he sends his Apsaras to seduce him.

The truly ascetic man is interested in the realization of the truth, however, and not in becoming a second Indra. Heaven is of no importance for him. Evidently, the natural laws of procreation have been arranged in such a way that man is kept on a lower level than the gods, for otherwise the human race could not survive on the present stage of the spiritual evolution. There must be some exceptions, however. For them the philosophy and practise of yoga and Tantra have been invented. But there is no security that they fulfil what they promise. Otherwise, the achievement of continence would become too easy.

The three classes of animals that are depicted on the three-sided tablet 2762 (M-468) can be compared to the three classes of adepts distinguished in the Tantric scriptures: The paśu or the cattle-type as the lowest, the vīra or the hero-type in the middle and the divya or the divine man as the highest. They can also be related to the three upper castes. The bull is the representative of the common people and the servants, the tiger of the nobility, the unicorn of the brahmins. Only the brahmin or the divine man knows the true Soma as is said in ṚV X.85.4.

The inscription written on each of the sides reads 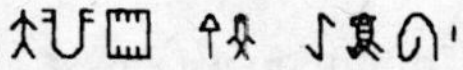.
It corresponds to the last verse of the Vena-hymn, R̥V X.123.8:

> *drapsaḥ samudram abhi yajjagārti*
> *paśyan gr̥dhasya cakṣasā vidharman*
> *bhānuḥ śukreṇa śociṣā cakānas*
> *tr̥tīye cakre rajasi priyāṇi*
> *When the drop (of the Soma) comes to the ocean*
> *looking around in the vastness with the eye of a vulture,*
> *then the sun rejoices in the clear light*
> *and reveals the lovely names in the third sky.*

The four signs of the first line can be read as the drop of the Soma coming to the ocean or as the eye of the vulture looking around in the vastness. The first sign is equal to the drop and the eye, the second to vastness and ocean, the third to the Soma or the vulture, the fourth to coming or going around. The second and the third sign of this line can also be read as the sun. Clear light is equal to the two signs of the second line. The lovely names are equal to the cup-sign, the field-sign to the sky, the man-sign to us, the poet or brahmin, who is able to understand the lovely names and to write them down as the signs of the Indus script.
Patañjali mentions one more cakra, the fourth, in sūtra III.34. By concentrating on this cakra one achieves knowledge of the mind. The place of the mind is the head, but in order to get knowledge of the mind the thoughts must be directed to the heart. The heart resides likewise in the midst of the body as the sun is in the midst of the planetary system. The planet that corresponds to the heart is therefore, in Western and Eastern astrology alike, the sun. The fourth cakra is called anāhata in Śiva Saṃhitā V.83. This means 'not (being) beaten'. It refers to the beat of the heart that is itself not beaten, but works out of its own free will. Herein it is equal to the cosmic man described as the One in R̥V X.129.2:

> *There was neither death nor life in those days,*
> *nor the distinguishing signs of day and night;*
> *breathless breathed of its own free will the One,*
> *apart from it there was nothing else.*

The One can be identified with the sun, called Savitr̥, the instigator, since he is the eye and the heart of the creator.

To sum up we can say that Patañjali is very reluctant in regard to the cakras and the planets and that he is totally silent about the Kuṇḍalinī, whereas in the scientifically educated West it is the Kuṇḍalinī and her way through the cakras that find the greatest interest nowadays. One of the reasons for that might be, that the Western man, feeling dried up by the emptiness of solely abstract thought taught in schools and universities, is looking for something more concrete that might give him a hold in an inhospitable world.
Patañjali being himself a scientific man, though not in the sense of a modern scientist, can meet with this demand only partially. Seeing the hubbub now made in the West with the cakras and Tantra, Patañjali's reserve in regard to these things can only be applauded. Obviously, he is not interested in the symbolism of the Kuṇḍalinī and the cakras nor in the spheres of the universe, but in expounding how the highest samādhi can be achieved. At his time science had a different outlook than today. Many of the problems we are facing today have come about by modern science. It may not seem reasonable to look for a solution of these problems in the teachings of the ancients, but Patañjali is certainly an exception, as his teachings have even been useful in promoting computer technics. He also cautioned against the dangers of super-human powers that are now acquired in another way by modern science, often without any scruples in regard to the results.
Perhaps because out of fear of these powers Patañjali enjoins merely a male god to meditate on, but consequently he did not take notice of the origin of the yoga in the Indus Valley, where the goddess, the mistress of all these powers, was worshipped, too. His negligence led to the suppression of the female part of the mind. In this way, the Puruṣa, who is male and female, eludes the full understanding of the yogi who follows Patañjali's teaching. His yoga must hence be re-examined under the premise of androgyny. Then it could be helpful indeed in bringing about a new harmony between man and woman, in their personal as well as in their social relations. Harmony means literally 'put together'. We arrive at this aim by putting the sherds together that are called arma in the Veda, the sherds that have remained from great civilizations like that of the Indus Valley. Patañjali's aim of the reabsorption of the guṇas can then be achieved by some of us without suppressing the female half or their being, except if it appears in the modern amazons who can accept men only if they give up manhood for their sake.

IX. CHESS AS A COSMIC DIAGRAM

In his commentary on aṭ-Ṭogra'i's *Lāmīyat al Aǵam* the poet and biographer Ṣalāḫaddin aṣ-Ṣafadi († 1363) writes that the game of chess (Arabian šaṭranǵ) was invented by the Indian Sessa ibn Dahir and not by the famous Arabian chess-player al-Sūlī, as it was generally believed. Inspite of this invention chess was still played according to the rules of the Persian king Ardšir ibn Babeq, whose chess-board was divided into ,12 squares according to the months of the year and furnished with 30 pieces according to the days of the month.[1] This chess was played with dice, whose opposite eyes amounted to seven, the number of the planets, one was opposite six, two opposite five, three opposite four. The die decided, which piece the player had to move.

Aṣ-Ṣafadi points out that the die expressed divine decision and determination. There was, however, enough room left for an ingenious player to move the stones in such a way that he could overcome his opponent, no matter how the die had fallen. Aṣ-Ṣafadi adds that the cosmic interpretation of the game was taught by the followers of al-Ašari (a philosopher who lived in the 10th century). He then refers to sheikh ibn Tamimaḫ, who had told him that chess with dice (the Persian šaṭranǵ)as he thinks) would be better than the Indian chess without dice, because the latter lacked divine decision and predestination.

In the next sentence, however, aṣ-Ṣafadi says, that the šaṭranġ invented by Sessa was valued higher than the other (the Persian šaṭranġ)by the wise men of that time. He does not give any reason to explain this judgement, but the lexicographer Ibn Ḫallikān, who lived about 50 years earlier than aṣ-Ṣafadi, mentions in his vita of al-Sūlī that the Indian king Śehrām, to whom Sessa disclosed his invention, preferred it to anything else he knew, because it was a means for studying war, for establishing religion, for increasing the prosperity of the country and for

---

[1] The Arabian text together with a Latin translation was published by the mathematician J. Wallis in his Opera Mathematics I, Oxford 1695, p. 159 (reprint Hildesheim 1972). For a short biography of aṣ-Ṣafadi cf. C. Bockelmann, Geschichte der arabischen Literatur, Weimar 1898, I, p. 247, II, p. 31,32.

training the mind.[2] Both Arabian authors report that the king was so pleased with the invention, that he offered a boon to Sessa. Sessa asked for the amount of wheat which is obtained when the corn, that is put on the first square of the chessboard, is continually duplicated till the 64th square. The king felt almost insulted for being asked for such a trifle, and he enjoined Sessa to ask for something more valuable. But Sessa did not want anything else. Eventually, the king gave orders to his mathematicians to calculate the sum and to deliver the amount to Sessa. Some time later they informed him, that it would not be in his power to fulfil Sessa's desire, as the amount of wheat he was asking for, was more than the wheat extant in the whole world. After they had explained the matter to the king, he admired Sessa still more. At the end of his treatise, aṣ-Ṣafadi explains how easy it is to calculate this sum with the help of the Indian ciphers and he closes the chapter with the remark that the Indians excel in the world by three things: The book of Kalila and Damna (the Pañcatantra of Viṣṇuśarma), the game of šaṭranġ and the new ciphers.[3]

We can learn from this commentary firstly that India was held in high esteem in the Arabian world at that time and likewise in the previous centuries, for the Pañcatantra was translated into Persian in the 6th century.[4] Secondly, we are informed of an earlier chess game invented by the Persian king Ard(a)šir. The name is identical to Sanskrit ṛtakṣatra and to Greek Xerxes. Ardašir, the son of Babeq or Papak, lived at the beginning of the 3rd century. He was the founder of the Sassanide dynasty and made Zoroastrianism the religion of the state.[5] The game that he invented was interpreted as an image of the universe and of human life. The division of the basic line of its board into 12 squares is

[2] Cf. J. Wallis, op. cit. p. 163.

[3] One could add the gum arabicum that had been imported by Arabian traders from India already since the time of the great Egyptian dynasties.

[4] Cf. J. Hertel, op. cit. (1970), p. 20; R.C. Bell, Board and Table Games, Oxford 1969, p. 57.

[5] Cf. D.H. Teuffen, Die östliche Welt, Baden-Baden 1962, p. 416.

retained in the courier game, which was still played in the 17th century, but it could not prevent the success of Sessa's invention.
The name Sessa ibn Dahir has a historical background, too. Dahir or Dāhar was the name of the king of Sindh, who was defeated by the Omayyads in the year 712.[6] He had a son called Jaisingh, whose name may have been converted into Sessa by the Arabian writers. It may also be identical to Sanskrit śeṣa, the name of the snake, on which Viṣṇu rests after the dissolution of the world. Dāhar is the same as Hindī dohar, second. Dāhar was the second son hence. The Omayyads took the game with them to Baghdad. Jaisingh may also have told them the story of the king Śehrām, whose name can be explained as šah̲ Rām, king Rāma. He can be identified with the mythical king Rāma, the prototype of all Indian kings, or with king Candragupta, who won Sindh back from the Sakas in the 4th century.[7]
Aṣ-Ṣafadi's explanation of the word šaṭranġ is wrong, however. It is not of Persian origin and did not mean composed of six members (ṣaṣ + [ṭr]anġ) as the number of the pieces in modern chess made him believe, but it is based on the Indian word catur-aṅga. Catur-aṅga refers to the four members of the Indian army at the time of Alexander the Great, elephants, chariots, horses and infantry, or to the four kings of the game. There was no queen originally.
But catur-aṅga is older even than this. The eight squares on the basic line, the zoomorphic symbolism of the gamesmen and their arrangement in the form of a swastika make it likely that it was known already in the Indus Valley. Dice have been found in Mohenjo Daro and in Lothal together with conic stones which look quite similar to the later Indian catur-aṅga chessmen,[8] and it was in this area that the Arabs became ac-

[6] Cf. R.C. Majumdar, Northern India during AD 650-750, in: History and Culture of the Indian People, vol. II, Bombay 1954, p. 164.

[7] Cf. M. Edwardes, Illustrierte Geschichte Indiens, München 1961, p. 83.

[8] Cf. J. Marshall, op. cit., pl. XIII, XCII, CLIII. M. thinks it "quite possible that dice were used in conjunction with board-games" (p. 552).

quainted with the game. H. Rosenfeld has refuted that chess with dice was invented later than chess without dice.[9]

Two men seem occupied in playing dice or chess with dice on the lower register of tablet 8526 (B-24). This is confirmed by the inscription of the tablet 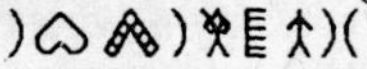 that agrees with verse 9cd of the dice-hymn X.34:

divyā aṅgārā iriṇe nyuptāḥ śītāḥ santo hṛdayaṃ nirdahanti
The heavenly charcoals (of the dice) thrown in the channel
burn the heart though they are cool.

For divyā, heavenly, we get the two curved lines, aṅgārā, charcoals, that is homophonous with aṅgiras, fore-father, corresponds the man-sign. Iriṇe, in the channel, is identical to the sign for woman. Nyupta, thrown, from the root vap, to sow, is equal to the guardian-sign, because warriors are known for playing dice in their leisure-time. The dice were also part of the ritual, an aspect that has been omitted in the Vedic hymn. In this connection the sign can be read as Rudra who is the creator of the seed of the father of the sky in ṚV I.71.5. For śītāḥ, cold, we get the following curved line, since it is homophonous with sītā, furrow. Santo is rendered by the curved line at the end. Hṛdaya, heart, is identical to the pictogram, for nirdahanta, burn, we get the triangle sign, because it can be read as the fire-sticks.

The last four signs are also found in the inscription of the motifless seal 1471 (M-331): . The first sign renders the oblong Indian dice, the number-signs are equal to their eyes (1-4), heavenly is written by the moon-sign with a stroke denoting running (at the sky), the channel, in which the dice were thrown, is equal to the compound whose last element is repeated after the number-sign for one to stress the bad cast. Nyupta, thrown, is equal to the horn-sign. The horn may have been used as dice-box.

---

[9] Cf. Die Beziehung der europäischen Spielkarten zum Orient und zum Urschach, Archiv für Kulturgeschichte 42, 1960, p. 24. Among the followers of this theory is P. Thieme (op. cit. vol. 2, p. 425). As dice are not mentioned in the earliest accounts of chess, he concludes that they did not exist. But this is again an argumentum ex silentio, that we have come across already in regard to the words 'writer' and 'writing' in the Veda (cf. chapter I.1)

In the Vedic hymn only dice made of the vibhītaka-nut are mentioned. They had no eyes, but dice with eyes were certainly known to the Vedic poets , as the nuts are said to have the same effect as the Soma found in Muñjavat, a Vedic writing for Mohenjo Daro. The dice-board is called channel and written by the sign for woman, as it is similar to the sacrificial mound, the vedi. In the Mahābhārata the chess-stones are compared with an army, the chess-board with the battle-field.[10]

The four players of the catur-aṅga chess, two of whom are allied, can also be compared to the two priests and the sacrificer and his wife sitting at the vedi, though its form is not a square as that of the chessboard.[11] The four kings correspond to the political situation of that time, one king ruled in the Indus Valley, one in South India, one in Mesopotamia, one in Egypt.

According to the Indian tradition chess with dice has either come from Kaśmir or from Sri Lanka,[12] which was ruled at that time by the Rakṣasa king Ravaṇa. Kaśmir is very near to the Indus Valley and the Rakṣasas could be relatives of the Indus people. The position and form of the figures of catur-aṅga are rendered by Raghunandana[13] in the 16th century in the diagram at the right:[14]

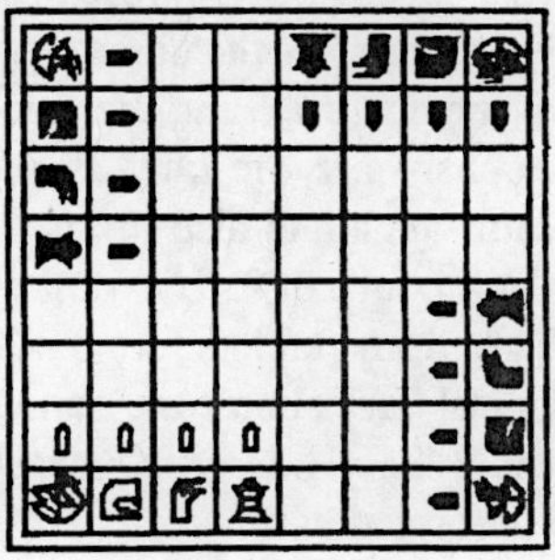

[10] Cf. K. de Vreese, The Game of Dice in Ancient India (The Vibhīthaka Game), Orientalia Neerlandica, Leiden 1948, p. 353.

[11] The vedi appears as a sign on seal 5076 that has been discussed in chapter IV.

[12] Cf. W. Jones, op. cit., p. 160.

[13] Raghunandana explained the rules of chess in his Smṛtitattva, an adaptation of the Caturaṅgadīpika of M. Śulapāni living in the 15th century. Cf. S.Y. Wakankar, A Survey of Sanskrit Works on the Game of Chess, Journal of the Oriental Institute 33, Baroda 1986.

[14] The diagram was taken from E.B Székely, Das Spiel des Asha, Frankfurt 1981, p. 120.

The gamesmen of catur-aṅga are arranged from right to left in the same direction as the signs of the Indus script. The piece next to the king is an elephant represented by its trunk, then follows a horse with its head resting on its fore-legs, the last one is a ship.[15] All these gamesmen can be regarded as vehicles or ministers of the king, but the elephant is the most dignified. He represents the governor or general and is the forerunner of the queen in modern chess that was not necessary in catur-aṅga. Indeed, a queen is out of place on a battle-field.[16]

Moreover, the piece of the king has female features. The cross that we find on his head today is much older than the Christian symbol. It represents the sun (cf. chapter XI). The form of his body is equivalent to the vedi that is also represented by the chessboard as a whole. Nowadays we may prefer the horse to the elephant on account of its speed. Instead of the horse we find the unicorn on the Indus seals. The unicorn and the elephant are the only animals which are on a par with the lion.[17] In catur-aṅga and also in modern chess the horse is of lesser importance. On account of its outward appearance in the diagram it could also be a hare. Some tablets found in Harappa that are carved in the shape of this animal have almost the same form as this chess-piece, tablet 3421 (H-333) and 3425 (H-335) for instance. The sign for the horse  can also be interpreted as a hare.

On tablet 3425 the two signs  are written on the body of the animal. They are identical to the two signs of the centaur-seal 7040 (K-50) that we have discussed in chapter III.2. The motifs of the hare and the centaur are related, because both are symbols of fertility. The original form of the horse in catur-aṅga could have been a centaur.

The last figure, the ship, is not part of the four-membered Indian army, but it was of great importance in the Indus Valley. Later on the horse-drawn chariot became more important than the ship and took the place

---

[15] A terracotta in the form of an elephant's trunk and a horse-head have been found in Lothal. Cf. S.R. Rao (1991), pl. CXXX.

[16] Except in the case of the amazons, where the queen replaces the king. For the root of the word amazon cf chapter I.1, note 39.

[17] Cf. D. Schlingloff, op. cit. p. 53.

of the elephant, which was transferred to the place of the ship.[18] The horse-drawn chariot is a symbol of the superiority of the later Āryans over the remnants of the urban population of the Indus cities and the Dasyus. The exchange and replacement of the pieces is a deviation from the ancient cosmic order, however, and makes a philosophical and psychological interpretation of the game more difficult. Nowadays the chessmen seem to be only profane actors in a profane game, but chess could not have been used as a simile for human life, if the figures had no cosmic and psychological background.

This was realized by the Arabian philosophers in regard to the older form of chess, but their explanation is limited to their religion. Székely's explanation of the symbolism of the game on the basis of the teaching of Zoroaster as the armies of Ahura Mazda and Ahriman seems to be more justified, [19] because the game was brought to the West through a Zoroastrian king, but since the origin of the game is in India its explanation must also be based on Indian philosophy.

Instead of the planets, that do not play an important role in the ancient Indian philosophy, the five elements can be taken for comparison. They are contained in the 25 tattvas of the Sāṃkhya system referred to in the Gītā, where Lord Kṛṣṇa says in 7.4:

Earth, water, fire and air, ether, mind, intellect and ego-sense -
in this way my Prakṛti is divided into eight parts.

---

[18] For the revirement of the chessmen cf. H.J. Maßmann, Geschichte des mittelalterlichen Schachspiels, Quedlinburg 1839 (Leipzig 1983), p. 35-39. H. Rosenfeld (op. cit. p. 27) explains the ship on account of Bengali influence. The Persian name of this piece, rokh, English rook, could indeed be derived from Bengalī rōkh, tenacity, which can be regarded as an attribute of this piece. G. Wahl thinks it possible, that the Persian name could mean unicorn and derives it from Sanskrit ratha, car (cf. Der Geist und die Geschichte des Schachspiels, Halle 1798, p. 190,196), but tha cannot become kha, except through a mistake in reading of the Bengalī script, where tha and kha are very similar. On p. 192 Wahl explains the piece as a camel or dromedar, the ship of the desert. This is quite near to the centaur.

[19] Op. cit. p. 39. His identification of the officer chessmen with "cosmic powers", the pawns with "natural powers" (p. 43) is quite arbitrary, however.

These elements are not identical to the eight officers or the pawns of modern chess, but they could be related to the lines of the chessboard. Eight is one third of the 24 tattvas of the Sāṃkhya, the 25th, the Puruṣa, is separate.

We have already pointed out that the chess-officers were originally arranged according to dignity. The most dignified officer, the elephant or unicorn, is most adequate to represent the intellect, the ship must then represent the mind. In modern chess mind and intellect have changed their places: The mind in the form of the car dominates the intellect. For the horse or centaur remains the ego-sense, which is quite appropriate to it, because the ego is proud like a horse. The zik-zak movement of the piece could have been borrowed from the hare. This animal is known for its sexual appetite, which is also a feature of the centaur and the ego. The hare is out of place on a battle-field, but in its form of a horse it can be identified with the rising sun that shines over the two opposite armies as described in ṚV X.121.6. The horse is also known for its readiness to sacrifice itself and this quality is sometimes also found in the ego.

In the enumeration of Gītā 7.4 only the five gross elements of the Sāṃkhya are mentioned. They correspond to the five senses of perception, whereas the subtle elements (the tanmatras of the Sāṃkhya) correspond to the motoric senses, as we might call them. In chess, both groups are symbolized by the pawns. As there is no queen in ancient Indian chess, we find only four pawns instead of five in one set, but if we take the king as representing two figures on account of his male and female aspects, we get five pawns here, too.

The elements and the senses can now be arranged according to consistency: The ether, to which ear and language belong, agrees with the pawn of the male aspect of the king, the air and feeling and grasping with the pawn of the female aspect of the king, the fire and seeing and going with that of the elephant, water and tasting and generating with that of the ship, the earth and smelling and secreting with that of the horse or centaur. Elements and senses with mind, intellect and egoty form the 'lower nature'. It is different from the 'higher nature'. Beyond both is the Puruṣa identified with Lord Kṛṣṇa in Gītā 7.5,6:

This is my lower Prakṛti, another is to be realized as my higher Prakṛti;
this is the life-force, o hero, by it this world is supported.
This (higher Prakṛti) is the womb of all beings, thereof you can be sure,
and likewise am I the origin and the dissolution of the whole world.

The commentaries differ a great deal with regard to the meaning of the 'life-force' or jīva-bhūta, literally what has become life, but with the help of the chessmen it is quite easy to find an equivalence for it, which is appropriate to the meaning of the Gītā. The life-force is the female aspect of the Puruṣa called Aditi and Virāj in ṚV X.90.5 and X.72.4 and is equal to the female aspect of the king. Through Sessa's invention it became the general, and reappeared as the queen in modern chess.[20] The king is the witness like the primordial spirit in ṚV X.129.7 and Gītā 9.10. The role of the general in Sessa's invention is similar to that of the Prakṛti in the Sāṃkhya system, but this is merely accidental. Sessa did not want to help the human mind to transcend nature, he brought it even more under her sway.

Sessa did not only introduce the general, but he also removed the dice, and he formed two battle-lines of the four lines of catur-aṅga. In this way he totally changed the aim of the game, which was formerly centred on winning an empire, while today the players only have to try to put the opponent's king check-mate, which is equal in life to killing him. In catur-aṅga a king could either be killed or be captured and return to the battle-field with the help of the allied king, in modern chess the game ends with check-mate. The removal of the dice was in accordance with the laws of Manu, however, who enjoins the king in IX.225 to banish the player of dice from the town. W. Jones remarks in this connection that Manu's prohibition was not applied to catur-aṅga played with dice being "openly taught by ancient and modern brahmins".[21]

---

[20] According to Bell (op. cit. p. 59) the general was placed in front of the lines and moved one square forward and backward. In catur-aṅga the elephant could move an unlimited number of squares in all directions like the queen.

[21] Cf. op. cit. p. 165.

Although Sessa's invention was a great improvement in the opinion of the king of that time and is in our opinion as well, he did something as blameworthy as the snake in Paradise. That snake was cursed because it offered man the opportunity to become wise as the creator of man, while Sessa induced humanity to give up the gods that manifest their will through the dice and to depend solely on their own intellect. But he was neither cursed nor punished, neither by a god nor by a king, he was rewarded and praised. Nowadays we realize more and more that his invention is quite similar to the box of Pandora.

Moreover, Sessa was instrumental in making humanity forget that there is something behind the screen of the world called the cosmic man or Puruṣa in ancient India. He was not punished by the Puruṣa, as the conception of the cosmic man has nothing to do with the rational image of a punishing godhead in monotheistic religions. Sessa could not remove the chessboard itself, however, he could only teach mankind to make another use of it, just as modern technology makes another use of the long-known invention of the wheel. This was not the introduction of spokes - they can be found on early Indus pottery and in the related Indus sign already -, but firstly the use of horses instead of oxen, and then of motor-power instead of horse-power. Sessa's invention could not change the original symbolic value of the chessboard, however, that can be compared to a yantra in the sense of a diagram. In the Veda a yantra is a machine, a vehicle or a thread. In ṚV I.34.1 it is identified with the thread in the clothes of the Aśvins. This shows that yantras could also be woven. Accordingly, the chessboard-design is found on clothes and pottery. It is significant that the Veda mentions the yantra together with the Aśvins who are related to day and night, represented in the white and black colours of the fields and the chessmen. Besides, the Aśvins are in close relation to the Dawn, one of the Vedic equivalences of the great goddess, the life-force of the Gītā. Lord Kṛṣṇa says in Gītā 18.61:

The Lord dwelling in the heart of all beings, Arjuna,
moves all of them by his māyā, as if they were mounted on a yantra.

If human beings are regarded as puppets, the yantra is the string, through which they are moved, and the Lord is the player, but normally Indian puppets are mounted on sticks as in the Chinese and Indonesian phantasmagoria. Hence it is more likely that yantra means diagram here, and the diagram, on which the figures are mounted and moved like puppets, is the chessboard. Of course, we do not like to look upon ourselves as chessmen, on the contrary, we prefer to believe that we are like gods. This we do on account of the capacity of our mind to imagine several movements in advance, or a sequence of movements, by which the opponent is put check-mate. It is possible to be a good player without knowing anything about the symbolic meaning of the chess-game, one does not even have to bother oneself about it, as it is excellently proved by the chess computers. A philosophic mind wants to know, however, what is behind the visible world and what is the original meaning of the chess-diagram. In this regard Lord Kr̥ṣṇa says in Gītā 7.7:

There is nothing higher than me, o acquirer of wealth!
On me all things are strung like a heap of pearls on a thread.

According to the Gītā the aim in life is to realize the thread going through the hole of the pearls. Only then can we feel the hand of the Lord moving our steps. This is also intended by the swastika-form of the diagram of the chessboard of catur-aṅga.[22] As soon as we have realized the string of the pearls in the structure of the diagram, we get the pearls on the thread and the victory of the game in a deeper sense. We really become 'acquirer of wealth', as Arjuna is called here. If we do not find the string of the inner meaning of the game of the world, we are merely figures on the chessboard moved by an indiscernible fate, still more, when we play it without dice, though the player does not realize this. It is the ego with its feeling of attraction and rejection and its pride of being godlike that prevents him from finding the reality of the string or swastika whose two bars are equal to male and female or good and evil (cf. chapter XI).

---

[22] This similarity was seen by S. Levitt, but he did not pay heed to the Indus civilization at all. (Cf. Chess - Its South Asian Origin and Meaning, Annals of the Bhandakar Research Institute, Poona 1993, p. 539).

To sum up we could say that Sessa's main contribution to the development of the human mind lies in the removal of predestination. He was successful in making man believe that he himself is the master of his fortune. In the same way Maya tricks man into believing that he is the doer in life. Indeed, we do not expect that a game will lead us beyond illusion, though we suffer over and over again, when we are losing. Even cheating the opponent is part of the game. Herein chess is quite in agreement with many stories of the Pañcatantra, and our enjoyment as spectator or listener is even enhanced, when truth and virtue are not on the side of the winner. We can learn from this, how to manage our life, as the Pañcatantra says in the introduction.

The negative aspect of chess is pointed out in the Buddhist story of a deceitful king, whose chessboard split up in the middle, whereupon the king sank down into the abyss of the earth, which opened under him as in an earthquake. The story is illustrated on the stūpa of Barhut (100 ante our era).[23]

The support the game offers to the shrewd and the wicked together with the removal of divine predestination may also explain, why there is nowadays no famous Arabian and only one famous Indian player. Chess in its modern form was not very successful in its motherland nor in the land that brought it to the West. But ethnology and psychology have found out recently that the trickster is also a divine image, provided he knows what is behind his tricks. Sessa seems to have known that. He has revealed his true nature by asking for a reward impossible to fulfil. It is the intuitive element contained in chess as in mathematics, through which Sessa's invention excels the borders of the rational mind that gives it a divine character, in spite of its being centred on the human ego. Therefore, Sessa deserved the reward he asked for.

---

[23] For the story and a picture of the stūpa cf. H. Rosenfeld, op. cit. p. 29,30.

X. THE DEVELOPMENT OF THE BRĀHMĪ AND THE TAMIL SCRIPT

The Brāhmī is the first Indian letter script. Its oldest remnants are found on stone-edicts of the Buddhist emperor Aśoka who ruled in the 3rd century ante our era. The language of the edicts is mostly Prākr̥t or Pali. It is not very reasonable, however, to assume that the Brāhmī script was invented for the purpose of writing Buddhist messages, the more so as it was named after the daughter of the creator Brahmā. It is more likely that Aśoka made only use of the script that was known for several centuries.[1] This can also be inferred from the fact, that there are a lot of variants in the letters of the edicts, though no definite historical development can be given for it. Notably, we find the same form of the letter ta in the 1st century after our era and in the 3rd century before, whereas in 2nd century of our era it is similar to that of the Gupta script.[2]
In the course of the excavations at Mohenjo Daro four sherds have been found that belong to the Kuṣāṇ period according to J. Marshall.[3] It is not exactly known, at what time the Kuṣāns, whose homeland was in Central Asia, came to India, but probably they ruled in the 2nd century.[4] Like the Sassanides in Persia the Kuṣān kings promoted Zoroastrianism, but they were supporters of Buddhism and of Śivaism also. In the time of Kaniṣka the Mahāyāna Buddhism was inaugurated. The tolerance the Kuṣāns had for all religions is reflected in the monograms of their coins.[5]

---

[1] Cf. H. Haarmann, op. cit. p. 524.

[2] Cf. G. Bühler, 17 Tafeln zur indischen Paläographie, Straßburg 1896, pl. II.

[3] Op. cit. p. 127.

[4] Cf. M. Edwardes, op. cit. p. 405. The first king of the 'Great Dynasty' of the Kuṣāns must have lived before the founder of the Sassanide empire, because he would not have been able to usurp the throne in the presence of such a rival.

[5] The coins of the first Kuṣān king do not show Sassanide influence (Göbl, op.cit. vol. III, pl.1,1-3). Göbl's argument for dating the Great Dynasty of the Kuṣāns to 231-330 (op. cit. vol. II, p. 269-301) does not considerate the religious and political facts sufficiently. The Constantin medaillon with the Persian goddess Ardoxšo, that he regards as the main proof for his theory, can be a reprint of an earlier stamp.

A coin of Kaniṣka II who was contemporaneous with the Sassanides deserves special attention, as it can be read as a bilingual. On this coin we find the Brāhmī letter kha above the monogram of the triratna.[6] If this monogram is read as the Vedic niṣka for jewel and put together with the Brāhmī letter, we get the name of the king. Kha, as in khan, lord, is the Mongolian rendering of the initial letter of his name. Niṣka denotes the breast ornament of Rudra in the Veda and can also mean golden coin. That the Kuṣān kings regarded themselves as incarnations of Śiva, is obvious from the motif of many of their coins, where they depict themselves as this god or where an image of the god standing before his bull is depicted on the reverse.[7]
The Mahāyāna Buddhism is a synthesis of Hindu and popular beliefs with the teaching of the Buddha. At this time we find the first images of a standing or sitting Buddha,[8] which becomes the characteristic of the style of Gandhāra henceforward.[9] Kaniṣka distributed not only coins with the motif of the Buddha and of Śiva with his bull, he also wrote a poem in Sanskrit.[10] This is another proof of his endeavour to live in agreement with the Indian tradition. His attitude can be compared to Alexander's politics of reconciling the Greeks with the Persians.[11] Hence we can expect that inscriptions from the Kuṣān-period reflect the manifoldness of the religious life of that time.

---

[6] Cf. Göbl. op. cit. vol. III, pl. 1,13. The triratna consists of three pearls and the foot-print of Nandi, Śiva's bull.

[7] Cf. Göbl. op. cit. vol. III, pl. 1. This motif was still used in the 5th century. Cf. E.J. Rapson, Indian Coins, Straßburg 1897, pl. II, no. 15.

[8] Cf. M.L. Carter, Petroglyphs in Chilas II, in: A. Gail/G. Mevissen, op. cit. p. 349. C. gives the first century as the date of a Kaniṣka-coin with the motif and the name of the Buddha and the monogram of the Persian god Pharo (effulgence). This is certainly too early.

[9] Cf. H. Goetz, Indien, Baden-Baden 1960.

[10] Cf. Edwardes, op. cit. p. 75.

[11] Cf. F. Altheim, Zarathustra und Alexander, Frankfurt 1960.

Marshall believed that the four sherds with Brāhmī inscriptions he found in Mohenjo Daro contain nothing but names. His translation is in accordance with this presumption. In one case he admits that the inscription could not be deciphered with certainty and gives no translation at all. But in the other cases the translation is no less uncertain and based only on a few letters. The transcription may not be correct either. But if we abandon his unfruitful assumption, we arrive at reasonable translations, though they are not entirely free from ambiguity. But this is a well-known trait of the Indian scriptures from the very beginning. One inscription can even be related to the Bhagavadgītā.

As I have no access to the original sherds, I can only give the inscriptions as published by Marshall on plate XC,1-4 of his excavation report. They have to be read from left to right. The language is Sanskrit, but the endings could also have been taken from Prākr̥t, as was the rule in the time of the Mahāyāna Buddhism.[12]

1 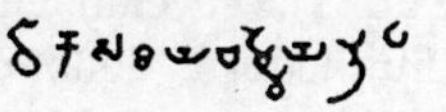 2 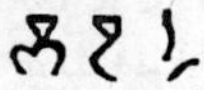

3 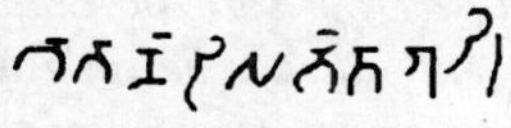 4 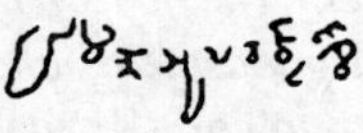

1 Dvikāla-deya dharmmya-dr̥ḍha

Most of the signs are uncertain here, especially the first one and the last two. The first sign could be ḍva + i, which can become dvi, the fourth sign I read with Marshall as 'de'. That the following three letters are to be read as dharmmya is sure. The last sign could be a circle and be read as ṭha being equal to ḍha. Then the penultimate sign can be read as dr̥. The translation of this reading is: *At two times (morning and evening) must be given by the man steadfast in the law.* This recalls Gītā 17.20. The inscription could have been written on the pot of a man, who wanted to follow this injunction. Translating only two words of the inscription Marshall renders it as *the gift (deyadharmma) of - the name is missing.*[13] Taken as a compound deyadharma means 'the

[12] Cf. M. Mayrhofer, Handbuch des Pali, Heidelberg 1951, p. 13.

[13] Op. cit. p. 317.

duty of giving' in Buddhist literature according to Monier-Williams. It does not make any sense in this connection.

2 Of this inscription only two or perhaps three letters are preserved, the rest is obliterated. The first letter is bha like the first letter of the third inscription, but as it has two additional strokes it should be pronounced as bhe. The second letter could be ḍa. On account of two additional strokes it should be read as ḍe. The third letter is probable na as the third letter of the third inscription. Hence we get: *Bheḍena, (given) through Bheḍa.* Bheḍa means ram. It is also the name of one of the mothers of the war-god Skanda. Perhaps the pot was used in a ritual. Marshall translates bhaṭata, Pali for mendicant, without taking notice of the additional strokes.

3 Tata-nandi (bhata-nandi) satata-khādako [bhavet/bhavisyati].

The first two letters are repeated in the second half, the fourth letter is identical to the last but one, the last one could be ko. The seventh letter looks like Devanāgarī ga, but it is kha + a. The fifth letter is doubtless sa. The translation is then: *The joy of the father (the son) or Bhata-nandi (who is fond of a good meal, bhatta) may always be an eater (may always have enough to eat).* Khādaka means debtor also. For this meaning we would get the variant: *Bhatanandi will always be (your) debtor*. Marshall reads the first letter as bha and is satisfied with translating the first four letters, which he renders as *bhatanaṃdi, either the donor or the owner of the vessel.*

4 Raramanidoha-cañcumān. Or: Rādhāmanidoha-cañcumān.

This inscription is the most difficult. It was not translated at all by Marshall. The first letter has perhaps been duplicated for intensification, the third letter is most probably identical to the last but one and the fourth to the last. The fifth letter is probably da + o. The ligature is most likely ñca. This transcription is equal to: *Versed in milking cows*. The pot might have belonged to a herdsman. For the alternative reading we get: *Famous through the yielding of the gem of Rārā*. Rārā can be changed into Rādhā. Both renderings may refer to the story of Kṛṣṇa or to a man with this name.

It is clear from these readings that the Brāhmī had a religious function like the Indus script. This function may have diminished in the course of time, but it is never totally lost. Otherwise the script did not deserve to be called after the name of the daughter of the god Brahmā. Aśoka, too, used it for religious aims.
The similarity of the Brāhmī and the Aramaic alphabet can be explained by their development from the same source, the Indus script.[14] This is not in contradiction to the historical fact that the Phoenicians invented the first letter-script and that this script was used for commercial activities. Furthermore, the letters of the Devanāgarī have been arranged according to the cakras, the subtle centres of the body, in Tantric scriptures,[15] and Tantra has its origin in the Indus Valley religion, as is evident from several tablets with sexual motifs (cf. chapter III.7 and V). The line that we find on top of the Devanāgarī letters can also be explained through its derivation from the Indus script that was read from bottom to top, i.e. from the motif upwards.
I shall now introduce a list of the Brāhmī letters together with a key-word related to a sign of the Indus script. The employ of the first letter of a word for the alphabet is called acrophony. The key-words are not fixed. There are other words equally suitable for being used as prototypes. The signs of the Brāhmī and their number have been taken from Bühler's list. In case of a missing number the corresponding sign could not been ascertained in the Indus script. This happens very seldom, however. Mostly it is the case with cerebrals, that normally do not occur at the beginning of a word in Sanskrit. As a rule only a part of the Indus-sign is adopted and frequently it is written inversely.

---

[14] This was supposed by S. Langdon. Cf. The Indus Script, in: J. Marshall, op. cit., p. 433. Perhaps there were some intermediate links between the Indus script and the Brāhmī, but the variations are solely on the side of the Brāhmī, the Indus script remained almost constant through the centuries (cf. chapter I.6).

[15] Cf. J. Woodroffe, The Garland of Letters, Pondicherry [9]1989.

No.	Brāhmī	Key-word	Translation	Indus-Sign	Notes
1	𑀅 a	asu	life		womb
2	𑀇 i	indu	drops (of Soma)		
5	𑀉 u	u	to weave		
7	𑀏 e	eta	gazelle		horn
8	𑀑 o	oj	to sprout		
9	𑀓 ka	karma	work		
10	𑀔 kha	khā	well		beam for a well
11	𑀕 ga	gam	go		
12	𑀖 gha	gharma	kettle		
13	𑀘 ca	candra	moon		
14	𑀙 cha	chāyā	to cover		wheel
15	𑀚 ja	jāya/jnāna	woman/wisdom		
23	𑀢 ta	tantu	thread		
24	𑀣 tha	(ra)tha	car		
25	𑀤 da	dakś	to be potent		
26	𑀥 dha	dhanus	bow		
27	𑀦 na	na	not		
28	𑀧 pa	patra/pada	cup/foot		
30	𑀩 ba	bandha	deposit		
31	𑀪 bha	bhṛ	carry		
32	𑀫 ma	matsya	fish		
33	𑀬 ya	yā	to move		move (like a car)
34	𑀭 ra	rad	scratch		
35	𑀮 la	liṅga	sign/genital		mortar
36	𑀯 va	vas	to shine		flower; spring
37	𑀰 śa	śaru	arrow		
39	𑀲 sa	sarpa	snake		
40	𑀳 ha	hara	Śiva		

The Brāhmī alphabet has no relation to the zodiac as the Greek (cf. chapter III.2). The order of the consonants and vowels, which are recorded separately, depends solely on the place of articulation here. The signs are purely geometrical. The letter a is explained as a derivation of the Phoenician sign 𐤀 by Monier-Williams.[16] In the Semitic languages it stands for alpum, bull, but there is no word for bull in Sanskrit that begins with an a. If we take aśva, horse, instead, as I proposed earlier, the horns are missing. Hence it is more advisable to affiliate it to a sign that can be explained as a womb. The womb gives life and is also related to the goddess of the earth called Aditi which is an aspect of the goddess Brāhmī. In the Greek alphabet it has become the letter K, which can be affiliated to the centaur (written kentaur in Greek), which is closely related to the mother-goddess (cf. chapter III.2).

The sign for a is written as अ or अ in the Devanāgarī script, which was invented in the 7th century. The first sign can be explained as an udder, the second as a bosom, both attributes of the mother-goddess. At the same time as the Devanāgarī alphabet the symbol for the mystic syllable ॐ (spelled OM or AUM) must have been invented, which is a symbol of the Puruṣa, as it is explained in the Māṇḍūkya Upaniṣad. Its main part is the letter U that is derived from an Indus sign that can be explained as to weave. The whole sign may be regarded as a tree. The tree is compared to language in the Veda and the Gītā as expounded in the preface of this volume. Like the syllable OM it consists of three parts, the crown, the stem and the root. The fourth part or the 'unspoken' language is indicated by the anunāsika, the nasal. It can be explained as a drop of Soma or as the seed called bindu in the Tantric Saṃhitas. The process of speaking can be compared to the sexual act and to creation: In the beginning was the Word. Meditation is the inversion of the creative process. To attain this aim the Gītā enjoins in 15.3,4 to cut the tree of language off at its root:

---

[16] Cf. A Sanskrit-English Dictionary, Delhi 1990 (reprint), p. xxvii.

> The shape of this tree cannot be perceived here,
> it has neither beginning nor end nor permanence;
> this many-rooted aśvattha tree one should cut off
> with the sharp knife of non-attachment
> and then go to that highest place,
> from where, when it is reached, one never returns,
> meditating on the original Puruṣa,
> through whom this world was manifested of yore.

The cutting of the tree is not a cruel act here. The aśvattha tree is a parasite that suffocates other trees using them as host for its roots. Creation in general and its image in the invisible tree of language is supported by those who are not attached to it, whose work consists in non-working, as the Gītā formulates it in the fourth chapter. Writing is an activity that is well suited for carrying out the teaching of the Gītā into practise. That may be the reason, why the Devanāgarī and the Tamil script were both invented in the 7th century, in a time of reviving the eternal Dharma.

According to the Māṇḍūkya Upaniṣad the first letter A of the syllable AUM that represents the waking state is qualified as the beginning and as attainment. Their relation to the mother-goddess is hinted at in the next sentence, where someone who knows the function of this letter is said to attain all his desires. All desires are granted by the mother-goddess in the Veda.

The letter U is qualified as elevation (or eminence) and participation in both (in the waking and the sleeping state). It is called the dream state, because life is a dream for the Upaniṣad. The dream state is elevated to the waking state like an adult is more eminent than a child. This state is, after all, a state of transition. Someone who knows the meaning of this state will have nobody in his family who does not know the absolute Brahman, but he seldom has a family, because he knows that the world is transitory.

The letter M related to the sleeping state is qualified as measuring and dissolution. This refers to the devouring aspect of the mother-goddess. But even after the whole world has dissolved, the germs for a new creation remain like the seed kept in a pot. Likewise the sleeping state is the measure of the waking and the dream state. Somebody who knows this is not effected by dissolution and death.

The fourth state that is equal to a drop of Soma or immortality can be compared with the cup-sign in the Indus script, because it includes all other signs. Somebody who knows this identifies himself with the cosmic air, he is not confined to the air in the pot of his body, as is said in Gauḍapadas Kārikā (commentary) to the Upaniṣad.[17]

Whereas the Devanāgarī claims divine origin, nothing is reported of the Tamil script in this respect, it has not even a name. It is almost unanimously accepted nowadays, however, that the Devanāgarī like the Tamil script and all other North and South Indian scripts were derived from the Brāhmī.[18]

In the Tamil script the acrophonic method is not applicable, because several consonants of its alphabet do not occur at the beginning at all. Tamil is ornamental in structure like the South Indian art and hence more focused on the end of the word and to extensions by suffixes.[19] But the letters, consonants as well as vowels, can be arranged according to a symbolic method of classification entirely independent of their alphabetic order. We arrive then at the following pattern:

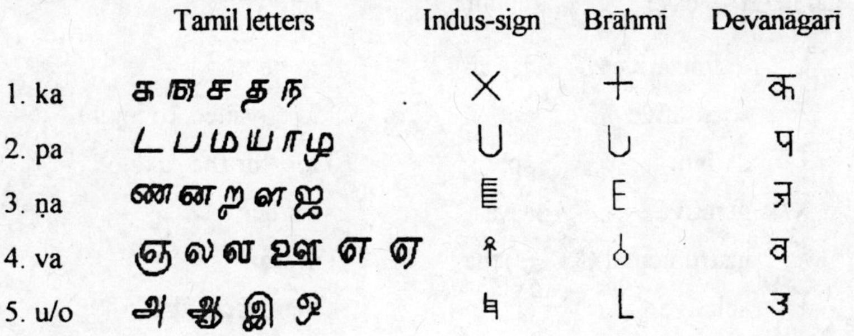

[17] Cf. E. Richter-Ushanas, Das Stillhalten der Fackel, Bremen ²1985.

[18] Cf. H. Haarmann, op. cit. p. 523.

[19] Cf. P. Jothimuththu, A Guide to Tamil, Madras 1965.

According to the symbolic value of the Indus pictograms the first group is identical to the jaws, the second to the cavern of the mouth, the third to the teeth, the fourth to the tongue and the fifth to the skull. As the sound of the vowels is formed here, the skull is identical to the element ether. Likewise the other four groups can be affiliated to the other four elements: the jaws to the earth, the cavern of the mouth to the waters, the teeth to the fire and the tongue to the air, as it moves in the air of the cavern of the mouth. The tongue is also a symbol of fire in the Veda and correspondingly 'pavana' in Sanskrit means air as well as fire.

The five classes can also be divided into male and female: The first and the third class are female, the second is male, the fifth belongs to both sexes. In this way it becomes obvious that the Tamil script represents the whole cosmos like the Devanāgarī and the Brāhmī. That the Devanāgarī is estimated as higher than other Indian scripts is equally unjustified as the demand of the North Indians for supremacy over the South. To replace it by a Dravidian fundamentalism would be equally silly, of course.

Like the letters of the Brāhmī the Sanskrit case endings can be derived from the Indus script:

final letter	case	ending	reference
	nominative	as (aḥ)	to be
	accusative	am	to advance, to injure
	dative	abhi	for, for the sake of
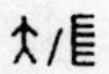	genitive	asya	his/her
	instrumental	(s)ena	servant
	ablative	āt	then, from that

It can be deduced from this list that the case endings were originally separate words or particles as in agglutinative languages. It must be noted, however, that the Indus signs were not used as case endings by the writers of the Indus script themselves.

XI. THE SWASTIKA

'Swastika' is the Indian name of the gammadion cross. It is perhaps the most popular symbol in India and is painted above the entrances and on the walls of many temples and houses. Its meaning is peace and happiness. Its name is derived from Sanskrit svasti, welfare, prosperity, luck. It is therefore connected with god Viṣṇu, the maintainer. It has a similar meaning in Buddhism, where it is found on the back of the feet of the Buddha. From the 3rd century ante to the 4th century after our era the swastika appears on Indian coins together with the motif of the cosmic tree or the pyre.[1] It was hence related to life and death. Its earliest appearance, however, is on seals and tablets from the Indus Valley, which is another proof for the persistence of this civilization.[2]

The swastika has not been found in India only, but also in the Near East, in Egypt and in Scandinavia and in the areas inhabited by the Celts. Though it is generally believed that the symbol came into being independently in all these regions, it cannot be altogether precluded that these peoples were influenced by the Indus civilization. This does not mean, however, that the swastika is an Āryan sign, as its adaptation by the nationalistic movement in Germany may suggest. We have pointed out in chapter I.1 that the population of the Indus cities was mixed.

It is not unlikely that the meaning of the swastika in India today is identical to that it had in the time of the Buddha or the Indus civilization, since the Indian mythology and philosophy has not changed very much in the course of the five millennia that are known to us historically. This is mainly due to the caste system which was most probably invented by the founders of the Indus civilization.

The Indian name for caste, varṇa, means colour. This is explained in the Bhagavadgītā in a psychological sense: The caste depends on the natural inclination of a human being, and this determines his profession.

---

[1] Cf. E.J. Rapson, Indian Coins, Straßburg 1897, plates III,9,12.

[2] The first swastika has been found on a stamp seal from Mehrgarh, dated 2600 ante approximately. Cf. Vergessene Städte am Indus, fig. A 69.

According to Ṛg-Veda X.90.13, where the origin of the castes is described for the first time in Indian literature, they were produced from the body of the Puruṣa, when he was sacrificed by the gods in the primordial sacrifice, from which the world came into being:

The brahmins were born from his mouth,
the warriors were born from his arms,
the land-owners were born from his thigh,
the servants came forth from his feet.

As the swastika is one of the oldest symbols of the Indian civilization, it could be understood as a representation of the rules of Dharma, the holy order, established together with the sacrifice of the Puruṣa. The four castes would then be equal to its branches and its centre to the divine state that everybody should strive for according to the injunction of the Bhagavadgītā. It would then be possible to restore the so far hypothetical original meaning of the swastika with the help of the Veda in the same way as we have done it with the signs of the Indus script in the foregoing chapters of this book.

There have been found about 50 seals and tablets with the swastika motif in the Indus Valley, but of them only one seal and four tablets have an inscription: Seal 1311 and the tablets 1580 (M-482), 2717 (M-488), 3306 (H-182) and 3317 (H-242). In addition, there are the tablet 2733 (M-1415) with the motif of a Latin cross, of which nine copies exist and the tablet 2720 (M-461) with the motif of a variant of a St. Andrew's cross, of which 16 copies are illustrated in the Corpus of Indus Seals and Inscriptions. On tablet 2078 (M-419) and 2624 (M-1389) the swastika occurs with a grid motif. On tablet 1623 (M-443) and on the stone slab 2707 (M-1356) it appears with another geometric design.

According to the Indian concordance the swastika is used as a sign in the inscription of the tiny Harappa seal 3500 rendered there as |||⾌ |||卐卄. In the Finnish concordance the swastika is replaced by the field-sign 凸 that occurs also on the two otherwise identical Harappa tiny seals 3482 and 3486 (H-911). Seal 3500 is not illustrated in the Corpus of Indus Seals and Inscriptions I and II, but the careful study of the illustration given by Vats in his manual suggests that the tree-sign ᛉ is written here. In any case the inscription can be read according to

I.160.1, where Heaven and Earth regarded as female are personified as two plates (dhiṣaṇā):

Heaven and Earth, who give welfare to everybody,
bear according to the Law the seer of the sky;
between Heaven and Earth, the two well-bearing plates,
walks the pure sun-god according to the Law.

Heaven and Earth as two female entities are rendered by the banner-sign, the hand-sign and the three strokes can be read as to carry according to the Law valid for the three castes. The land-owners and the servants are regarded as one caste here (cf. chapter II). The sun-god or seer of the sky is written by the horse-sign. If there is a swastika in the inscription, it would represent the sun-god, too.

The inscription of tablet 2733 with the motif of the Latin cross 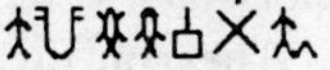 corresponds to the first verse of R̥V X.10, the dialogue between Yama and Yamī, who are brother and sister and are said to be the first human beings. In the first verse Yamī says to her brother, after he has come back from a long journey:

May I win the friend for friendship;
may the gracious one, who has gone to many places
across the ocean, generate a grandson for the father,
thinking of the contimuation of life on earth.

The Vedic verse does not keep to the sequence of the signs. The literal translation would be: The man, who has gone across in all directions of the earth, I may win as friend for generating a son. The last line is equal to the motif of the cross that can be explained as a fertility symbol in this context. Her brother is most fit in the eyes of Yamī for this purpose, because he has seen the whole world and because all other men in the place where she lives have died in his absence, probably by some natural calamity. This could refer to the inundation of the Indus cities. Yama and Yamī would then be the only survivors and their cohabitation was necessary for saving the Āryan race from total annihilation. In this way, the last become the first.

The first man-sign with an additional triangle meaning to walk stands for Yama, the cross-sign and the field-sign render all directions of the earth which include the oceans, because otherwise one cannot go in all directions. Yamī is equal to the bee-sign, the crowned fish-sign that can also be read as Mitra, renders friend. The cup-sign can be read as to generate, the last man-sign as son or grandson. Yama is not only the first man, but also the god of Death. This aspect of the Latin cross has been adopted by Christianity.

In case of the bull-seal 1311 (M-1225) the swastika on the back has to be included in the reading of the inscription 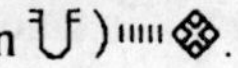. Then it agrees with ṚV I.105.10:

Those five bulls standing in the midst of the sky
as a deed the gods are to be praised for,
they have disappeared together -
admit this, heaven and earth!

The midst of the sky is equal to first sign, the five bulls or stars to the second, to disappear (or to wane) to the curved line. The cup-sign represents the gods, the swastika their deed. Hence it is a symbol of heaven and earth here, summoned by the poet as his witnesses.

The inscription of tablet 3306 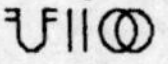 that is repeated on the reverse can be read according to ṚV X.125.7: *I pervade heaven and earth*. The intersected circles can be read as heaven and earth, the two long strokes as pervade, the cup-sign as the personal pronoun of the goddess Vāc. The motif of this tablet, the deity and the tiger, is similar to the motif of the goddess in the tree and the tiger. The drum of the deity may also be interpreted as a drawn-up skirt as we find it on pottery painting from the Harappa cemetery and on Mesopotamian seals depicting the goddess Ištar as a prostitute.[3] It is identical to the *brotherless woman*, as the Dawn is called in Ṛg-Veda I.124.7. The sun is compared in X.101.11 to a man with two women in bed, i.e. to a male prostitute.

The St. Andrew's cross  following the two signs 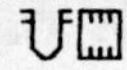 on the tablets 2720 (M-457 to M-463 and M-1409 to M-1414) can be regarded as a fertility symbol like the Latin cross. The field-sign can be read as the sieve for purifying the Soma rendered by the cup-sign. Hence the inscription can

---

[4] For an illustration cf. Vergessene Städte am Indus, fig. 183. For the goddess Ištar as a prostitute cf. U. Winter, Frau und Göttin, Göttingen 1983 (plates).

be affiliated to R̥V. IX.83.1: *Your sieve has been stretched out, Brahmaṇaspati, you pervade the limbs on all sides.* Brahmaṇaspati, the lord of the hymns, is equal to the cup-sign.

On the reverse of these tablets a motif that can be described as a snake coiling up a tree or a pillar standing in a railing is inscribed The coils are six, together with the railing we get the number seven. Therefore they can be identified with the cakras of the Kuṇḍalinī. Seven goddesses are mentioned in relation to the Soma in IX.9.6.

The signs for heaven and earth in the middle suggest the affiliation of the inscription of tablet 3317  to R̥V I.160.3:

sa vahniḥ putraḥ pitroḥ pavitravān
punāti dhīro bhuvanāni māyayā
dhenuṃ ca pr̥śnīṃ vr̥ṣabhaṃ suretasaṃ
viśvāhā śukraṃ payo asya dukṣata
The car-driving son illuminates both parents,
the wise purifies the beings by his magic power;
from the speckled cow and the well-seeded bull
he milks all days their milk and seed.

The first sign can be read as the car of the sun driving in all directions, the second sign is equal to the first-born, the son. The horse-sign can be read as magic power and as to illuminate. The woman-sign and the rhombus-sign are equal to earth and heaven. The hand-sign renders to milk, the field-sign can be read as all days here. The last two signs are equal to the well-seeded bull and the speckled cow. Milk and seed is supplemented by the Vedic poet. The swastika is equal to the sun.

The same verse is referred to by the inscription 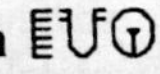 of tablet 1580, whose last two signs are identical with that of seal 3317. Here the hand in a circle renders to milk all days. In the motif an acacia tree is found together with the swastika. It refers to the cosmic tree and to the tree, out of which the Soma was produced, through which the sun obtains its magic power. The motif of the crocodile with a fish in its mouth on the reverse of this tablet depicts the law of nature: The big swallows the small. It is equal to the dark aspect of the sun. It can only be overcome by the sacrifice of the male part of the Puruṣa, as it is reflected in the Greek word 'androgyn': The male stem aner (Sanskrit nr̥) is declined, the female stem gyn remains as it is. The same motif is found on the ship-tablet 2828 (cf. chapter VII,2). Instead of the crocodile a bird can be the catcher and eater as in the inscription of the unicorn-seal 1194 (M-22) , which can be read as the bird catches the mouse, but if the first sign is taken as a symbol of the Soma, it can be affiliated to R̥V IV.26.6:

Stretching out the eagle brought from afar
the stalk that intoxicates and makes happy;
he embraced it tight, when he brought it
with the help of the gods from the highest sky.

Here the law of nature is replaced by a higher purpose that can be realized by initiation. The crocodile or eagle becomes the teacher or guru then, the food the disciple. Both are divine, but the disciple must be 'swallowed' by the teacher to get rid of his ego-sense. The ego-sense is the offering then. With regard to this sacrifice the word guru, literally meaning 'heavy', can be derived from the root gr̥̄, to swallow. The heaviness of the guru is caused by the disciples he has swallowed, as it were. That means that the institution of guruship has its origin in the Indus culture like the caste-system. The guru is described as swallower and being swallowed in the Uśanas-story of the Mahābhārata. In a similar way the nature of a true guru is described by Sri Ramakrishna:[4]

One day [when making a walk] I heard the croaking of a bull-frog and I thought that it must have been seized by a snake. When I came back after some time the croaking had still not come to an end. I went nearer and saw that a small water-snake had seized the frog and now it could neither swallow it nor get rid of it. Therefore the state of suffering of the frog did not cease. It came to my mind that if the snake would have been a big one the frog would have been silent after three croaks. As it was only a water-snake both had to suffer.

Similarly, somebody's ego-sense is removed, when he meets a real guru. When the guru is unripe', both have to suffer, the guru and the disciple. The ego-sense of the disciple is not removed and he is not released of the clutches of attachment to the world. When he has come across an unripe guru, the disciple will not attain liberation.

---

[5] Cf. Tales and Parables of Sri Ramakrishna, Madras ^{2}1947, p. 272. The translation in this volume follows the Hindī version of Svāmī Mumukṣānanda in Śrīrāmakr̥ṣṇākathā Citramālā, Calcutta ^{3}1992, p. 41.

Ramakrishna's criticism refers only to the personal teacher of the ancient tradition, not to the members of organisations including that one established in his name. A teacher in a religious organisation will not suffer very much of his unripeness as it is known from the priests of the Christian church, after which many Indian religious organisations are modelled today. Indian religiosity has to answer, of course, the present needs.
Tablet 2717 with the inscription 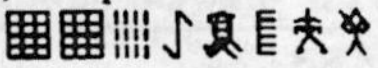 can be related to the first two verses of another cosmic hymn, X.190.1,2:

r̥taṃ ca satyaṃ cā_bīddhāt tapaso 'dhyajāyat
tato rātry ajāyata tataḥ samudro arṇavaḥ
samudrād arṇavād adhi saṃvatsaro ajāyata
aho rātrāṇi vidadhad viśvasya miṣato vaśī
Law and Truth have been born from the enflamed heat.
From that was born the night, from that the fleeting ocean.
From the fleeting ocean was born the year,
that separates day and night ruling over all that has blinking eyes.

The guardian-sign can be read as law and truth, the sign of the androgyn deity as enflamed heat, because it is the father of the sky whose tapas is enflamed as it were by his daughter, the Dawn. The woman-sign can be read as the night, the ocean as the horse-sign, because the Soma generally represented by this sign is compared with the ocean in the Veda. Fleeting is rendered by the stroke-sign. It refers to ebb and flood depending on the attraction of the moon. The year is equal to the twelve strokes representing the months, day and night is written by the two net-signs. On account of the retina they may also represent the blinking of the eyes.
On the reverse of the swastika-tablet 1623 we find 4x4 triangles in a circle. The motif recalls the Śrī yantra. In Praśna Upaniṣad 6.1 the Puruṣa is said to have 16 parts. Probably the grid motifs on tablets 2624 and 2078 have the same meaning as the triangle motif. On tablet 2773 the swastika on the reverse of this motif is replaced by the signs  They can be read according to R̥V X.125.8b: *I carry all the worlds.* The water-carrier with a vessel on the head represents the goddess Vāc, the three strokes are equal to the three worlds. Vāc, the goddess of language, is like the goddess of luck, Lakṣmī, a personification of the swastika.

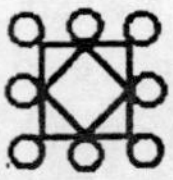

The motif of two intersected threads is found together with a swastika on a rectangular stone recorded under the number 2707 (cf. figure at the left). Both motifs are a symbol of luck.

We could end our investigation here, if not recently a cylinder seal from Seistan/Iran with Indus characters had been rediscovered in the British Museum, which I give the provisional number 9911*:[5]

The seal is broken and probably only a part of the inscription has been left. The second sign is heavily damaged. It is restored by itself, however, immediately after it is drawn. We arrive then at the following line . Knox regards the first sign correctly as a number-sign, but why should 12 persons be recorded on a tablet? Fortunately, the sign can also be interpreted as rain or the year consisting of twelve months. Taking it as such we are directed to ṚV VII.103, which we have come across already in relation to seal 2423 in chapter I.7. The hymn that is addressed to the frogs can be regarded as a rain-charm and the tablet is therefore a suitable amulet in a desert. The frogs are a personification of the brahmins. Their arms and feet can form a swastika. Maybe, a swastika was written on the opposite side of this cylinder as on seal 2078. In the first verse of ṚV VII.103 the frogs are described in the following way:

saṃvatsaraṃ śaśayānā brāhmaṇā vratacāriṇaḥ
vācaṃ parjanyajinvitaṃ pra maṇḍūkā avādiṣuḥ
After having been silent for one year
like brahmins that obey a vow,
the frogs invigorated by Parjanya
have started their speech.

For the 12 strokes we get saṃvatsara, year, the first man-sign is equal to the silent brahmin. For *vratacāriṇa*, observing a vow, we get the guardian-sign and the two strokes. Parjanya, the rain-god, is rendered by the second

[6] Cf. A new Indus Valley cylinder seal, South Asian Archaeology, Helsinki 1994, p. 375.

man-sign, for invigorated we get the woman-sign he holds in his right hand. The derivation of the name Parjanya is somewhat obscure, but most likely it can be deduced from the root pr̥c, to fill. This has a sexual connotation, too. The frogs starting their speech are rendered by the third man-sign and another woman-sign combined with it.

Three seasons are mentioned in the Puruṣa-hymn R̥V X.90.6, five in the cosmogonic hymn R̥V I.164.12. They could be referred to by monogram on top of the Seistan seal, which could be explained as an image of the cosmic tree. Knox compares it with the monogram  on the top of the cylinder seal 7733 (Sibri-2) and the triangle motif on tablet 1623. The main motif on the seal from Sibri, a lion attacking a zebu, has much similarity with one of the main motifs of Akkadian seals. Apart from the astrological meaning (cf. chapter I.1 and III.2) it could be explained as an illustration of the fight of the elements. The lion would symbolize the fecundating power and the zebu the fecundated. In R̥V V.83.3cd we read in this connection:

From the distance the thunder-cries of the lions arise,
when Parjanya creates the rain-clouds.

Parjanya is compared to a bull in verse 1 of this hymn. The bull and the lion are both aspects of the godhead. Therefore, the goddess Durga is identified with the lion in a later Indian story, where she fights a buffalo. The crocodiles above and below the motif on Sibri-2 are a symbol of fertility, too. On the top of Sibri-3 with the motif of a lion facing a zebu we find a small animal which Knox thinks to be a scorpion, but which is most likely a frog. Whatever it is, both animals belong to the rainy season.

To sum up, we can say that the swastika is a symbol of the sun and that it represents the cosmic tree as well as the cosmic game (līlā), whose rules are repeated in the ancient Indian chess of catur-aṅga. Though we had only very little material to study, we have nevertheless arrived at a comprehensive and consistent result.

There is one question left, however: How could an emblem, whose meaning is peace and welfare, be used for bad purposes, as it happened in Germany 60 years ago? The reason for this lies in the structure of creation. With three quarters the Puruṣa is the immortality in heaven, with one quarter only he is the universe according to ṚV X.90.3. Male and the female is within this one quarter and within it is good and evil. Creation begins, when the Puruṣa burns up evil, says the Bṛhad Āraṇyaka Upaniṣad in I.4.2.1, but obviously he did not burn up it totally. In the time of the later Veda, the Āryans believed that the Dasyus were the evil that the Puruṣa had left to them to destroy. In a similar way, Hitler and his followers thought the Jews were the evil that had to be annihilated. They did not believe in the cosmic man, but carried the philosophy of Darwin into practice. The Gītā was equally important for them, Himmler, who was in charge of the holocaust, read it before sleeping. Mahatma Gandhi who lived at the same time understood the Gītā in a completely different way and was killed for that. There were only two years between Hitler's and Gandhi's death. The war between the species that Darwin called selection went on with other prototypes then. The outward war is mirrored in the inward war between the male and female half of our being. This war is a sacrifice, too, and beyond it there is the primordial and permanent sacrifice of the cosmic man. This was not realized by Darwin and the evolutionists who have adopted his teaching.

In Christianity, the permanent sacrifice was replaced by a historical sacrifice. But what can history achieve in the face of eternity? The only true solace in this eternal struggle is to realize that it is imaginative and that the thing real (the thing-in-itself in the words of the German philosopher Kant) cannot be effected by it. This is the teaching of Indian philosophy since ancient times. It must have been the teaching of the Indus priests and seers as well.

BIBLIOGRAPHY

Allchin, F.R.
The Legacy of the Indus Civilization, in: G. Possehl, South Asian Archaeology Studies, Oxford 1992

Allchin, B. and F.R.
The Birth of Indian Civilization, Harmondsworth 1968

Altheim, F.
Zarathustra und Alexander, Frankfurt 1960

Antiquitates Indogermanicae,
Gedenkschrift für Hermann Güntert, Innsbruck 1974

Atre, Sh.
Lady of Beasts - The Harappan Goddess, Purātattva 16,1986

Bell, R.C.
Board and Table Games, Oxford 1969

Bhargava, P.L.
Vedic Religion and Culture, New Delhi 1994

Bhartṛhari,
Poems, transl and ed. B. S. Miller, London 1967

Bhattacharji, S.
The Indian Theogony, Cambridge 1970

Bockelmann, C.
Geschichte der arabischen Literatur, Weimar 1898

Boehmer, R.M.
Die Entwicklung der Glyptik während der Akkad-Zeit, Berlin 1965

Borger, R.
Babylonisch-Assyrische Lesestücke, Rom 1979
Assyrisch-Babylonische Zeichenliste, Neukirchen-Vlyn 1978

Brooks, R./Wakankar, V.S.
Stone Age Painting in India, London 1976.

Buber, M.
Die Sprache der Botschaft, München 1964

Bühler, G.
Indische Paläographie, Straßburg 1896
(tr.) The Law of Manu, Sacred Books of the East XXV, Oxford 1888

Buren van, E.D.
The Sacred Marriage in Early Times in Mesopotamia, Orientalia 13,1944

Carter, M.L.
Petroglyphs at Chilas II: Evidence for a pre-iconic phase of Buddhist art in Gandhāra, in: South Asian Archaeology, Stuttgart 1993

Charpentier, J.
Die Suparṇasage, Leipzig 1920

Chia, M.
Taoists Secrets of Love, New York 1984
Churchward, J.
Mu, Der versunkene Kontinent, Aitrang 1990
Dales, G.F.
New Inscriptions from Mohenjodaro,
Kramer Anniversary Volume, Neukirchen-Vlyn 1976
Dandekar, R.N.
Harappan Bibliography, Poona 1987
Vedic Mythological Tracts, Delhi 1979
Deimel, A.
Sumerisches Lexikon I, Rom 1947
Deppert, J.
Rudras Geburt, Wiesbaden 1977
Dumézil, G.
Le problème des Centaures, Paris 1929
During-Caspers, E.C.L.
Another Face of the Indus Valley Magico-Religious System,
in: South Asian Archaeology, Stuttgart 1993
Dvivedi, H.P.
Jīvema śarada śatam,
in: Hindi Gadya Padya Samgraha, Calcutta 1960
Edwardes, W.
Geschichte Indiens (History of India), München 1961
Eggeling, J. (transl.)
Śathapatha Brāhmaṇa,
Sacred Books of the East XIII, Oxford 1882-1900
Edzard, D.O.
Die Inschriften der akkadischen Rollsiegel, AfO XXII (1968/69)
Eliade, M.
Yoga, Frankfurt 1985
(ed.) Encyclopedia of Religion, New York 1987
Falk, H.
Quellen des Pañcatantra, Wiesbaden 1978
Soma I and II, Bulletin of the School of Oriental and African Studies 52, 1989
Falkenstein, A.
Das Sumerische, Handbuch der Orientalistik, Leiden 1959
Der Mythos von Inannas Gang zur Unterwelt, FS W. Caskel, Leiden 1968
Feldhaus, F.M.
Die Technik der Antike und des Mittelalters, Hildesheim 1971
Fleet, J.F.
The Kaliyuga Era of B.C. 3102, JRAS 1911

Franke-Vogt, Ute
Die Glyptik aus Mohenjo-Daro, Mainz 1991
Frankfort, H.
Cylinder Seals, London 1937
Frawley, D.
Wisdom of the Ancient Seers, Delhi 1994
Gadd, C.J.
Seals of Ancient Indian Style found at Ur,
Proceedings of the British Academy, London 1932
Gail, A.
On the Beginning of Figurative Representation in Indian Art,
in: South Asian Archaeology, Stuttgart 1993
Geldner, K.F.
Der Rig-Veda, Massachussetts 1957
Geldner, K.F./Pischel, R.
Vedische Studien I-III, Stuttgart 1889-1901
Gesenius, Wilhelm
Handwörterbuch über das Alte Testament, Berlin 1962
Gheraṇḍa Saṃhitā
with English translation ed. by R.B.S. Chandra Vasu, Delhi 1975
Göbl, Robert
Dokumente zur Geschichte der iranischen Hunnen in Baktrien
und Indien, Wiesbaden 1967
Götz, H.
Indien, Fünf Jahrtausende indischer Kunst, Baden-Baden 1960
Gonda, J.
The so-called secular, humorous and satirical hymns of the Ṛg-Veda,
in: Orientalia Neerlandica, Leiden 1948
Vedic Literature, Wiesbaden 1975
Grassmann, H.
Wörterbuch zum Rig-Veda Wiesbaden 51976
Gundel, H.G.
Der alte Vordere Orient, in: R. Elze/K. Repgen,
Studienbuch Geschichte, Stuttgart 1974
Haarmann, H.
Universalgeschichte der Schrift, Frankfurt 1990
Hale, W. E.
Asura in Early Vedic Religion, Delhi 1986
Haṭha Yoga Pradīpikā
with English translation ed. by P.Sinh, Delhi ^{2}1975
Haussig, H.W. (ed.)
Wörterbuch der Mythologie, Stuttgart 1984

Heidel, M.
The Meaning of Mummu in Akkadian literature, JNES VII 1948
Heimpel, W.
Das untere Meer, ZA 77 (1987)
Tierbilder in der sumerischen Literatur, Rom 1968
Herer, J.
Hanf, Frankfurt 1993
Hertel, J.
Rathaspṛś oder rathaspṛh, Indogerm. Forschungen XXXI
Tantrākhyāyika, Darmstadt ²1970
Hillebrandt, A.
Das Altindische Neu- und Vollmondsopfer, Jena 1879
Vedische Mythologie, reprint Hildesheim 1965
Hiltebeitel, A.
The so-called Proto-Śiva Seal from Mohenjo Daro, Anthropos 73,1978

Rāma and Gilgameš, History of Religions 19,1980
Hinze, O.M.,
Tantra Vidya, Freiburg 1983
Höfler, O.
Zwei Grundkräfte im Wodankult, Antiquitates Indogermanicae, Innsbruck 1974
Hoffmann, K.
Der Injunktiv im Ṛg-Veda, Heidelberg 1967
Hüttner, J.Chr.
Die Gesetze des Manu, Husum 1981
Humbach, H.
Methodologische Variationen zur arischen Religionsgeschichte, Antiquitates Indogermanicae, Innsbruck 1974
Jacobi, H.
Über das Alter des Rig-Veda, Kleine Schriften, Wiesbaden 1970
Jacobsen, T.
The Treasures of Darkness, New Haven 1976
Jansen, M.
Die Indus-Kultur, Köln 1986
Non-contemporaneity of the contemporaneous in the Indus Culture, in: G. Possehl (ed.), South Asian Archaeology Studies, Oxford 1992
Janssen, H.P.M.
On the Origin and Development of the so-called Lajjā Gaurī in: South Asian Archaeology, Stuttgart 1993
Jensen, P.
Die Kosmologie der Babylonier, Berlin 1890/1974

Jha, N.
Vedic Glossary on Indus Seals, Varanasi 1996
Jothimuththu, P.
A Guide to Tamil, Madras 1965
Jones, W.
On the Indian Game of Chess, Asiatic Researches, Calcutta 1788/90
Joshi, J.P./Parpola, A.
Corpus of Indus Seals and Inscriptions I, Helsinki 1987
Keel, O.
Das Hohelied, Zürich 1986
Keith, A.B.
Rig-Veda Brahmanas, New Delhi [3]1981
Keith, A.B./Macdonell, A.
Vedic Index of Names and Subjects, London 1912
Kenoyer, J.K. (ed.)
From Sumer to Meluhha, Madison 1994
Around the Indus in 90 Slides,
www.harappa.com/indus/90.html, Harappa 1996
Kenoyer, J.K./Meadow, R.H.
Harappa excavations 1993: The city wall and inscribed materials, in: South Asian Archaeology, Helsinki 1994
Kjærum, P.
Failaka/Dilmun, The Second Millenium Settlements, Aarhus 1983
Knox, R.
A new Indus Valley cylinder seal in: South Asian Archaeology, Helsinki 1994
Kosambi, D.D.
Ancient India, New York 1965
Myth and Reality, Bombay [3]1992
Koskenniemi, S./Parpola, A./S.
A Concordance to the Indus Inscriptions, Helsinki 1973
Koskenniemi, S./Parpola, A.
A Concordance to the Texts in the Indus Script, Helsinki 1982
Kramrisch, S.
Indische Kunst, Köln 1965
Kubitscheck, W.
Grundriß der antiken Zeitrechnung, München 1927
Lahiri, A.K.
Vedic Vṛtra, Delhi 1984
Lal, B.B.
Antecedents of the Signs used in the Indus Script, in: G. Possehl, South Asian Archaeology Studies, Oxford 1992

Langdon, S.
The Indus Script, in: J. Marshall, Mohenjodaro and the Indus Civilization, London 1931
Lengjel, L.
Das geheime Wissen der Kelten, Freiburg ²1981
Levi, S.
La Doctrine du Sacrifice dans les Brahmana, Paris 1966
Levitt, S.
Chess - Its South Asian Origin and Meaning,
Annals of the Bhandakar Research Institute, Poona 1993
Lingat, R.
The Classical Law of India, Berkeley 1973
Macdonnell, A.
Vedic Mythology, Straßburg 1898, reprint New Delhi 1981
Mackay, E.J.H.
Further Excavations at Mohenjo Dharo, New Delhi 1937
Chanhu Dharo Excavations, New Haven 1934
Majumdar, R.C.
Northern India during AD 650-750, in: The History and Culture of the Indian People, Vol. II, Bombay ²1962
Mahadevan, I.
Recent Advances in the Study of the Indus Script, Purātattva 9, 1973
The Indus Script, Bombay 1977
The Sacred Filter Standard Facing the Unicorn,
in: South Asian Archaeology, Helsinki 1994
Marshall, J. (ed.)
Mohenjodaro and the Indus Civilization, London 1931
Maßmann, H.J.
Geschichte des mittelalterlichen Schachspiels,
Quedlinburg 1839 (reprint Leipzig 1983)
Mayrhofer, M.
Kurzgefaßtes Wörterbuch des Altindischen, Heidelberg 1963
Handbuch des Pāli, Heidelberg 1951
Métraux, A.
Ethnologa of Easter Island, Honolulu 1940
Meyer, J.J.
Trilogie altindischer Mächte und Feste der Vegetation, Zürich 1937
Misra, S.S.
The Aryan Problem, Delhi 1992
Mode, H.
Das Frühe Indien, Stuttgart 1959
Monier-Williams, M.
A Sanskrit-English Dictionary, Delhi 1990 (reprint)

Moreau, J.
Die Welt der Kelten, Suttgart 1958
Nissen, H.J.
Frühe Hochkulturen im Nahen und Mittleren Osten, in: Vergessene Städte am Indus, Aachen 1987
Oberhuber, K.
Der Kyklop Polyphem in altorientalischer Sicht, Antiquitates Indogermanicae, Innsbruck 1974
O'Flaherty, W.D.
Woman, Androgynes and Other Mythical Beasts, Chicago 1980
Tales of Sex and Violence - Folklore, Sacrifice, and Danger in the Jaiminīya Brāhmaṇa, Chicago 1985
Oppenheim, A.L.
Mesopotamian Mythology II, Orientalia 4,1948
Parpola, A.
Decipherment of the Proto-Dravidian Inscriptions of the Indus Civilization, Copenhagen 1969
The Sky-Garment, Helsinki 1985
Deciphering the Indus Script, Cambridge 1994
Parpola, A/Shah, S.G.M.
Corpus of Indus Seals and Inscriptions II, Helsinki 1991
Pathak, P.V.
The Lady of Beasts or the Lord of Beast, Purātattva 21, 1990
Pierwszy, T.
Słownik Języka Polskiego, Warszawa 1978
Pisani, V.
Kamm und Scham, in: Antiquitates Indogermanicae, Gedenkschrift für H. Güntert, Innsbruck 1974
Porada, E.
Alt-Iran, Die Kunst in vorislamischer Zeit, Baden-Baden 1962
Possehl, G. (ed.)
South Asian Archaeology Studies, Oxford 1992
Pusalkar, D.
History and Culture of the Indian People, Bombay ^{4}1965
Ṛg-Veda and Harappan Culture, in: Mélanges d'Indianism,Paris 1968
Rau, W.
Zur vedischen Altertumskunde, Mainz 1983
Ranke-Graves, R.
Griechische Mythologie, Hamburg 1960
Ranke-Heinemann, U.
Eunuchen für das Himmelreich, München 1990

Rao, S.R.
Dawn and Devolution of the Indus Civilization, New Delhi 1991
Lothal and the Indus Civilization, London 1973
Rapson, E.J.
Indian Coins, Straßburg 1897
Rawson, Ph.
Tantra, München 1974
Richter-Ushanas, E.
Die Dreigestalt des Seins und ihr androgyner Ursprung, Bremen 1983
Bhagavadgita - Gesang des Erleuchteten, Bremen [5]1998
Das Stillhalten der Fackel - Mandukya-Upanishad
mit Gaudapadas Karika, Bremen [2]1985
Die sakrale Liebe im Alten Orient, im Alten und Neuen Testament
und im Rig-Veda, Bremen 1987
Im Wandel das Bleibende - Acht Upanishads, Bremen [3]1990
Raja Yoga, Patañjali's Yoga Sutra, Bremen [3]1991
Der Fünfte Veda/abridged The Fifth Veda, Bremen 1992
The Symbolic Conception of the Indus Script, Bremen [2]1992
Der Kosmische Mensch und die Indus-Kultur, Bremen 1992
Bhartrihari - Hundert Gedichte über die Liebe und die Entsagung, Bremen 1992
Eros und Mythos, Das Hohelied Salomos, Bremen [2]1996
Two Systems of Symbolic Writing, http://alf.zfn.uni-bremen.de/~ushanas
Die Schrifttafeln der Osterinsel, in print.
Ries, J.
Cross, in: M. Eliade (ed.), Encyclopedia of Religion, New York 1987
Riemenschneider, M.
Die Welt der Hethiter, Stuttgart 1954
Rosenfeld, H.
Die Beziehung der europäischen Spielkarten zum Orient
und zum Urschach, Archiv für Kulturgeschichte 42,1960
Roxburgh, W.
Flora Indica, New Delhi 1971, [1]1832
Sälzle, K.
Tier und Mensch, Gottheit und Dämon, München 1965
Sarianidi, V.
Recent Archaeological Discoveries and the Aryan Problem,
in: South Asian Archaeology, Stuttgart 1993
Scherer, A.
Gestirnnamen bei den indogermanischen Völkern, Heidelberg 1953
Schirra, R.
Im Tal des Indus (television spot), Baden-Baden 1994

Schlingloff, D.
Die Einhorn-Legende, Christiana Albertina AF 1970/71
Schneider, U.
Der Somaraub des Manu, Wiesbaden 1971
Schott, A./Soden von, W.
Das Gilgamesch-Epos, Stuttgart 1980
Schrader, F.O.
Indische Beziehungen eines nordischen Fundes, ZDMG 13, 1934
Shende, N.J.
The Ṛeligion and Philosophy of the Atharva-Veda, Poona 1985
Śiva Saṃhitā,
with English translation ed. by R.B.S. Chandra Vasu, Delhi 1979
Sladek, W.R.
Inanna's Descent to the Netherworld, Ann Arbor 1974
Soden von, W.
Akkadisches Handwörterbuch, Wiesbaden 1965
Speiser, E.
The Epic of Gilgamesh, ANET, Princeton 1955
Śrīmad Vālmīki Rāmāyāṇa with Hindī translation,
ed. by C.D.P. Śarma, Allahabad 1958
Srinivasan, D.
The Indus Valley Proto-Śiva, Archives of Asian Art 29, 1975
Staal, F.
Rules without Meaning, New York 1989
Svāmī Mumukṣānanda
Śrīrāmakṛṣṇākathā Citramālā, Calcutta [3]1992
Székely, E.B.
Das Spiel des Asha, Frankfurt 1981
Taimni, I.K.
The Science of Yoga, Madras 1961
Teuffen, D.H.
Die östliche Welt, Baden-Baden 1962
Thakur, U.
The History of Suicide in India, Delhi 1963
Thieme, P.
Kleine Schriften, Wiesbaden 1971
Thompson, R.C.
The Epic of Gilgameš, Oxford 1930
Tilak, L.B.G.
The Orion or Researches into the Antiquity of the Veda, Poona 1955
Tillner, E.O.
Die Edekal Höhle im Ambukuthy Crack am Battery Rock, Jahrbuch der Gesellschaft für vergleichende Felsbildforschung, Graz 1981/82

Tosi, M.
Die Indus-Zivilisation jenseits des indischen Subkontinents, in: Vergessene Städte am Indus, Aachen 1987
Vats, M.S.
Excavations at Harappa, Calcutta 1940
Velankar, H.D.
The Story of Naciketas, in: Mélanges d'Indianisme, Paris 1968
Vergessene Städte am Indus, Exhibition-Catalogue, Aachen 1987
Vreese, K. de
The Game of Dice in Ancient India (The Vibhītaka Game); Orientalia Neerlandica, Leiden 1948
Waerden, B.J. van der
Das große Jahr und die ewige Wiederkehr, Hermes 80, 1952
Wahl, G.
Der Geist und die Geschichte des Schachspiels, Halle 1798
Wakankar, S.Y.
A Survey of Sanskrit Works on the Game of Chess, Journal of the Oriental Institute 33, Baroda 1986
Wallis, J.
Opera Mathematics I, Oxford 1695 (reprint Hildesheim 1972)
Werner, K.
Yoga and Indian Philosophy, Delhi 1977
Whitney, W.D.
Atharva-Veda Saṃhitā, reprint Delhi 1993
Wilhelm, F.
Indien, Fischer 17, Frankfurt 1967
Wilhelm, G.
Neue Akkadische Gilgameš-Fragmente aus Ḫattuša, ZA 78
Winternitz, M.
Geschichte der indischen Literatur, Leipzig 1908
Woods, J.H.
The Yoga-System of Patañjali, Delhi 1983
Woodroffe, J.
The Garland of Letters, Pondicherry [9]1989
Wolf, W.
Die Welt der Ägypter, Stuttgart 1954
Yardi, M.R.
The Bhagavadgītā as a Synthesis, Poona 1991
Zaehner, R.C.
The Bhagavadgītā, Oxford 1969
Zimmer, H.
Altindisches Leben, Berlin 1879 (reprint Hildesheim 1973)
Zwart, H.J. de
Purūravas and Urvaśī, in: Orientalia Neerlandica, Leiden 1948

SEAL INDEX WITH VEDIC REFERENCE

SIGN-DICTIONARY

This dictionary is based on the sign-list of the Finnish concordance I. Bold numbers indicate singularities. Signs that do not occur in the seals and tablets discussed in the fore-going chapters have been supplemented by examples given at the end. In case of a different meaning of the signs they have been quoted in the dictionary with the number of the seal given in brackets. The list of signs is complete, but the meanings are not. The sign-dictionary is an illustration of the rule that the same sign can have different meanings and different signs the same meaning. That does not mean that there are no identities. But for many signs a variety of equivalents is given. They are related with each other through the pictographic form. This is irritating only for somebody who is not trained in reading a word-script. In many cases it is not easy to find the exact Vedic equivalence and it seems likely that a better rendering will be discovered in the course of the translation of further seals and tablets. Therefore the dictionary has a preliminary character and will have it, as long as a large number of seals has not been excavated.

001  to carry (in the womb), to bring goods (servant), generous, curative (Varuṇa, Dawn, Indra, Lopāmudrā), tribe of the Bharatas 49; 53; 100; 114; 121; 170; priest (1360); follower of Indra (Bharata) (2018); Agni (7037); to work (as messenger) (2134)

002  man, avenger, guard 49; 69 (2)

003  seed-giver and carrier of the two worlds (Viśvarūpa) 132

004  Varuṇa as measuring architect, creator (3254; 3086)

005  = 004; Varuṇa (2242); single god (3086)

006  = 001 benevolent (Urvaśī), take the heart (prostitute), bear the Soma (amṛta), having strong limbs, having many forms (Rudra), Varuṇa, daughter of the sun 44; 58; 68; 117; 172; 250 god(dess) of dice (2751); priest (3480); Mudgalānī (0357)

007  goddess Vāc touching the sky with the tuft of her hair (7142)

008 to carry goods (in a bag) 169

009 having long hairs (woman, bridegroom) 116

010 long-haired (keśī) 134

011 god (Indra), lord, asura (Rudra), goddess (daughter of the sun), car-driver (Purūravas) 42; 49; 69; 105; 170; magician (2083); speakers of the truth (3047); holy (2821)

012 deity, god, goddess, parents (being regarded as divine), man making furrows (Agastya) 46; 99

013 'guardian' (of the world, of the law, of the door), Rudra, Vāstoṣpati (lord of the house), long-haired, friend (of Rudra), warrior, law, truth, form (of the unborn), to guard, to throw (dice), to observe a vow, to urge to speed 42; 69; 109; 132; 133; 138; 168; 173; 206; 224; 249; 250; power (1373); ecstasy (2390)

014 Indra as club-bearer (2448); god (1393)

015 'man' (often following 324), god, husband, son, brahmin, guardian of Soma (Vāyu), friend (of Soma), Parjanya, Yama, owner (of a ship), male personal pronouns 32; 57; 85; 88; 96; 105; 169; 171; 193; 198; 207; 245; 250

016 man with phallus, god (Dakṣa), potent, impotent 85; 88; 126; 224, father (9002)

017 to move, to insert (the virile member) 120; to know the way (2134); to get hundreds of joys (0433)

018 the twin-gods (Aśvins) 118

019 god wandering on the earth in human disguise (Indra) 128

020 ~ 019 god wandering on the earth in human disguise (Indra)

021 man whose foot is bound in a snare 198

022 warding off difficulties (keep them at a distance), wandering seer, walking man 68; 134; 245

023  car-driver (0357)

024  cosmic man, androgyn, enflamed heat (tapas) 38; 109; 249; Virāj (2285)

025  rising up (storm-winds, sati, sattā) 58; defend (5075)

026  exposing the limbs to everybody (Dawn) 155

027  to swear with ten (= three) fingers (2751)

028  man with comb (barber): speaking much or be silent (frog) 250

029  the merchant Nodhas presenting his goods (2366)

030  man/frog invigorated by Parjanya (2351)

031  Varuṇa as measuring magician (2203)

032  Indra cutting down Vṛtra like a tree (3498)

033  wise man, wandering man (Indra), man with measuring line (Varuṇa), to hide (behind a wall) 69; 104; 138

033  man with a staff and a bag: cosmic man 38

034  cosmic man passing on all sides (2285)

035  Varuṇa standing between heaven and earth (4166)

036  Gandharva (rainbow) (3113)

037 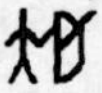 bow-man, archer (Rudra, Indra, Purūravas), Varuṇa (with pure strength) 173; 188; 212

038  man with two bows: divine warrior (Indra; Rudra) 55; 188

039 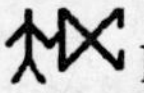 Ṛbhu (divine craftsman) (2088)

040  Viśvārūpa (2475); to pervade the worlds (2595)

041  man with navel, androgyn cosmic man 38

042 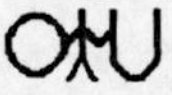 priest appearing as carpenter (3599)

043  man/priest offering Soma, man with phallus 51; 99; 120

044 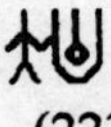 Agastya calling the Soma (0809); priest pressing the Soma (2238)

045  seer who knows the womb/the birth in advance 98

046  dog, pet animal of the hierodules 172

047  (dog-like) gazelle 170

048  composite animal, centaur (Gandharva) 44; 137

049  markhor 41; Asura (9002)

050  claw: to hold tight 248

051  thigh (Urvaśī) 172

052  = 051

053  woman spreading her thighs (Uttānapad) 38

054  aiming at a target (arrow, word), piercing like an arrow (phallus) 168; 170

055  speckled seer (frog) 70

056  = 057

057  seer, poet, teacher, brahmin, muni, man, star, god (Vāyu, Varuṇa, Viṣṇu, Pūṣan, Soma, Gandharva), Purūravas; Urvaśī (with 101), effulgence, mightiful, smooth-running (like a fish in the water), to believe, personal pronoun (of the seer) 41 (2); 57; 65; 85; 94; 110; 112; 134; 136; 171; 174; 184; 194; 198, 207; 214; light (5075); fame (3046); Dawn (2366); pure (2171); eloquent (3327)

058  born in the water (fish = son) 171; saps of the Soma (6022); adorer of the Soma (2340)

059 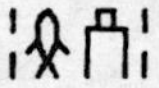 seer (Soma) at the back of the sky covered with water (1373)

060  being in the womb: having various forms, sun at the sky 114; 138; rainbow (the lovely) (2451)

061 seer like a bird in the egg-shell 98

062 = 061

063 god, goddess (Varuṇa, Soma, Vāc), girded with the wind (i.ę. naked) 58; 88; 108; 130; 133; Puruṣa (1362)

064 radiating sun-god (2171)

065 fish with gill (mouth): Varuṇa, Purūravas 56; 138; 167; effulgence of the sky (3113); to move (0600)

066 track of the bird/of the seer (2432)

067 god, seer, light, muni, friend (Mitra), Varuṇa 51; 68; 111; 132; 136; 138; 218; 245; head of somebody (1052)

068 Soma among the stars, radiant being with tiara (Āryan) 57; 128; king of all beings (6021)

069 'bee', fly, eagle, seer, adorer, sweet Soma, goddess Vāc, Yamī, to meditate, to polish, one-eyed, unmanly 34; 68; 70; 97; 111; 129; 136; 156; 168; 171; 173; 245; lover (2417); sacrificial cow (3584); light (6020)

070 dancing seer, beautifully winged bird 72; 108

071 divine man: hero 131; wise, knowing (2477)

072 people (9002)

073 bird (svarga - go to heaven), eagle 173; 248

074 sun-bird (1342)

075 falcon (on the nest), bird in egg-shell (helpless young woman) 130; 173

075 bird (eagle) in the nest 43; 49

076 duck (hierodule) 171

077 bird defending its egg: virgin 185

077 bird of the sky (6023)

078 cakravāka-bird 172

079 eagle (1431)

080 sun-bird 107

081 Dawn awaking the world like a cock (1207)

082 horse, leader of a horse (magician), calf of the year, Soma (ocean), sun, (man with) magical power 33; 45; 59; 111; 169; 171, 185; 218; 244; 247; 248; 249; Asura (2621)

monster (scorpion), opposite of (2821)

083 man with magical power (Agastya) making furrows 46

083 (the sign has to be turned by 90 ° to the right), sun-horse placed at the sky (2500)

084 'crab', bull (well-born), cow, to seize (to kill), to grasp (to understand), to enclose, to separate, to sacrifice 49; 52; 58; 100; 112; 129; 171; to reveal (3113)

085 turn away the eye (2687)

086 touching ape (1052)

087 'bee' or 'eye with lashes', offspring, fertility, to flash up 171; 173; witch (3004); be grateful (2398)

088 hiding ichneumon (0433)

089 to mount the air (Tantric sexual metaphor) (2390)

090 (the sign has to be turned by 90 ° to the left) sleeper (3280)

091 (golden) wings (2451, 2002)

092 to guard (to chase away) (1544)

093 club (1151)

094 Soma-twig 110, to protect (2038)

095 tree (of Soma), stalk, to draw (up), to stand, to exist, to ask 45; 57; 107; 110; 132; 138; friend (2451); win the friendship (3047); to awake (1207); to throw (6047); wrong (2805)

096 hand, tree, pillar, tribe, man, god, husband, centaur, bull, to drink, to support, to stand, to exist, to guard (guardian), to put on, to hold up, to push, to milk, to be gracious 49; 51; 56; 97; 102; 105; 120 (2); 129; 135 (2); 173; 183; 198; 226; 247; friend (6022); to shot (2018); to bring forth (5023); withstand (5075); to watch (6023)

097 pillar (man) and comb (woman): androgyn 131

098 to stand and to move 53

099 thornless, straight way (2710)

100 pot painted with flowers, thorny or blossoming flower 104; 184; 188; 198; bold (7122)

101 'banner', thunderbolt, lightning, skilful, donation, Urvaśī (with 057) 41; 49; 71; 171 (2); 173; Pūṣan (0145); magic power (3254); measuring line (3254); mistress full of power (3584)

102 the goddess Vāc (2431)

103 measuring Varuṇa (2038)

104 Urvaśī, heaven and earth 170; 244; pole of sacrifice (1360)

105 Apsaras and Gandharvas 134

106 'comb, teeth', woman, goddess (Vāc, Dawn), Apsaras (water-woman, Urvaśī), Lopāmudrā, witch, womb, earth, tuft of hair, things desired, channel for the dice, sacrificial mound (vedi), night, speech, butter, cow, belt, time, resoluteness, having barbs, pregnant, lovely, foolish, dangerous, not being, to take across, female pronoun 54 (3); 68 (2); 97; 102 (2); 105 (4); 112; 120; 137; 168 (2); 172; 184; 195; 196; 198; 204; 224; 247 (3); 249; 250; dislike (7122); to milk (2727)

107 roost, to carry 107; 133; to rise from the dark (3573); to stand (0600)

108 barley (6021)

109 golden bow (of Soma) in the pressing boards (2621)

110 flower (woman), dancing girl 104; 112

111 woman spreading her thighs like a flower its petals (5023)

112 Dawn following the path (of the truth) (2597)

113 flower and pillar (male and female) 42

114 cord between the male and female aspect of the world (2246)

115 filled stalk (Soma), long life (with cup-sign) 132; 171; seed-giver (1067); extract the thread (2597)

116 cord stretched through the midst of creation (2093)

117 (cosmic) tree, lord of the trees (Soma), standing (trunk) and moving (leaves) 52; 188; 206

118 heart 224 (2), everything (2049)

119 Agni, Agastya, tree, peg 46 (2); 98; 112

120 Agastya, Soma plant 131; 137; 207; 212

121 tree on a hill: Agastya (aga-sthya) 48

122 pillar, flower-bud 67; 130

123 channel for throwing the dice 224

124 suitor 116

125 flower-bud (dice) of the vibhītaka tree (terminalia) 45; Dawn (5075)

126 to grasp a flower-bud (Prajāpati, Purūravas) 107; 169

127 go ahead, be the first, be like, first personal pronoun 43; 51; 55; 65; 71; 99; 106; 108; 112; 114; 136; 168; 183; 247, morning (3584); to win (2070); highest (2070); newly (2264); some (6047)

128 one, thirteenth (month), drop of Soma (of poison, of honey), eye (of the die), first personal pronoun, negation particle 42; 44; 45 (2); 57; 114; 128; 135 (2); 138 (2); 155; 173; 183; 198; 218; 224; rock (4141); rain (6021)

129 two, both, or (possibilities, entities, persons, things), drops of Soma, dew, eyes (to look), seed, trace, to distribute, together with, only, above (sky, divine, venerable), prefix, demonstrative and personal pronoun 44; 56; 57 (3); 69; 70 (2); 96; 100; 102; 104; 111; 112; 114; 128; 130; 134; 135 (2); 136 (2); 168 (2); 171; 173; 188; 198 (2); 206; 207; 224; to cut off (1052); eagle (2018); let swell (2038); mighty (3046)

130 three (worlds, Asuras, Ṛbhus), seed, eyes (of the die) 41; 51; 94; 114; 130; 172; 193; 224; 249

131 Soma-drops, children and grandchildren 56; 102; 224; 226

132 seed, stars, tribes, many 53; 106; 135; rain (1321); creature (6023); wolf and thief (5075); world (1207)

133 six (worlds, days) 45; 58; 67; 69; 105; height and depths (5075); heaven and earth (7027); many (hundreds) (8451)

134 seven (streams, sons) 49; 114

135 seven (women) 97

136 seed (2267)

137 Navagvas (nine seers) (3047)

138 ten sons (3734)

139 vertebra of a snake 53; chair (7080)

140 = 139 (7080)

141 drive away, dispel (5075)

142 vertebrae of a snake 53

143 seven places of the earth (2355)

144 nine planets (3693)

145 pert girl (2224)

146 = 130

147 drop, eye (1616)

148 plaits (1130)

149 seed (0217)

150 twelve (months), year, many (thousand) 57; 70; 249; 250

151 having eyes, feet, mouths on all sides (3086)

152 snake, stalk, bridge, phallus, corpse (to sleep), stream, river, to live, one (= hundred), third personal pronoun, negation (without) 49; 52; 53; 67; 97; 100; 134; 137; 155; 206; night (5075); to be born (7016); quick (2134)

153 two (things, persons), streams (of Soma), winds, wood, pressing boards, path, places (Gandhāra), earth, Purūravas (with 373), to hold together, to pervade, to be higher, to cross, to spread, negation 41; 49; 57; 67; 68 (2); 71; 72; 95; 105; 112; 114; 126; 130 (2); 134; 168; 172; 173; 196; 212; 250; fire-wood (2049); back (2455); space (5075); to forgive (make smooth) (0809); to pervade (6024); to cut off (2465); always (2044); everywhere (6024)

154 run around (the pressing boards) 119

155 winds (mind), three heroes, rivers, men (fingers), virile members, threefold (law), rain, Trita, thrice, plurality 58; 100; 128; 130; 131 (2); 133; 135; 138; 167; 170; 188; 198; 244; to cross (1544); to search much (7037); brazen (2821); great (0108); near (1400)

156 three steps, house (7102)

157 finger pointing to heaven and earth (2617)

158 four (fingers); streams of Soma or rain, erect (the virile members), to move up and down 32; 107; 120

159 streams of water, five tribes, five reins 51; 69; 71; 196

159 joined (horses) 71

160 to cross (the ocean), earth (of Chanhu Daro) 51; 114; 142

161 harness the broad (car) (3573)

162 to turn to 132; son (2265; 6208)

163 seven streams (2070)

164 to draw (the bow), cast (the die) 107; 224 (6), broad (0104); sky (7080)

165 new pot (2049)

166 = 170

167 rainbow (2417)

168 rainbow (1400)

169 crescent of the moon (new-born child), (reddish) moon, Soma, quarter, ecstasy 44; 51; 57; 66; 106; 116; 133; 198; womb (2617); poison in the cup (3004); all the gods (Soma-drinkers) (2043)

170 ~ 169; cutting the thread of the seer (moon) 109; Soma (4141)

171 long-haired (2656)

172 = 152

173 long-haired (3004)

174 pressed Soma (2238)

175 running moon 224

176 ship 168; forge (in the fire-plate) (2002)

177 forge together (in a fire-plate) (2002)

178 rising sun (2031)

179 wool, stream (of Soma), snakes (riches) 40; 108; to be in the grip of somebody (7122)

179 stream, hair, top of the tongue, sky, double wall, all the worlds 41; 49; 51; 68; 70; 112; to take a seat (2821)

180 tooth in the mouth, running drop (of Soma) 49; 100

181 heaven and earth, rainbow, Gandharva, Vena (beloved), heavenly 135; 198; 206; 224 (cf. 349)

182 sacrificial mound (vedi) 188

183 golden veil, embracing belt 128; 207

184 crescent of the moon, Asura, veil 32; unveil (9002)

185 wind (2233)

186 dice-board 45

187 hand with fingers 71; (desire for the) daughter (2316)

188 father of the sky desiring his daughter (2267)

189 swelling breast (1046)

190 'bow' (rightful ruler, guardian; Asura), female genitals, (to) cause, everywhere 55; 107; 137; 168; mortal (nomad) (2390); mistress full of power (3573); artful (3327)

191 magic of the dice (7122)

192 legs spread apart, to go, to go to heaven (enthusiastic), horn 38; 52; 53; 207

193 = 152

194 = 192 to evade 98

195 hill with cloud 58

196 field and mountain (1400)

197 to measure out, to flash up (lightning), to stand, to go (to look) around, fleeting 58; 110; 168; 218; 249

198 highest step at the sky (2044)

199 creeper 207

200 snakelike way 213

201 two snakelike ways (1102)

202 thread 69

203 thread, (hood of) snake, wool, first-born of the snakes (Vṛtra), wind, reed (rod), father-in-law (fore-father), magical power, Kuṇḍalinī 41; 49; 55; 56; 69; 105; 168; 169; 170; virgin (3047)

204 fire-sticks: to burn 224 (2); stretch out (2018)

205 (~ 192 and 204) fire-sticks (Agni), corner (inside), to go 68; 114; 128; 212; to extend (1373)

206 to fall on the knee (to pray, to ask) (1470)

207 safety device (2629)

208 coat of mail: mighty power 57

209 to follow, be occupied, to rise, to draw up, female personal pronoun 100; 169; 171; 207; 213, voluptuous one (8451); virgin (1130); to set (3693)

210 'nose', 'beak', male organ (seed-giver), witch (Apsaras), colour (caste), weapon, to incite, greedy 42; 46; 53; 102; 106; 121; 134; 138; impulse (1067); fixed place (1108); man (2398); light (3427); Indra (3498); effulgence (2656); face (= nose) (2475)

211 to look down (6023)

212 'step' (~ 192), to creep near, to divide, to go, to jump, thigh 107; 114; 129; 172; to separate (6047)

213 sitting ape, Vr̥ṣākapi, Dāsa 104; 126; 128, 188

214 grasping ape (2191)

215 = 216

216 gods drinking from the fire 57; to spend power (hill) (3046)

217 (~ 212; 218) to run for (to choose), having many forms (like a bag) 53; 134; path of the truth (2477)

218 (~ 212) Agni, to assault (violate), wandering soul (to be burnt) 104; 129; 137,198

219 horn: dice-box 224

220 domestic Agni (fire under a roof) 198

221 domestic Agni during the night (1274)

222 = 221 (2134)

223 to pour out (0435)
224 firm (hill) (3736)
225 mountains (1343); firm (1130)
226 teeth 51
227 'lance', (spear of the) Maruts, Indra, pillar, phallus, power, to dismiss, to urge, to carve, to write, to mount, to stay, to insert, to guard, to protect, to awake, far-reaching, clear 58; 66; 94; 112; 130; 132; 135; 155; 167; 183; 198; 218; Dāsa (phallus-worshipper) (1400); husband (1046); law (1321); to ejaculate (2617); to excel (1362); to flow (3254); strong (3046)
228 Uttānapad, she, who spreads her legs apart (for giving birth), Aditi 85; 88; to be grateful (1321)
229 speed (wings of a wind-mill), sky in cohabitation with the earth 98; 109; mount the car (of the sky) (0144)
230 sky in cohabitation with the earth 142
231 pointing to heaven and earth (2264)
232 drum of the strong men (the winds) (2727)
233 harmful cast of the die (7122)
having two wings: eagle (2018)
234 (wearing) ornaments: woman, intoxicated muni 133; 172
235 to separate 142; mother (3599)
236 to separate and to cohabit 143, to measure out (0104)
237 to measure out by the sun 55
238 (= 228) woman, womb (having manifold progeny), resistance, to incite, to create, to enclose (Varuṇa, Aditi), to seize (cf. 084), to separate 58; 85; 88; 99; 112; 114; 130; 136; 204
239 to bring forth 171
240 cosmic egg, egg born by the mother-goddess 88
241 after it was born (cosmic egg) it became the only lord of the universe (2151)

242 = 238

243 touch the vulva 126

244 Parśu (rib) (0108)

245 plough with the hand, ship (with oars), anoint with magical power 38; 107; 195

246 to fight, to take revenge 49

246 to reach, to seize, (all) directions 51; 131; 245

247 eight sons of Aditi (the planets) (1393)

248 Uttānapad (spreading the leg), lover (Vasiṣṭha) 38; 173

249 living in the house (3407)

250 conjoined halves (of heaven and earth) 67; pathfinder (6022)

251 rain like honey falling (from the sky) through the guardians of the way/the truth (0144)

252 ~ 247; eight sons in the body of Aditi (2083)

253 ruler (3427)

254 guardian of the road (mountain) putting on a cloud (0104)

255 to hold at the top (3721)

256 yoked (car) 41

257 flagstaff (flag drapsa caus. from drā, to move), joy (of the New Year) 168

258 six worlds (7142); world (four directions) (1536)

259 'crossing', path, town, earth, universe, all 58; 107; 111; 114; 132; assembly (meeting) (3427)

260 (~ 259) town = queen (of the country); car of the sun 108; 247; universe (1102)

261 highest step (of Viṣṇu) standing at the sky (2535)

262 ten fingers of the two arms (2340)

263 = 289 (9002)

264 car of the sun (3738)

265 sieve (3713)

266 dice, everything 45; 67

266 field of sacrifice, oblong die, day 100; 224; 247; earth (4166)

267 skin of light (3296)

268 pressing boards 41

269 Soma standard, lunar mansion, sacrifice, immortality, activity, meadow 66; 88; 96; 112; 114; 183 (2)

270 being born in a pot on the place of sacrifice (2265)

271 safety device (1452)

272 pressing board (1444)

273 'net', pressing board, sieve, sacred action (to spin), ocean, melted butter, day and night, sky, cloud, rain, blinking of the eyes (retina), here and there 70 (2); 72; 129; 137 (3); 138; 206 (2); 249 (2); rib (0108); earth (6023); standard (2088)

274 place (of Manu, of the sacrifice), pressing boards, pressing stones, sieve for purifying the Soma, third sky of sacrifice 130; 173 (2); 218; 246; universe (5023); abundant (2018); back of the desirable (2455); to unite (7016), to hold tight (8451)

275 homestead 42

275 place, sieve (= 274), design 34; 168

276 house, castle (with 385) 97 (2); 198

277 brick-work, fire-sticks 169

278 head (~ 292) 51

belly (1343)

butter-face (1130)

279  'field', earth (place of sacrifice), creation, law, truth, cloth (house), stable, Ādityas 44; 56; 57; 121 (2); 135; 168; 245; car (2049); body (2390); hide (3480); right (2805); everything (1052)

280  humidity, phallus with seed (fertility) 38; 119

281  place the earth under the sun like a hide (2331)

282  sky (1391)

283  amulet (equal to gold), immortality (gained by the script), breast ornament (to rule) 42; 53; 72; 198; innermost heart (0809); hide (3069); true power (3599); true order (6120); golden/brazen (7080)

284  hammer (weapon of Indra) 52; jointly (3002)

285  banner (3130)

286 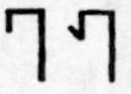 shadoof (with a hook), look down, draw from the water 119; 134; 171; to protect the step (0600); to water the earth (6021)

287  draw the seed up (4057)

288  draw the seed up (2118)

289  cut off the bald head (2465); destroyer (9002)

290  head (of the father) of the world (2595)

291  (decapitated) head, lord, Vasiṣṭha, Purūravas, Mitra and Varuṇa, to supersede 90; 97; 138; 170; 208; the first (2366)

292  tower, top (of the tower), son (the highest aim), upside 90; 212; law (2264); cow-shed (2597)

293  to rise from the dark (3584)

294  Soma at the top of the sky (2355)

295  (Soma) placed in the vat by the ten fingers (2530)

296 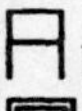 block, obstacle (evil) 198

297  back of the sky (2185)

298  beauty (curtain), (antagonistic) power 120 (2)

299 hold together the two worlds, to speak together 132; 171; to proclaim (1342)

300 hard bed (keep awake), safety device, ladder (to mount) 45; 57; 112; 133

301 to protect (0600), to solve the snare (0158)

302 to forge together (9501)

303 ichneumon (8451)

304 earth, hide, food 55; 58; 114; 204

305 earth as a hide (2242)

306 loom 45, offering (0443)

307 offering mixed with butter (0443)

308 measure out (3069)

309 back of the Dawn, kuśa-grass 129; ear-field (2191); womb of the good deed (6047)

310 wave of the ocean (receptacle of water) (2455)

311 two world-halves, two girls (1582), to make friendship, to have pity (7122)

312 Soma (in the vat) (2018)

313 (often following a number-sign) cup, vessel, jar (with Soma), draught (of Soma, of nectar), phallus (Indra), being, fertility, river-bed, born in the womb (child), to cry, to carry (in the womb) 49 (3); 54; 67 (2); 68; 71; 95; 100; 107; 120; earth (1206)

314 stem of a tree with seed drawn upwards (image of ūrdhvaretas) 212

river with water 32; heaven with stars (1206)

315 the three worlds 196; seed in a vessel (6208); drop falling in the womb (3002); three vats (2448)

316 Soma running down, fluids of the womb 112; 198

317 lovely (vulva) (1403)

318 'mortar' for pressing Soma, Soma, Soma-ritual (law), Soma-standard, Soma-stalk, Soma-vat, cloth of Soma, honey, gift of immortality, woman, man and woman in cohabitation, Varuṇa, to press the Soma, to unite, to squeeze, to sacrifice, enjoy, generous 42; 53; 55; 56; 57; 67; 72; 100; 106; 112; 118; 128; 130; 132 (2); 135; 138; 168; 198; happiness and pain of the womb (0108), yo-jana (distance to travel by a carriage in one day) (1400); juvenile waters (1544); ocean (3254); garment for the Soma (2621); priest (3480)

319 four naves (of the Soma-standard) 68

320 phallus: yearning 54; father (6047)

321 breast ornament, measure out the earth 99; 105; earth (3069); concealed (2432)

322 pressing stone (1452), Agni growing in his own house (6120)

323 to carry in the womb (0145)

324 'cup', god, goddess, lord, master, father, pot, vessel, vat, sky, phallus, vulva, womb, (swelling) udder, heart, ship (of the ritual), life, giver of treasures, draught of immortality, daughter of the sun, sun, well-seeded bull, mare, cow, highest name, lovely names, (magic, creative) power, strength, share of Soma, friend, husband, abyss, Kuṇḍalinī, Vāc, Viśvakarman, Soma, Indra, Agni, Varuṇa, Mitra, Śiva, Asura(ship), Rudra, Viśvarūpa, Gandharva, to be, to stand, to promote, to rule, to wish, to adore, to create, to generate, fill with desire, helpful, fit for men, divine, everything, whole, all, best, personal pronoun (male and female)
34; 40; 41; 42 (2); 46; 49 (3); 50; 55; 56 (2); 57 (3); 58; 67; 68 (2); 69; 70; 71; 85; 88; 94; 96 (2); 97 (2); 98; 99; 104; 105; 106 (2); 107; 108; 111 (2); 112 (3); 114 (3); 119; 126; 128 (2); 129;

130; 131; 132 (2); 133; 134 (2); 135 (2); 136; 137 (2); 138; 143; 155; 168 (2); 169; 170 (2); 171 (2); 172 (4); 173; 193 (2); 198; 207; 212; 218; 245; 246 (3); 247; truth (3047); wrath (7122); guardian in the highest heaven (2246); rule (1130); give milk (1342); reborn (2366); to surpass (1151); grateful (0144)

325  hair of a horse-tail (Indra), Soma running in the vat, sieve, seed and womb, youth (Urvaśī), female wolf, fecundate the womb (to increase, to sow), female personal pronoun 49 (2); 51; 57; 106; 112; 121 (2); 142; 169; 170; 172; 198; virgin (6208); womb of the true order (0158); fragrant garment (3113); to bring forth (1536); stainless (6022)

326  Dakṣa (creator), (primordial) being, god (Rudra, Indra); Asura 85; 88; 107; track of the sun (1342); Vaiśvānara (the sun) (2185)

327  Viśvarūpa (god who has three bellies, three udders and three faces), goddess carrying three gods in her womb 68; 130; Varuṇa (3069)

327  births of the gods, drops of rain 32 (cf. 314); 44; 171; Viśvakarman (0156)

328  Varuṇa's pot turned upside down 0453, 0441

329  Urvaśī united with Purūravas 171

330  divine womb (2662)

331 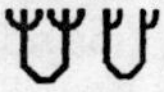 (mostly preceding 324) womb (swelling), cup (with poison), fertile (rich in seed), well, body (limb), two hands put together (to desire, to understand, to cry), female self 46; 57; 68; 111; 119; 129; 135; 136; 170; 171; joy (8451); cow (1342); be afar (separated) (1400); to colour (in a pot) (1582); to turn away (2687)

332 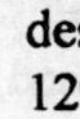 forbidden womb (2465)

333 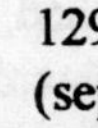 to lick the butter (1108)

334  udder of the womb (2432)

335 to carry the gods (in the womb) (5054)

336 well-ruling king (0443)

337 stars fastened at the sky (3032)

338 queen of the sky (2431)

339 pillar of the divine chair (1320)

340 covering of the two plates (heaven and earth) (1262)

341 sitting in the upper part of the sky (1548)

342 rainbow, (path of the) sun, vastness, ocean 102; 218; cross the air (3296)

343 Dawn bringing the sun (6020)

344 sun going around the sky, far-reaching protection, halves of the world 106; 132 (2)

345 (~ 344) conjoined halves of the world 67, plates of heaven and earth (2171)

346 balance, balanced (wise) 54

347 car, ship 41; 51; 71; 195

348 drops of Soma 51

349 heaven and earth (in cohabitation), the worlds, quarters of the sky, rush together, to be bent (like heaven and earth) 49; 51; 69; 105; 114; 130; 133; 170; 212; creation (2246); vastness of the space (6024)

350 sweet drops of rain falling from the sky on the earth (2398, 1321)

351 pointing to heaven and earth (2805)

352 seed of the sky, three heavens and three earths 107; 129

353 bubbles, having three bellies (Viśvarūpa) 54; 132

354 bound to the sacrificial post (Śunaḥśepa) 119

355 aim 107; earth (0104)

356 earth (peoples), womb 52; 53; 142

357 to give birth to twenty children at once (2615)

358 to excel the earth by the width of ten fingers (1362)

359 to radiate (2455)

360 sun with rays, vulva 105; 119

361 club (2584)

362 daughter of the sky (1360)

363 eye, bosom, wheel 172 (2); 193 (2); 198; circle (2185)

364 swelling breast (1349)

365 navel, bosom, (angry, wise) eye 100; 172; 173; 188

366 forbidden womb 104, plate (7027)

367 head and navel 99

368 water of the ocean 196

369 die (7122)

370 breast 112; place (1400)

371 Mātariśvan (2043)

372 night (6024)

373 king, king of the gods (Indra), Mitra and Varuṇa, Asura, Purūravas, queen, hero, sun, wheel, rim with spokes, to rule 49; 51; 52; 53; 96; 113; 114; 136 (2); 138; 169; 173, 198; mightiful (1444)

374 two ways of the sun going round the earth (2261)

375 Puruṣa (2554)

376 splendour (1151)

377  midst of the sky, to dwell 114; 246; place of the good deed (0158); human habitation (3573)

378  bottomless space (2435)

379  sun at the sky, truth, 'all-shaped' car of the sun-daughter, sun-like one who has sacrificed these worlds 57; 66; 183

380  womb, mouth, sun, truth, long-haired, to speak 32; 69; 70; 100; 109; 111; 135; 189; time (2687); world (1274)

380  'rhombus', womb, breast ornament, ocean, sun, mouth (Purūravas), earth, Dawn, Mitra, whole 32; 51; 66; 95; 112; 134; 135; 138; 168; 195; 212; 247; Māna (father of Agastya) (2265); world (2083); woman (2597); to embrace closely (8451); unimpaired (0158)

381  womb (3327)

382  to pervade heaven (3488)

383  under the sun (3480)

384  light of the sun (6022)

385  'womb with hand', flower, vulva (to let bloom), iron wall 46; 97; 98; be at rest (7122)

386  bottomless space 212; swelling womb (2398)

387  sap of Soma churned by the air (Vāyu) 134

388  cosmic tree in the bottomless space 213

389  head of the cow (7037)

390  bull (Indra) (3046)

391  to separate the earth 0262

392  Vasiṣṭha (1183)

393  hammer in the house (Purūravas) 170

394  Vṛtrahan, killer of Vṛtra (Indra), guardian, Ṛbhu, to create, to make, to measure out the earth, to milk (the sky), to stem apart, to rule (the world), to be limited (to a circle) 49; 53; 56; 58; 69; 99; 107; 111 (2); 138, 193; 212; 247; Tvaṣṭṛ (0145); midst of the fountain (2432); air over the trees (4141); Dawn (2477); magic power (3254); to cover the earth (1362); to know (everything) (2477); to want (2727)

 vulva 41

395  being distributed on many places (1332)

396  broken (counted as a sign)

397  illegible (counted as a sign)

Examples

0104 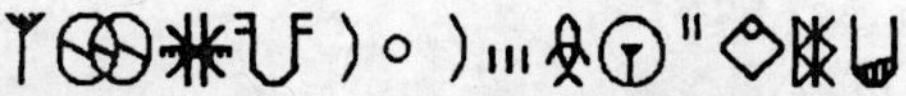 V.85.1,4

Who has measured out (2) the earth (1) through the sun (3) and placed the sun (5) at the sky (4), Varuṇa (6) waters (7) the broad (8) earth (9) and the sky (10), and when he wants milk (11), the mountains/guardians of the road (12) put on a cloud (12) and the winds (13), the mighty men (14), arise (14).

0108  X.86.23

Parśu (4), the rib (2,3), the daughter (6) of Manu (5), gave birth to twenty children (1) at once (1); great (8) happiness (7) she felt, (though) pain (7) came (9) to her womb (7) (through the ape) (10).

0144 unicorn  V.63.1

Guardians of the way/the truth (1), you mount the car (3) in the highest heaven (2); for him, to whom you are grateful (7), Mitra and Varuṇa (4, 5), the rain (1) flows down from the sky like honey (1).

0145 unicorn  X.125.2

I carry in my womb (1) the swelling Soma (2), Tvaṣṭṛ (3), Pūṣan (4) and Bhaga (5).

0156 unicorn  X.81.2
What was the fundament (1) and what was the pillar (1), and how was it erected (1), how combined (1), when Viśvakarman (2) created (3) the earth (4)?

0158 unicorn  X.85.24
I solve (1) you from Varuṇa's (1) snare (1), with which the dear Savitṛ (2) has bound you (1); in the womb of the true order (3), at the place of the good deed (4), I deliver you unimpaired (5) to the husband (6).

0217 unicorn  VII.33.13
Through the moon-like Urvaśī (1,2) the gods (3) (Mitra and Varuṇa) lost their seed (4) in a vessel (3), from that vessel (7) Agastya (5), was born (6).

0262 unicorn  V.85.1
Who has separated the earth (1) and placed it at the sky (2) under the sun (3), is Varuṇa (4), the king of the universe (4).

0357  X.102.2
The woman (3) Mudgalānī (2) was the car-driver (1) in the race (4) for the cows (5).

0433 two rhinos 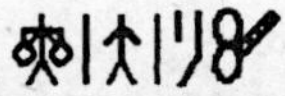 I.126.6
Who hides herself like (2) a female ichneumon (1), the voluptuous (4) one gives me hundreds of joys (3).

0435 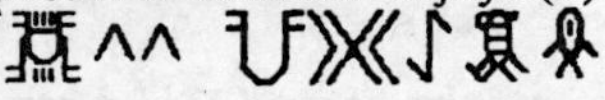 V.85.3,5
I will sing of Varuṇa's (1) great magic power (2), with it as measuring line (3) he has measured out the earth (4) through the sun (5).
He has poured out (6) in the vessel cast upside down (7) the sky, the earth and the intermediate space (7).

0441  V.85.2,3
By his magic power (4) Varuṇa (2) has expanded the air (1) above the trees (3).
He has poured out in the vessel cast upside down the sky, the earth and the intermediate space (5).

0443 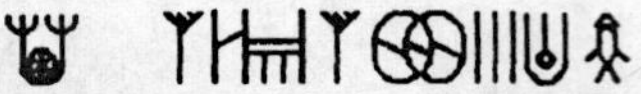 III.59.1,4

Mitra (1), (who calls himself friend), unifies (2) mankind (3), Mitra bears (5) heaven and earth (4), Mitra give (7) the offering mixed with butter (6); Mitra is the well-ruling king (7).

[On tablet 1595 the separate sign is replaced by the motif of an hare-like antelope that is an image of the well-ruling king.]

0600 zebu 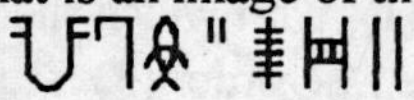 I.159.3

You (heaven and earth) (1) protect (2) the truth (2), you preserve (2) all what stands (3) and (4) moves (5) and you protect the step (6) of a truthful son (7).

0809 bracelet 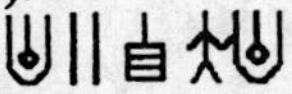 I.179.5

I directly call (1) the Soma (1) drunken with my innermost heart (2), the wrong we did (4), he may forgive us (3).

1046 unicorn 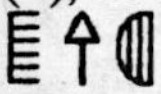 X.102.11

By the swelling breast (1) the wife (3) wins her husband (2).

1052 unicorn 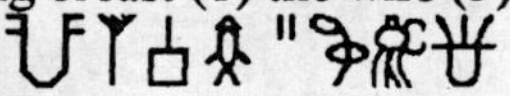 X.86.5

The ape (2) has touched/broken (2) my (3) beautiful painted things (1), I (3) will cut off (4) his head (5); Indra (8) is higher (7) than everything (6).

1067 unicorn 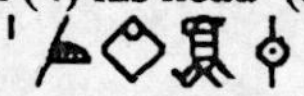 X.129.5

There were seed-givers (1), there were powers (2), and the place (3) of the impulse (4) was at the bottom and the granting one (5) was above (5).

1084 unicorn  I.181.1

The Aśvins (1) brought up the pearls from the ocean (2) like priests (3) (the Soma).

1102 unicorn 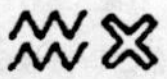 X.88.15

In the universe (1) there are two paths (2).

1108 unicorn 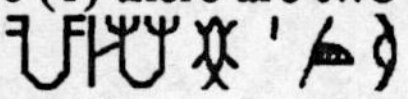 I.22.14

At the fixed place (2) of the Gandharva (1) the seer (4) lick the food (the Soma) (3) with prayers (5) that is like butter (like immortality) (6).

1130 unicorn 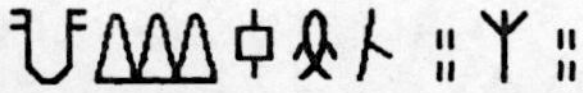 X.114.3
The virgin (2) with four plaits (1) who is beautifully adorned (3), whose face is of butter (4), has firm (5) rules (6).

1151 unicorn 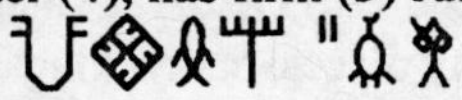 II.33.3
Rudra (1), the bearer of the club (2) and (3) of lightning (4), surpasses (7) in splendour (6) all that have been born (5).

1183 unicorn  VII.33.13
Vasiṣṭha (1) was born from the seed of the gods fallen into a vessel (2), Agastya (3) was also born from that vessel (4).

1206 unicorn 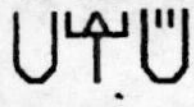 V.85.5
Varuṇa (2) stands between the two vessels of heaven (1) and earth (2).

1207 unicorn  V.80.2
The beautiful (woman) (1) awakes (3) the world (2) (like the cock) (1).

1262 unicorn 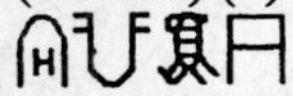 IX.69.5
With his power (2) the Soma (3) decorates the back of the sky (1), the covering of the two plates rich in water (4).

1274 unicorn  X.88.6
The domestic Agni (3) is the top (2) of the world (1) in the night (3) and the rising sun (3).

1320 bull 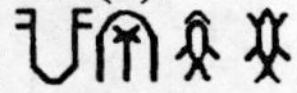 V.62.7
The pillar of the divine (4) chair (3) of Mitra (1) and Varuṇa (2) is embellished with gold (3).

1321 bull 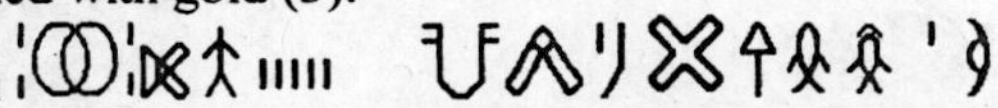 V.63.1
Guardians/eyes (2) of the truth (1), Mitra (3) and Varuṇa (4), whose laws are true (5), you (9) mount (8) the car (6) of the highest sky (7); for the man (11), to whom your are grateful (12), the rain (10) brings the sweetness of the sky (13).

1332 zebu  X.125.3

I am the queen of the sky (5), the collectrice of treasures (1), I am the knowing one (3), the first to be honoured (2); I was distributed by the gods on many places (4), being at many places, many things enter me (4).

1342 rhino  I.164.7

Here (1) he shall proclaim (2) it, if he really knows it (4), the track (3) left by that beloved bird (the sun) (5); from its head the cows (6) give milk (7).

1343 rhino  I.32.1

Indra (1) killed Vṛtra (2), he (3) drilled up (3) the waters (4), he (5) tore the bellies (6) of the mountains (7) asunder (6).

1349 unicorn 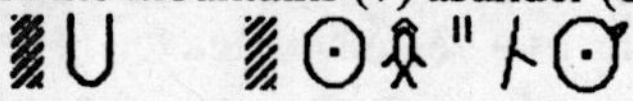 IV.33.10

I, the river (7), will bow (2) to you (3), the mighty seer (4), with swelling breast (1), like a young woman (5) who surrenders to her lover (6).

1360 crocodile 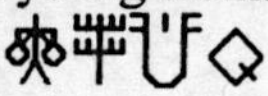 I.92.5

The daughter of the sky (1,2) has set up her speckled light (3) like a priest (4) the pole of sacrifice (3).

1362 elephant  X.90.1

The Puruṣa (4) covered (3) the earth (3) completely (2) and excelled (5) it by the width of ten fingers (6).

1373 elephant 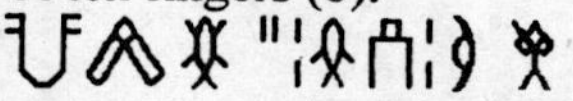 IX.69.5

By his power (1) the Soma (2) adorns the back of the sky (3), he (5) extends (6) the cover rich in water (3) over the two (4) plates (7).

1391  I.160.2

The two (2) halves of the sky (1) are like two pert girls (3,4) clad in beautiful colours (5) by the father (6).

1393  X.72.8

Eight sons (4) were born from the womb (5) of Aditi (4), seven (1) sons (2) she brought to the gods (3).

1400
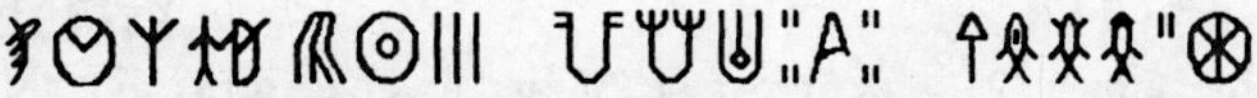 X.86.19,20
I walk looking around (1), discriminating between (2) Ārya (3,4,5) and Dāsa (6); field and mountain (6), how many yojana (7) are they (9) afar (8)? Come to the place (11) that is nearer (10), Vṛṣākapi (12), Indra (13) is higher (14) than everything (sun and rainbow) (15,16).

1403 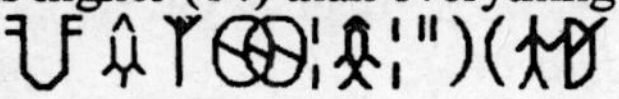 X.123.7
Upright the Gandharva (2) was standing (1) at the sky (3), bearing his wonderlike weapons (1); clad in a fragrant garment (4), looking like the effulgence of the sky (5), he revealed (6) the lovely (7) names (8).

1431 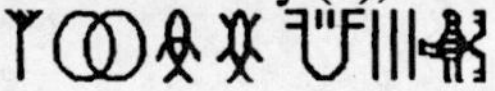 IV.26.4
This bird (1), you winds (2), stands beyond all birds (1), since he brought (7) to the earth (6) the Soma (3) cherished by all the gods (4, 5).

1444 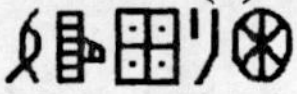 X.85.4
Secured by locking arrangements (4), guarded by mightiful powers (1) you are, Soma (5), hearing only (2) on the pressing stones (3).

1452 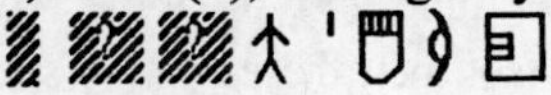 X.85.4
Secured by safety devices (1) you are, Soma (2), hearing only (4) on the pressing stones (3); the Soma of the knowing ones (7) nobody (4, 5) enjoys.

1470 unicorn  V.63.2
We ask for (4) your rain (1), Mitra (3) and Varuṇa (4), as offering of immortality (5).

1536 bull 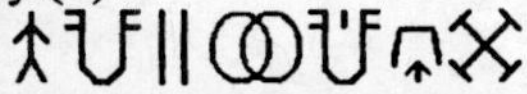 X.125.7
In the head (2) of the world (1) I bring forth (3) the cosmic (6) father (7) pervading (5) all the worlds (4).

1544  I.105.11
The beautifully winged (stars) (5, 6) are sitting there in the middle (4) of the ladder to the sky (3); they chase (2) the wolf (1) away (2), that wanted to cross (8) the juvenile waters (7).

1548 unicorn 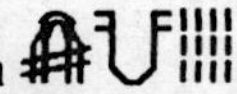 I.164.12

He is called the father (2) with five feet (3) and twelve forms (1), the humid one (2) sitting in the upper part of the sky (3). [The five feet are the three heavens and the two ways of the sun crossing it]

1582 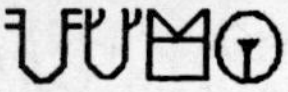 I.160.2

The two halves of the world (1) are like two pert young girls (2), clad in coloured garments (3) by the (cosmic) father (4).

1616 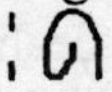 X.123.8

When he runs as drop (2) to the ocean, he looks from the sky (1) with the eyes (2) of a vulture.

2002 unicorn 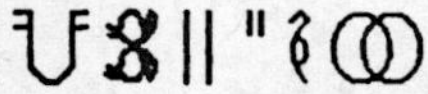 X.81.3

Heaven and earth (1) were created by the one god (6) by forging (2) them together (3) with arms (4) and wings (5).

2018 unicorn  IV.27.3,4

When the eagle (1) flew over the sky (2) and the winds (3) carried the abundant (4) away, when Kṛśanu (5), the archer (5), draw the bowstring (5) and shot him (6) as quick as thought (6), then the eagle (7) stretching out (8) brought the Soma (9) to Indra's followers (the Bharatas) (10).

2031 unicorn 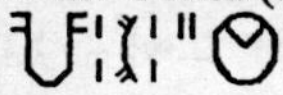 X.88.6

From Agni (4), the head (2) of the earth (1), the rising sun (3) is born (4).

2038 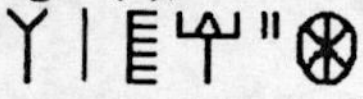 VII.49.3

In whose midst (2) king (1) Varuṇa (3) walks (5) the divine waters (4) shall protect me (6).

2043 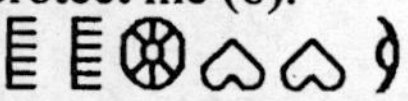 X .85.47

May all the gods (1) lead our hearts (2,3) together, may Mātariśvan (4), may the wise women (4,5) unite us.

2044 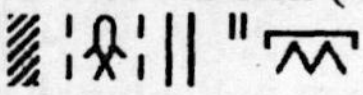 I.22.20

Viṣṇu's highest step (1) standing like an eye (2) at the sky (1) is always (3) seen by the seers (4).

2049  X.86.18

Vṛṣākapi (5) found three things (a dead ass, a knife, a plate) (1), a new pot (2) and a car (4) with fire-wood (3) - Indra (8) is higher than everything (6,7)

2070 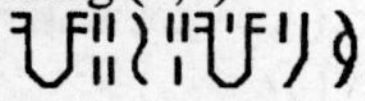 I.32.12

You, the only god (3) won (2) the Soma (1), you (5) set free the seven streams (4).

2083 unicorn  X.72.7,8

When you gods (4,5) like magicians (6) let swell (3) the worlds (2), you brought forth (7) the sun (1) that was hidden in the ocean (1).
Eight sons (8) were born from the body of Aditi (8).

2088 unicorn  I.110.5

The three Ṛbhus (1) have measured out (1) the standard (3) like a field (4).

2093  X.129.5

Across the midst they stretched out the cord.

2118  I.179.6

The seer (3) Agastya (4), who ploughed with pegs/drew up his seed (5), went to the gods/obtained the fulfilment of his desires (6, 7).

2134 unicorn 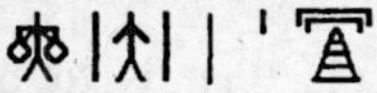 X.88.6

The domestic Agni (1) is the top of the world (2) and the rising sun (1), knowing the way (4) he does his work (5) quickly (3).

2171 elephant 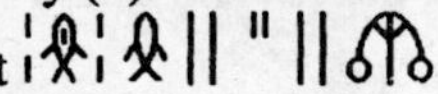 I.160.1

Between (3) the two (2) plates (1) walks according to the law (4) the pure (5) sun-god (6).

2185 unicorn 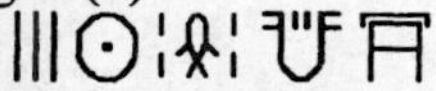 III.2.12

Agni Vaiśvānara (the sun) (2) has mounted the back of the sky (1), praised by the seers (3) he goes around in a circle (4) on the same path (5).

2191 unicorn 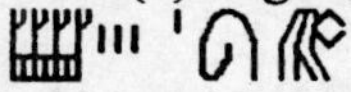 X.86.20

The ape (1) wants the top (3) of the sky (2) and the ears (4) of the ear-field (5). [He should take what is nearer].

2203 unicorn 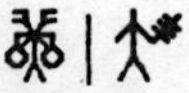 V.85.1
The magician (1) who measured out (1) the earth (2) is Varuṇa (1).

2224 unicorn 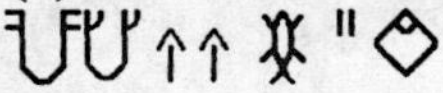 I.160.2
The two halves (2) of the world (1) are like two pert (4, 5) young girls (3), clad by the (cosmic) father (7) in coloured garments (6).

2233 unicorn 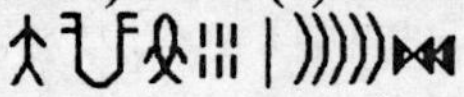 X.136.2,4
The munis (1) follow the path (3) of the wind (2), they (5) look down on all things (4), they are the friend (7) of this or that god (6).

2238 bull  IX.12.1
The Soma, the bright drop (2), has been poured out (by the priest) (1); for Indra (3) he has been pressed (4) at the seat (5) of the truth (6).

2242 unicorn  V.85.1
Who has separated (2) the earth like a hide (3) is Varuṇa (3).

2246 unicorn  X.129.5
Across the midst (1) they stretched out the cord (1), was this down or that above (2)? This creation (3), whether it was created or not (4), the guardian in the highest heaven (5) knows it.

2264 unicorn 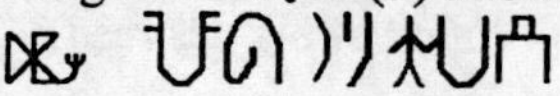 I.105.12
Newly (3) the Law (1) is established (1), that is to be praised (2); according to the Law (1) flow the streams (4), according to the Truth (6) the sun arises at the sky (5) - admit this, heaven and earth (7)!

2265 unicorn  VII.33.13
Who was born on the place of sacrifice in a pot (1), is the son (3) of Māna (2) (Agastya).

2267 unicorn  I.71.5
Having noticed that the the father of the sky (1) felt (sexual) desire for his daughter (1) he created (3) seed (2) for him.

2285 unicorn 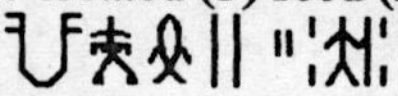 X.90.4,5
The cosmic man passed on all sides (1) over eating (4) and (2) non-eating (3), from him was born (6) the Virāj (5), and he was born by the Virāj.

2316 dancer  X.129.4
Sexual desire for the daughter (1) was in the beginning (2); the cord (3) between being (3) and non-being (3) was discovered by the seers (4).

2331 zebu  V.85.1,5
Varuṇa (1) has placed (2) the earth under the sun like a hide (2). He has measured out the earth (3,4).

2340 unicorn 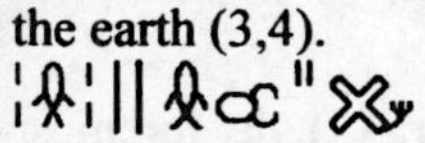 IX.71.5
The ten fingers (1) of the two arms (1) place (3) the Soma (4) in the womb of Aditi (the pressing-boards) (5), after the adorers have made the place ready (6).

2351  VII.103.1
Invigorated by Parjanya (1) the frogs (1) have started their speech (2).

2355 unicorn 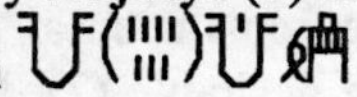 I.22.16
From there (1) the gods (2) may refresh us (with Soma) (1), from where Viṣṇu (4) went over the seven places of the earth (3).

2366 zebu 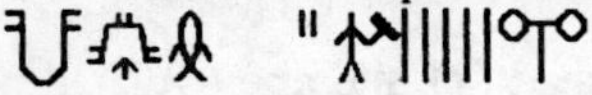 I.124.4
Who is like a ship (1) on the five streams (2) or (4) like Nodhas (3), she (the Dawn) (5) as the first (6) of those being reborn (6).

2390 bull 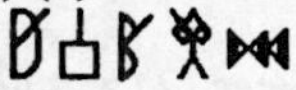 X.136.3
Intoxicated (1) through ecstasy (2) we have mounted the air (3), only our body (4) the mortals see (5).

2398 unicorn  V.63.1
Guardians/eyes (2) of the truth (1), Mitra (3) and Varuṇa (4), whose laws are true (5), you (9) mount (8) the car (6) of the highest sky (7); for the man (10), to whom your are grateful (11), (the womb) swells (12) with the sweetness of the sky (13).

2417 unicorn 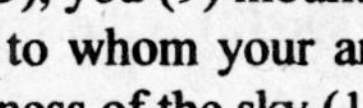 X.123.5
In the highest sky (1) the rain-bow (2) is born (3) by the water-woman (4) as her lover (5).

2431 zebu 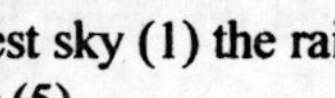 X.125.3
I (2), the queen of the sky (1), was distributed (4) over many places (3).

2432 unicorn  X.5.1

Agni follows the udder (1) in the womb (1) of the two (2) concealed (3); in the midst of the fountain (4) the track of the bird (5) is hidden.

2435 unicorn 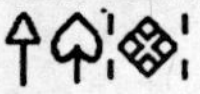 I.24.7

In the bottomless space (1) stands the tree (2) with its root above (3).

2448  I.32.3

Three (1) big vats of the Soma (1) Indra (3), the foremost (2), drank.

2451 unicorn 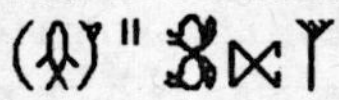 X.123.5

The friend (1) penetrated the womb of the friend (2), the lovely one (5) is sitting (5) on two (4) golden wings (3).

2455 unicorn 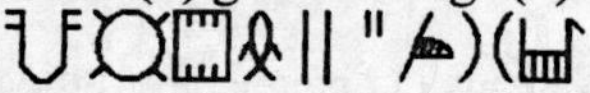 X.123.2

The lovely one (2) draws up (3,4) the wave from the ocean (1), born from the Soma (5) he saw (6) the back of the desirable (7); he radiates (8) from the top of the truth (9).

2465 unicorn  X.86.5

I (2) will cut off (3) his (bald) head (1), the ape (6) shall not enter my womb (4), because he has polluted my painted things/pots (4).

2475 unicorn 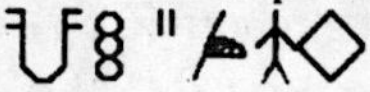 III.56.3

Viśvārūpa (1) has three bellies (4) and (3) three faces (2) and udders (5).

2477  I.124.3

She follows (1) exactly (3) the path of the truth (2), as if she knew it (4,5), and she (8) never misses (7) the direction (6).

2500 bull  V.63.7

Mitra and Varuṇa (bull) have placed the sun (2) at the sky (2) as a car to behold from all sides (1).

2530 unicorn 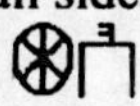 IX.71.5

Like a car (2) the ten fingers (1) have placed the Soma in the lap of Aditi (the vat) (1).

2535 zebu 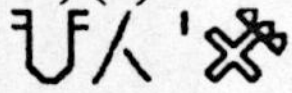 I.22.20

Viṣṇu's (4) highest step (1) stands (3) like an eye (2) at the sky (1).

2554 goat 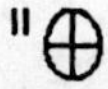 X.90.10

Out of him (the Puruṣa) (1) the goat (2) and the sheep (2) came forth.

2584 unicorn  I.32.1

Indra (4) killed Vṛtra (with his club) (1), he let the waters (of rain) (2) run, and (3) he (6) tore asunder (5) (the bellies of the mountains).

2595 unicorn  X.125.7

I am (2) in the head of the father of the world (1), pervading all the worlds (3,4).

2597 unicorn  III.61.1,4

Goddess, old and young (1), desired by all (2), you follow the law (1). Like a weaving woman (4) extracting the thread (3), the generous Uṣas (5) arrives, the mistress (7) of the cow-shed (6), the mother of the sun (8).

2615 tiger  X.86.23

Parśu (1), the rib (the wife) (1) of the ape (2), gave birth (1) to twenty children at once (3).

2617 unicorn  I.105.2

The woman (1) draws the seed (3) of her husband (4) in her womb (2), both ejaculate (7) the powerful streams (6), she gives her juice and milks the man (5) - admit this, heaven and earth (8)!

2621 unicorn 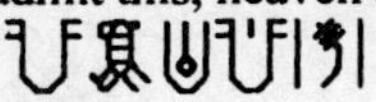 IX.99.1

For the golden one (1), the bold one (1) they bend (1) the power (2) for the bow (1); for the Asura (4) the mightiful (5) they weave a beaming garment (4) in front of the sieve (3).

2629  X.85.4

The Soma (3) is guarded (1) by safety devices (2).

2656 unicorn  X.136.1

The long-haired (1) appears as the effulgence (3) of the sky (2).

2662 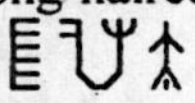 X.85.37

The men (1) sow the seed (1) in the divine womb (2) of the women (2) who love them (3).

2687 unicorn 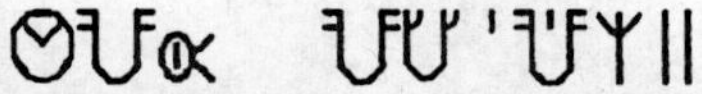 X.10.9
Day (1) and night (1) she would offer (2) her womb (3) to him (4), she would turn away (5,6) the eye (7) of the sun (8) for some time (9).

2710 graffito  X.85.23
Straight and thornless the ways shall be.

2727 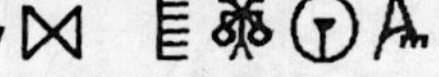 V.85.4
When Varuṇa (3) wants (2) to be milked (4), the hills clothe in a cloud (1) and strong men (5) let their water fall down (5).

2751 bull  X.34.12
I swear (2) by the god of dice (Varuṇa) (1) that I do not hide any treasures (bull in the motif).

2805 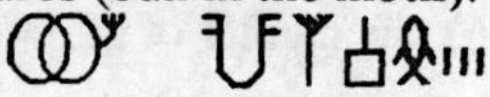 I.105.5
You gods (2), who are above in the three bright spaces of heaven (1), what is right (3), what is wrong (4), where has your former offer gone (5) - do admit this, heaven and earth (6)!

2821 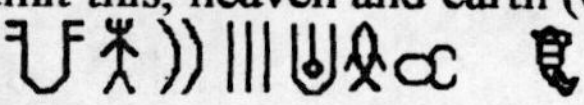 IX.1.2
Who kills (2) all monsters (1), who is loved (2) by all good men (3), takes his seat (6) in the brazen (5) womb (4), in the vat (4), at the holy (7) place (8).

3002 unicorn 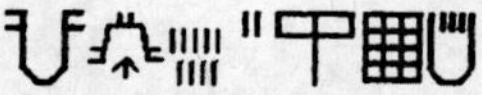 X.17.11
Day after day (2) the drop (1) is falling in the womb (1), drop and womb (1) that go jointly (4) together (3), the seven (5) divine (7) priests (6) I call.

3004 unicorn  X.136.7
Together with Rudra (2) the long-haired (1) drinks the poison (3) from the cup (3); the wind (4) has churned (4) it (5) for him, the witch Kunaṃnamā (6) has quenched (7) it (8) for him.

3032 unicorn  I.24.10
The stars fastened above (1) that appear in the night (2) have gone anywhere at daytime (3).

3046 unicorn 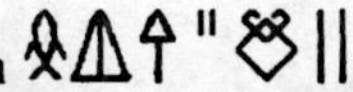 I.171.5
With the mighty winds (1) the mighty (3) bull (Indra) (2), the strong one (4), who spends power (5) may give us fame (6).

3047 unicorn  X.61.10
The Navagvas (1) won the friendship (2) of the virgin (3), the speakers of the truth (4) won her for (the union with) the truth (5).

3086 unicorn  X.81.3
Who has eyes on all sides (1), who has mouths on all sides (1), who has arms on all sides (1), who has feet on all sides (1), the single god (2) has created heaven and earth (2).

3069 unicorn  V.85.5
Varuṇa (1) has measured out (3) the earth (2) like a hide (4).

3113 unicorn 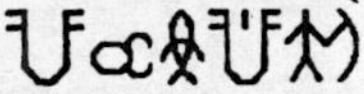 X.123.7
Upright (1) the Gandharva (1) is standing (1) at the sky bearing his wonderlike weapons (1); clad in a fragrant garment (2), looking like the effulgence of the sky (3), he revealed (4) the lovely names (5).

3130 unicorn  I.189.7
Like a banner (1) Agni (2) discriminates between two times (3,4).

3254  V.85.5,6
Varuṇa (2) is standing between heaven and earth (1); with his magic power (3) as measuring line (4) he (5) has measured out the earth (6) with the sun (7); (through him) the rivers (9) flow (10) into the sea (8) (without filling it).

3280  I.124.4
Like a fly (1) she (the Dawn) (2) awakes the sleeper (3).

3296 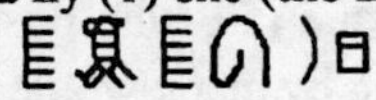 X.123.1
The lovely rainbow (2) incites, covered with a skin of light (1), the daughters (4, 6) of Soma (5) when crossing the air (3).

3327 tree 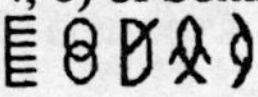 IX.26.1
The runner for the victory (the Soma) (1) the eloquent (2) have artfully placed (3) in the womb (4) of Aditi (5).

3407  I.28.3
The woman (2) living in the house (1) knows to press (3) the Soma (4).

3427 fish 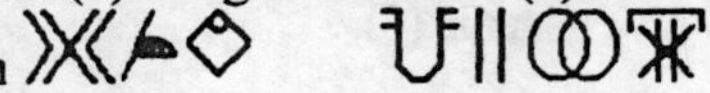 V.63.2
You are standing as rulers (1) over this world (2,3), Mitra-Varuṇa (4), like the light (6) of the sun (5) over the assembly (7).

3480 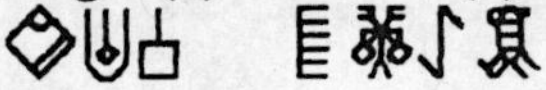 V.85.1,5
By his magic power (1) Varuṇa (3) has measured (2) out the earth (4), like a priest (3) he has spread (6) it like a hide (5) under the sun (7).

3488  X.125.6,7
I pervade heaven (1) and earth (2); my womb (4) is in the water (3), in the ocean (3).

3498  X.89.7
Indra (2) cut down to the earth (1) Vṛtra (3) like a tree (4), he opened a path/a bed (6) for the streams (5).

3573 three circles 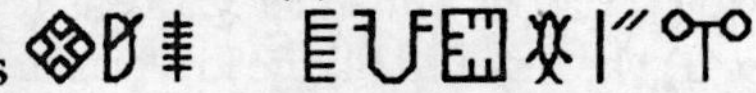 I.123.1
The broad (2) car (1) of the sacrificial cow (4) is harnessed (3) (on the sacrificial field (4) for the gods (6,7); the mistress full of power (9) has risen from the dark (8) taking care of human habitations (10).

3584 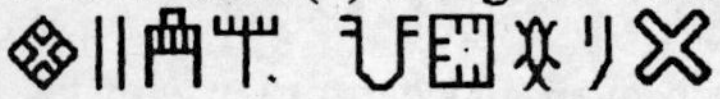 I.123.1
In the morning (2) the car (1) of the sacrificial cow (3) is harnessed (on the sacrificial field) (4) for the gods (6); the mistress full of power (6) has risen from the dark (8) taking care (7) for the human habitations (9,10).

3599 stone inscription 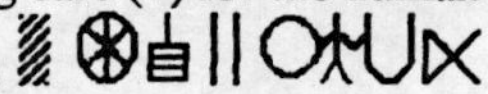 I.59.4
The two worlds (3) are like two mothers (1) for the son, praised by the priest like by a carpenter (3), he who is like the sun (5), who possesses true power (4), the wonderful Vaiśvānara is loved by many women (6).

3693 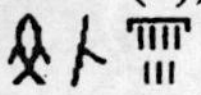 X.85.2
The Soma (3) was set (2) in the womb of all the stars/the nine planets (1).

3713 graffito 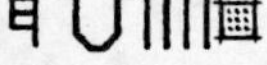 I.28.9
Pour the Soma (2) through the sieve (1), put it on the hide (4) of the cow (3).

3721  I.24.7
Varuṇa (2) holds up the tree (3) in the bottomless space (5) at the top (4).

3734 graffito  X.85.45
Ten sons shall be born in the womb (of the owner of the pot).

3736  X.114.3
The virgin (pot) whose face is like butter (1), has firm rules (2).

3738 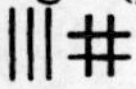 I.164.2
Three naves (2) are fixed to the car (1) that never grows old, that never rests (like the owner of the vessel).

4057 unicorn  I.179.6
The seer (1) Agastya (2), ploughing with pegs/updrawing the seed (3), obtained the fulfilment of his desires (4).

4141 unicorn 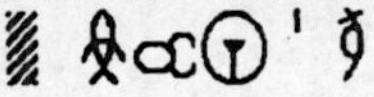 V.85.2
Varuṇa (5) has placed (4) the moon (1) on the rock (2), he has extended (4) the air over the trees (3).

4166 unicorn  V.85.5
Standing between heaven and earth (1) Varuṇa (1) has measured out the earth (2).

5023 unicorn  X.72.3
The universe (1) was brought forth (2) by the woman (3) who spreads her thighs like a flower its petals (4).

5054 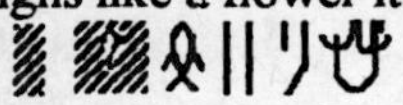 X.125.2
I (2) carry the gods (1), I give riches (5) to the Soma-presser (3,4).

5075 brazen implement

 X.127.1,6

The moonlike (2,3) night (1) appeared and looked around with many eyes (4,5), the immortal goddess (6) has filled the wide space (7), the heights and depths (8) with her light (9), she (10) drives away (12) the dark (11). Against the wolf and the she-wolf and the thief (13) defend us (14), be easy to withstand (15).

6020 unicorn 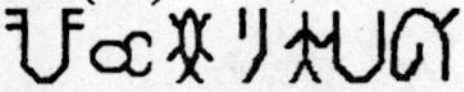 V.80.1,2

For the Dawn who brings the sun (1) the seers (2) keep awake with hymns (2); in the beginning of the days (3) the Dawn (6) holds up (5) her light (4).

6021 bull 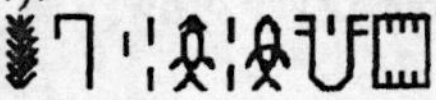 V.85.3

Varuṇa (3) has poured out (2) in the vessel cast upside down (2) the sky, the earth and the intermediate space (1); he (4) is the king of all that has been born (4), by him the earth is watered (6) like the barley (7) by the rain (5).

6022 goat 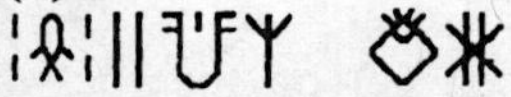 IX.101.10,14

The best path-finder (1) for finding the light of the sun (2), the stainless (4) friends (3) are the pressed (5) saps of the Soma (6).

6023 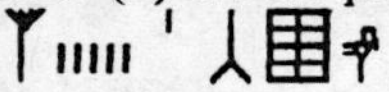 IX.71.9

The bird of the sky (1) looks down (3) on the earth (2), the Soma (4) watches (6) over the creatures (5).

6024  X.127.1,2

The night (2) has began (3), everywhere (4) the eyes (1) of the goddess, the stars (5,6), flash up; the immortal goddess (9) pervades (8) the vastness of the space (7).

6047 unicorn 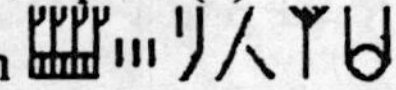 X.61.6

When the father (1) had thrown (2) his whole energy on his daughter, they lost some (4) seed (5) in separating (3), which fell on the earth in the womb of the good deed (6).

6120 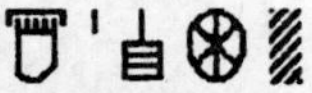 I.1.8
We adore (1) the king (2) of the assemblies, the radiant guardian/eye (4) of the true order (3), who grows in his own house (5).

6208 bull and unicorn 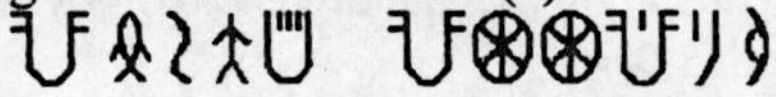 VII.33.13
Through the moonlike (1,2) virgin (Urvaśī) (3) the gods (6) Mitra (4) and Varuṇa (5) lost their seed in a vessel (7), from that the son (9) of Māna (8), the seer (10), was born (11).

7016 unicorn  X.88.16
The two (1) united (2) bear him, Agni (3), who has been born (4) from their head (3).

7027  I.160.1
Between the beautifully delivering (3) two plates (1,2), the goddesses (4) of heaven and earth (5), walks (2) according to the law (6) the pure sun-god (7).

7037 unicorn 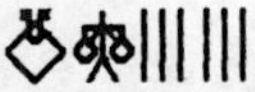 X.46.3
Trita (1) searching much (2) found Agni (3) on the head of the cow (4).

7080 bronze implement 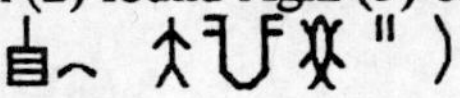 V.62.8
When the Dawn (3) flashes up (2), Mitra (5) and Varuṇa (4) mount the golden chair (6,7) in the sky (1).

7102 rhino  I.22.18,20
The highest step (2) of Viṣṇu's three steps (1) is always seen by the seers (3). (Viṣṇu is the favourite god of the vaiśyas, the land- and house-owners identified with the rhino on seal 2420; cf. chapter II. The first sign can also be explained as a house).

7122 unicorn  X.34.14
Make friendship (1) and have pity (1) with us (2), dice (3)! Do not harm (6) us boldly (5) with your cruel magic (4)! Your wrath (7) and dislike (8) shall both be at rest (13), somebody else shall be in your (10,11) grip (9,12)!

7142 sealing  X.125.7
I (2) pervade all the worlds (1) touching the sky with the tuft of my hair (2).

8451 unicorn  I.126.6
Who holds tight (1), who embraces closely (2), who hides herself like (4) a fẹmale ichneumon (3), hundreds (5) of joys (6) the voluptuous one (7) gives to me (8,9).

9002 bull  IX.71.2
Bold like a destroyer of peoples (1,2), unveiling his Asura-colour (3,4) he (4) comes to the place of the father (5).

9501 bull  X.81.3
Who has eyes on all sides (1), who has mouths on all sides (1), who has arms on all sides (1), who has feet on all sides (1), the single god (2,3) has created heaven and earth (4), he (7) has forged them together (8) with arms (6) and wings (5).

GENERAL INDEX